C0-DAL-632

WATERMELONS

Characteristics, Production, and Marketing

Donald N. Maynard, editor

ASHS Horticulture Crop Production Series
Jules Janick, editor-in-chief

Watermelon title, 2001
Muscadine title, 2001

Copyright 2001 by ASHS Press

(ISBN 0-9707546-1-2)

All rights reserved. No part of this publication may be reproduced or transmitted in any form or by any means, electronic or mechanical, including photocopy, recording, or any other information storage or retrieval system, without the written permission of the publisher.

This publication is designed to provide accurate and authoritative information in regard to the subject matter covered. It is sold with the understanding that the publisher is not engaged in rendering legal, accounting, or other professional services. If legal advice or other expert assistance is required, the services of a competent professional person should be sought. Neither the author nor publisher is responsible for errors or omissions. *From a Declaration of Principles jointly adopted by a Committee of the American Bar Association and a Committee of Publishers.*

ASHS Press
113 South West Street
Suite 200
Alexandria, VA 22314
phone 703.836.4606 • fax 703.836.2024
e-mail ashspres@ashs.org

This is the first volume of a new series on horticultural crop production published by ASHS Press. These books, written primarily for an American audience, will be of value throughout the world.

In the United States, watermelons have been traditionally associated with family outings in the long, hot days of summer. More recently, watermelons have become a year-round, everyday kind of fruit, but still retain the joy of summertime fun and good eating. Our national holidays—Independence Day, Memorial Day, and Labor Day—are intimately associated with this delectable melon. Watermelons are even more popular in other parts of the world and are grown and consumed in large quantities in Asia, especially China and Korea, and in the Middle East with Egypt and Iran being the leaders.

Watermelons are part of our artistic and popular culture. There are many examples of watermelon in art; a well-known example is Melons and Morning Glories painted by Raphaelle Peal in 1813 found in the collection of the National Museum of American Art in Washington, D.C. Watermelons lend themselves to competition. Who can grow the largest watermelon? Who can spit seeds the furthest? Which young woman will represent the industry as a watermelon queen?

Some of the leading watermelon experts in the United States have contributed to this volume. I am grateful to them for their support and to their good humor despite unforeseen delays. The usually unheralded work of reviewers is recognized with great thanks. Vince Rubatzky and Tom Williams provided excellent reviews and suggestions for improvement. Jules Janick's editorial work helped to pull it all together into a more readable work without sacrificing accuracy. Together, we have attempted to ferret out errors and inconsistencies, but if any remain, they are totally my responsibility. Finally, thanks to Brian Sidoti for careful proofreading and to Amy Dunlap for multiple revisions done with a smile and total dedication to the completion of this project.

Donald N. Maynard, editor

Contributing Authors

Kenneth R. Barker. Department of Plant Pathology, North Carolina State University, Campus Box 7616, Raleigh, NC 27695-7616. e-mail: kenneth_barker@ncsu.edu

Gerald E. Brust. SW Purdue Agricultural Research Center, Purdue University, RR6, Box 139A, Vincinnes, IN 47591-3043. e-mail: brust@purdue.edu

Frank J. Dainello. Extension Horticulture, Texas A&M University, College Station, TX 77843. e-mail: f-dainello@tamu.edu

Gary W. Elmstrom. Sunseeds, 7087 E. Peltier Road, Acampo, CA 95220. e-mail : gary.elmstrom@sunseeds.com

Edmund A . Estes. Department of Agricultural and Resource Economics, Campus Box 8109, North Carolina State University, Raleigh, NC 27695-8109. e-mail: edestes@ncsu.edu

Jorge M. Fonseca. University of Costa Rica, Centro de Investigaciones Agronomicas, San Jose, Costa Rica.

Timothy K. Hartz. Department of Vegetable Crops, University of California, Davis, CA 95616. e-mail: hartz@vegmail.ucdavis.edu

George J. Hochmuth. Horticultural Sciences Department, North Florida Research and Education Center, University of Florida, Quincy, FL 32351. e-mail: gjh@gnv.ifas.ufl.edu

Gerald J. Holmes. Department of Plant Pathology, North Carolina State University, Campus Box 7616, Raleigh, NC 27695-7616. e-mail: gerald_holmes@ncsu.edu

Donald L. Hopkins. MidFlorida Research and Education Center, University of Florida, 2807 Binion Rd., Apopka, FL 32703-8504. e-mail: dhop@gnv.ifas.ufl.edu

Edwin Kee. University of Delaware, Georgetown, DE 19947. e-mail: kee@udel.edu

Anthony P. Keinath. Clemson University, Coastal Research and Education Center, 2865 Savannah Highway, Charleston, SC 29414-5341. e-mail: tknth@clemson.edu

Richard X. Latin. Department of Botany and Plant Pathology, 1155 Lilly Hall, Purdue University, West Lafayette, IN 47907-1155. e-mail: latin@btny.purdue.edu

Amnon Levi. U.S. Vegetable Laboratory. USDA-ARS, 2875 Savannah Highway, Charleston, SC 29414-5341. e-mail: alevi@awod.com

Donald N. Maynard. Gulf Coast Research and Education Center, University of Florida, 5007 60th St. E., Bradenton, FL 34203-9324. e-mail: dnma@gnv.ifas.ufl.edu

James E. Motes. Department of Horticulture and Landscape Architecture, Oklahoma State University, Stillwater, OK 74075. e-mail: jimmotes@aol.com

David G. Riley. University of Georgia, P.O. Box 748, Tifton, GA 31793. e-mail: driley@tifton.cpes.peachnet.edu

Vincent E. Rubatzky. Extension Vegetable Specialist Emeritus, University of California, 20 Birchall Drive, Haddonfield, NJ 08033-2710. e-mail: VNVatNJ@aol.com

James W. Rushing. Coastal Research and Education Center, Clemson University, 2865 Savannah Highway, Charleston, SC 29414-5341. e-mail: jrshng.@clemson.edu

Nischit V. Shetty. Seminis Vegetable Seeds, 432 Ty Ty Omega Rd, Tifton, GA 31794. e-mail: nischit.shetty@svseeds.com

James W. Shrefler. Wes Watkins Agricultural Research and Education Center, Oklahoma State University, Box 128, Lane, OK 74555. e-mail: jshrefler_okstate@lane ag.org

William M. Stall. Horticultural Sciences Department, University of Florida, P.O. Box 110690, Gainesville, FL 32611-0690. e-mail: wms@gnv.ifas.ufl.edu

Susan E. Webb. Entomology and Nematology Department, University of Florida, P.O. Box 110620, Gainesville, FL 32611-0620. e-mail: sewe@gnv.ifas.ufl.edu

Todd C. Wehner. Department of Horticultural Sciences, Campus Box 7609, North Carolina State University, Raleigh, NC 27695-7609. e-mail: todd_wehner@ncsu.edu

Leo J. Zanoni. Asgrow Vegetable Seeds, 5111 East ML Ave. #B5, Kalamazoo, MI 49001-9558. e-mail: leo.zanoni@svseeds.com

TABLE OF CONTENTS

Chapter 1
An Introduction to the Watermelon 9
D.N. Maynard

Chapter 2
Origin, Distribution, and Uses 21
V.E. Rubatzky

Chapter 3
Breeding and Seed Production 27
T.C. Wehner, N.V. Shetty, and G.W. Elmstrom

Chapter 4
Biotechnology 74
Amnon Levi

Chapter 5
Cultural Management 78
G.J. Hochmuth, E. Kee, T.K. Hartz, F.J. Dainello, and J.E. Motes

Chapter 6
Nematode-induced Maladies 98
K.R. Barker and G.J. Holmes

Chapter 7
Diseases 109
D.L. Hopkins and R.X. Latin

Chapter 8
Insect and Mite Pests 131
S.E. Webb, D.G. Riley, and G.E. Brust

Chapter 9
Weed Management 150
W.M. Stall and J.W. Shrefler

Chapter 10
Harvesting and Postharvest Handling 156
J.W. Rushing, J.M. Fonseca, and A.P. Keinath

Chapter 11
Marketing 165
E.A. Estes

Chapter 12
Promotion and Merchandising 189
L.J. Zanoni

Appendix 1
Watermelon Organizations 197

Appendix 2
Watermelon Seed Sources 199

Appendix 3
Cucurbit Publications 202

Appendix 4
Production Costs 203

Appendix 5
Common Names in 15 Languages 215

Index 216

CHAPTER 1

AN INTRODUCTION TO THE WATERMELON

D.N. Maynard

In the United States, watermelons have been traditionally associated with family outings and summertime fun although recently, they have become a year round, everyday kind of fruit. National holidays —Independence Day, Memorial Day, and Labor Day—are intimately associated with watermelon eating making watermelons as American as apple pie and corn-on-the-cob.

TAXONOMY

Watermelon, together with cucumber, melons of various sorts, summer squash, winter squash and pumpkin are the principal food plants of the gourd family (Cucurbitaceae). These products, together with the less well-known winter melon, chayote, West Indian gherkin, and an array of edible gourds, constitute a taxonomic group of diverse origin and genetic composition with considerable impact on human nutrition. The term cucurbit denotes all species within the Cucurbitaceae.

Various cucurbits are found throughout the tropics and subtropics of Africa, southeast Asia, and the Americas. Some are adapted to humid conditions and others are found in arid areas. Most are frost intolerant, so they are grown with protection in temperate areas or to coincide with the warm portion of the annual cycle. Cucurbits are mostly annual, herbaceous tendril-bearing vines. Plants are mostly monoecious (separate male and female flowers on the same plant) and flowers are insect pollinated. Fruit are variously shaped, many-seeded berries.

The Cucurbitaceae contain about 118 genera and over 800 species and is taxonomically isolated from other plant families. Two subfamilies—Zanonioideae and Cucurbitoideae—are well characterized; the former by small, striate pollen grains and the latter by having the styles united into a single column. The food plants all fall within the subfamily Cucurbitoideae. Watermelon [*Citrullus lanatus* (Thunb.) Matsum. & Nakai] is assigned to the tribe Benincaseae, subtribe Benincasinae and is native to Africa.

MORPHOLOGY

Watermelon plants are annual, with long trailing thin and angular vines which bear branched tendrils and lobed leaves and separate male and female flowers. Dwarf or bush types have been developed, but have not attained commercial importance. Root systems are extensive. Rooting depth is related to cultural and irrigation practices. Roots may reach depths of 4 ft or more in dry land, unmulched culture; whereas they may be restricted to the top foot of soil in irrigated, mulched culture. Watermelon flowers, which are smaller and less showy than those of other cultivated cucurbits, are borne solitary in leaf axils and remain open for only 1 day. The plant is monoecious. Staminate (male) flowers appear first and greatly outnumber pistillate (female) flowers (Fig. 1.1). The flowers are pollinated mostly by honeybees. Fruit may range in size from about 2 to as much as 250 lb, but ordinary cultivated types are 8–30 lb. The preferred commercial size is 18–24 lb. Shape varies from round to oval to elongated. Coloration of the rind may be light green, often termed gray, to very dark green, appearing to be almost black (Fig. 1.2). In addition, the rind may have stripes of various designs which are typical of a variety or type, thus the terms Jubilee-type stripe or Allsweet-type stripe (Fig. 1.3) are used to identify various patterns. Seed color varies from white to black as well as brown, red, green, and mottled. Seed size varies from tomato seed size to pumpkin seed size. Seed count ranges from 3,000–5,000 seeds/lb in large-seeded types and from 8,000–10,000 seeds/lb in small-seeded types. Hybrid diploid and triploid watermelon seeds are frequently sold by count rather than weight. The tendency in varietal development for commercial production is to strive for seeds that are small, but are vigorous enough for germination under unfavorable conditions and are dark colored rather than white since white seeds are associated with fruit immaturity. Flesh may be white, green, yellow, orange, pink, or red. Consumers in developed countries demand red or deep pink fleshed watermelon, although yellow-fleshed watermelon are grown in home gardens and to a limited extent commercially.

HORTICULTURE

Watermelons require a long, warm growing season for best pro-

Figure 1.1. Staminate (male) watermelon flower (l) and pistillate (female) flower (r).

Figure 1.2. Watermelon fruit showing variation in shape, rind color and flesh color. (Source: National Garden Bureau, Downers Grove, Ill.)

Figure 1.3. Jubilee-type stripe (l) and Allsweet-type stripe (r).

Figure 1.4. Low tunnels in Arava, Israel, provide protection to lengthen the season or permit production in areas with cool climates.

duction and quality. The earliest varieties produce mature fruit in about 75 days, but commercially important varieties require about 100 days from seeding to harvest. The frost-free period can be extended by the use of transplants (see Fig. 5.5), row covers, or low tunnels (Fig. 1.4). Fruit maturation from pollination requires 26–45 days, but most commercial varieties are ready for harvest 30–35 days after pollination.

Internal quality of watermelon fruit is a function of flesh color and texture, freedom from defects, sweetness, and optimum maturity. Unfortunately, these criteria can not be assessed without cutting the watermelon. So, watermelons of inferior or marginal quality are sometimes marketed which may lead to a lack of consumer confidence in the product. The current supermarket practice of preparing cut and sectioned watermelon provides at least partial assurance of quality to the purchaser, but no indication of sweetness. In Japan, where watermelon prices are often as high as U.S. $50 each (Fig. 1.5), quality of whole watermelon fruit is assessed by magnetic resonance imaging (MRI) before marketing where soluble solids and flesh integrity can be determined nondestructively in seconds (Fig.1.6).

Figure 1.5. Watermelon for sale in Japan at U.S. $50.

WORLD PRODUCTION

Watermelons are grown throughout the world in areas where a long, warm growing season prevails. Asia is by far the most important production site with 72% of the world area and 77% of the world production (Table 1.1). Europe is a distant second with 11% of the world area and 7% of the world production. The area devoted to watermelon production is similar in Africa, North and Central America, and South America; but production is lower in South America because of lower yields. In Europe yields are considerably below the world average presumably because of less

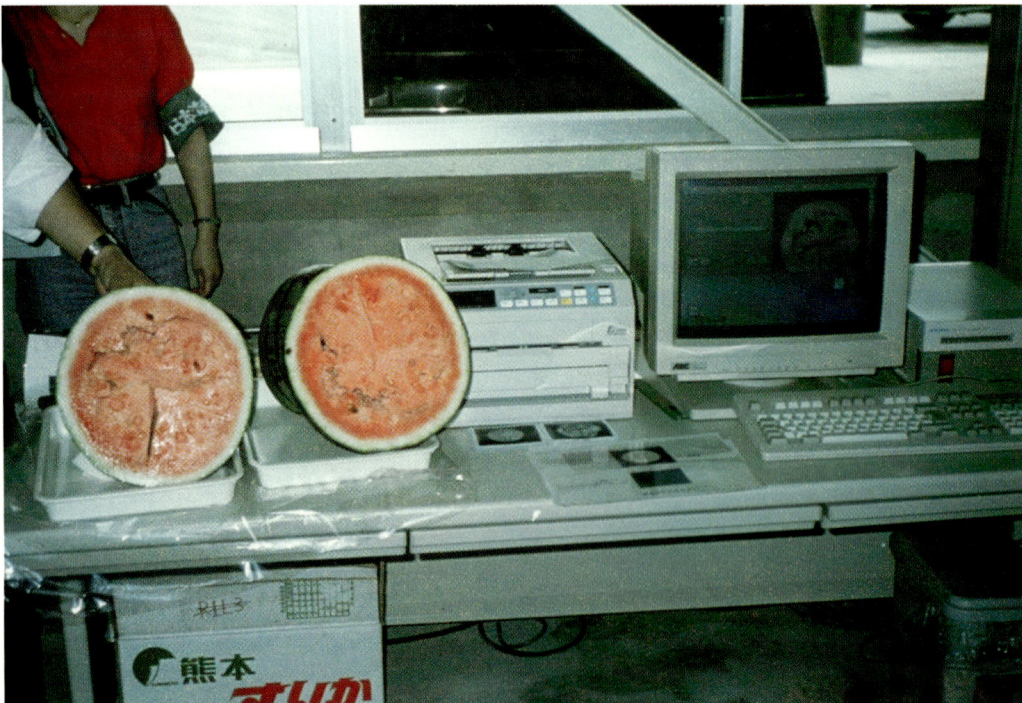

Figure 1.6. Watermelon quality determination in Japan by magnetic resonance imagery.

favorable climatic conditions while yields in Africa, North and Central America, and Asia are near or above the world average. Oceania contributes a very minor portion of the world watermelon production. Worldwide, watermelons are grown on over 6 million acres that produce more than 50 million tons of fruit. Although the magnitude of the watermelon industry is quite impressive, it accounts for only 2% of the world area devoted to vegetable production and contributes only 4% of world vegetable production.

With China accounting for 41% of world watermelon area and contributing 51% of world production, it is easy to understand why Asia is preeminent in the watermelon industry (Table 1.1). Also contributing to Asia's dominance are Turkey, the second largest producer; Iran, the fourth largest producer; and Korea Republic, the fifth ranking producer. Outside of Asia, only the United States and Egypt are included among the principal producing countries. There are no estimates of the farm gate value of the world's watermelon crop. However, one can project a rough estimate of annual world value exceeding $7.6 billion using the United States average price of $7.50/cwt for 1995–97.

Details of the United States watermelon industry in 1997–99 are shown

Table 1.1. World watermelon production, 1997.

Location	Area (1000 acres)	(%)	Yield (cwt/acre)	Production (1000 tons)	(%)
Continent					
Asia	4,310	72	183	39,374	77
Europe	689	1	115	3,968	7
Africa	373	6	158	2,952	6
North and					
Central America	291	5	193	2,798	6
South America	348	6	95	1,650	3
Oceania	12	<1	163	99	<1
World	6,024	100	169	50,841	100
Principal countries					
China	2,443	41	211	25,718	51
Turkey	353	5	237	4,188	8
United States	185	3	221	2,036	4
Iran	371	6	107	1,984	4
Korea Republic	116	2	221	1,282	3
Egypt	114	2	223	1,267	2
Others	2,442	41	144	14,366	28

Source: FAO Production Yearbook 51 (1998).

Table 1.2. United States watermelon production, 1997–99 averages.

Harvested area		Yield per acre		Production	
State	(acres)	State	(cwt)	State	(1000 cwt)
Texas	39,666	California	446	Florida	8,400
Florida	32,333	Delaware	403	Texas	7,115
Georgia	24,333	Arizona	345	California	6,963
California	15,566	Indiana	281	Georgia	5,061
S.C.	9,167	Florida	258	Arizona	2,566
N.C.	8,800	Maryland	244	Indiana	1,811
Others	45,018		147		7,291
U.S.	174,883		225		39,207

Source: Vegetables, 1999 Summary USDA Vg 1-2, 2000.

in Table 1.2. Because of the crop's special climatic requirements only 17 of the 50 states provide detailed data on watermelon production. However, the Census of Agriculture provides estimates of watermelon acreage by county (Fig. 1.7). The principal suppliers of U.S. watermelons are California, which has the highest yield per acre, and Texas, Florida, and Georgia, with the largest harvested area. Other states with high yields are Delaware, Arizona, and Indiana. Highest prices are obtained in Hawaii, where food is expensive because of shipping costs from the mainland and other production sites (Table 1.3). The well above-average price received by California growers is due in part to a high proportion of triploid (seedless) production which commands higher prices than diploids (seeded). The combination of high yields and prices accounts for the California crop having the highest value which exceeded $76 million annually for the period. Florida, Texas, and Georgia also had high annual returns from watermelons. Overall, the United States watermelon crop amounted to over 39 million cwt, from over 174,000 harvested acres, and has a farm value of over $286 million. The United States watermelon crop accounted for 9.2% of the harvested acres, 10.0% of the production, and 3.5% of the value of the United States fresh vegetable industry in 1999.

According to the U.S. Department of Commerce Bureau of the Census, 46.3% of the nation's watermelon acreage was irrigated in 1992. The proportion of irrigated watermelon land in the principal producing states varied from 11.5% in North Carolina (down from 17.7% in 1987) to 100% in Arizona and California.

WATERMELON CONSUMPTION

Watermelon consumption is designated as per capita use which measures disappearance of a product on a per-person basis. It is equal to total supply

Table 1.3. Price and value of U.S. watermelon crop, 1997–99 averages.

Price		Total value	
State	**($/cwt)**	**State**	**($1000)**
Hawaii	20.00	California	76,962
California	11.03	Florida	62,440
Maryland	9.00	Texas	41,229
Delaware	7.56	Georgia	26,183
Florida	7.51	Arizona	17,812
Arizona	7.13	Indiana	11,785
	6.05		49,687
	7.28		286,098

Source: Vegetables, 1999 Summary USDA Vg 1-2, 2000.

(production + imports + beginning stocks) less uses (exports + shrink and losses + ending stocks) divided by the total country population. Using this definition, per capita use for countries where data are available ranges from 0.4 lb in Djibouti to 155 lb in Israel with a worldwide average of 17 lb. Consumption in the world's leading producing countries varies from 17 lb in the United States to 138 lb in Turkey (Table 1.4). The data for several of these countries in terms of watermelon flesh consumption are exaggerated because a considerable quantity of watermelons are grown specifically for the seeds which are used as food in various ways. For the most part, the flesh of these varieties is not consumed because of very low total soluble solids. The

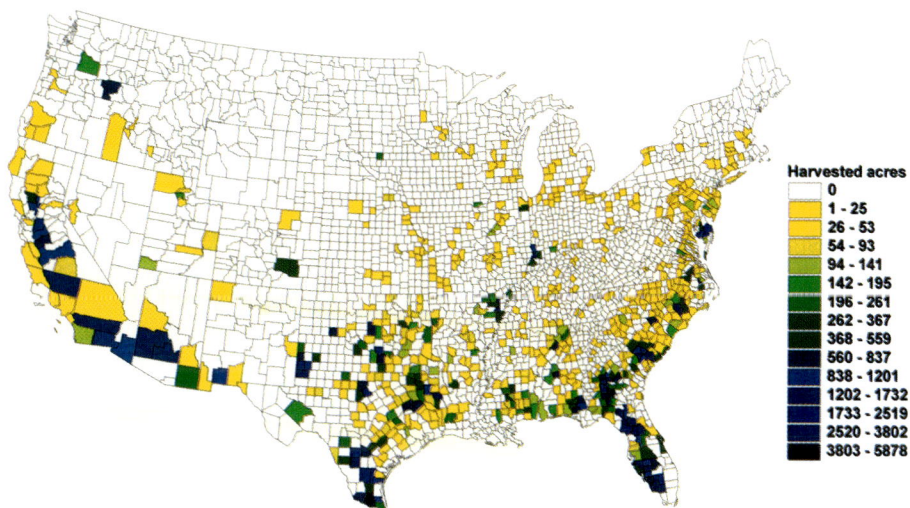

Figure 1.7. U.S. watermelon harvested acreage by county, 1997. USDA census of agriculture, 1997. (Source: G.J. Holmes and J. A. Thurman, North Carolina State Univ., Raleigh.)

Table 1.4. Per capita watermelon use in the principal producing countries, 1996.

Country	Consumption (lb)
Turkey	138
Iran	64
Korea Republic	42
Egypt	39
China	38
United States	17
World	17

Source: FAO Web Site www.fao.org.

data for Turkey includes melons other than watermelons which accounts in part for the large use reported there.

In the United States (Fig. 1.8), consumption ranged from 11 lb in 1980 to 17 lb in 1996. In general, consumption declined from 1960–80 and increased from 1980–98. The period of decline in popularity of watermelon was especially unwelcome because most individual produce items and total fresh produce use was increasing during 1960–80. Many factors contributed to these changes in consumption patterns. Most watermelons were sold as whole fruit at a time when family size was decreasing and watermelons had to compete for refrigerator space in the home. Furthermore, watermelons offered for sale were not always of consistent high quality and were not convenient to carry home and prepare for consumption. Product promotion was either lacking or haphazard at best so retailers and consumers were unaware of handling practices and use options.

A slow turnaround in consumer use of watermelons began after 1980 and hopefully will continue. The increased popularity of watermelons has been fueled first by the widespread availability of cut rather that whole fruit and more recently by precut, ready to eat portions. Watermelons are often featured on salad bars, another innovation that gained popularity after 1980. Quality was enhanced and became more consistent with the development and widespread production of varieties of

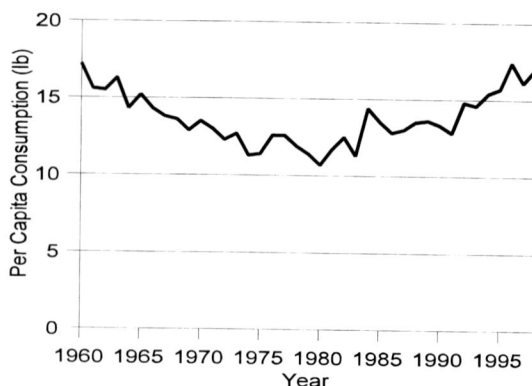

Figure 1.8. United States per capita consumption of watermelon, 1960–98. Source: USDA Economics Research Service.

the Allsweet type with 'Sangria' leading the way. Triploid (seedless) watermelons increased in popularity beginning about 1990 which also provided a tremendous boost to the watermelon industry. Fruit are generally of moderate size, have high sugar content and of course, are devoid of troublesome seeds. Other factors contributing to increased watermelon consumption are emergence of nearly year-round availability and increasing health consciousness among consumers. Last, but certainly not least, the National Watermelon Promotion Board (Orlando, Fla.) was established, with joint funding by growers, first-handlers, and importers to specifically promote the good features about watermelons to retailers and consumers. The general health benefits of all fruits and vegetables have been touted by the Produce for Better Health Foundation which runs the national 5-A-Day for Better Health Program in cooperation with the National Cancer Institute. Thus, no single factor has been responsible for the resurgence of watermelon popularity, but rather several factors have worked in concert to accomplish this feat.

Because of these recent events the watermelon industry is aware of the need to provide consumers with a consistently high quality, convenient

Table 1.5. Approximate nutritional composition of watermelon (Amounts per 3 1/2 oz).

Nutrient	Unit	Fruit	Seed
Water	g	92.80	5.70
Energy	kcal	24.00	567.00
Carbohydrate	g	6.40	15.10
Protein	g	0.50	25.80
Fat	g	0.16	49.70
Fiber	g	0.50	4.00
Ash	g	0.30	3.70
Vitamin A	IU	235.00	---
Vitamin C	mg	6.00	---
Vitamin B$_1$	mg	0.04	0.10
Vitamin B$_2$	mg	0.05	0.12
Niacin	mg	0.20	1.40
Calcium	mg	8.00	53.00
Phosphorus	mg	11.00	---
Potassium	mg	106.00	---
Sodium	mg	2.00	---
Magnesium	mg	10.00	7.40
Iron	mg	0.20	---

Source: Rubatzky and Yamaguchi, 1997.

product and must remain vigilant to insure that consumption remains high in the future. Watermelon consumers were characterized in a 1996 telephone survey of 300 households that was commissioned by the National Watermelon Promotion Board. Some of the important findings of this study were as follows.

• Within the past year 84.7% of the respondents had purchased cantaloupe, 76.0% had purchased watermelon, and 45.3% had purchased honeydew melons.

• There are two kinds of watermelon consumers. Traditional consumers purchase whole watermelon for picnics and special events. New use consumers purchase whole watermelon for special events and also cut melons and fresh cut watermelons in containers for everyday use. They also appreciate the convenience of icebox and seedless watermelons.

• Consumers are interested in watermelons for their nutritional value and as a healthy alternative to manufactured snack foods for their children.

• Fresh cut and whole watermelons do not compete for sales since they are bought for different reasons. Fresh cut watermelon is purchased by small families whereas whole watermelon are bought by large families or for special events.

• Consumers want reliable information on selection of a quality watermelon since many are uncertain of what criteria are important.

In a 1997 study of 99,501 households, watermelons were purchased by 25% of the sampled households in the last month and by 62% of the households in the last 12 months. Results of this type are useful in targeting promotion funds to further enhance the watermelon industry.

NUTRITIONAL COMPOSITION

Watermelon fruit are a dessert food so they are usually consumed with little thought about their nutritional contribution to the diet. Quality in watermelon fruit usually is not associated with nutritional composition, but with the visual impact of dark-red or intense-yellow flesh, the physical texture of the flesh that imparts crispness and an absence of fibers, the refreshing juiciness, and flavor largely determined by total soluble solids. In triploid watermelon fruit, the absence of hard and large rudimentary seeds is also an important quality component. Also, roasted watermelon seeds are consumed as a snack food in some cultures.

Traditional nutritional composition data (Table 1.5) indicate that the most striking feature of watermelon fruit is that it is about 93% water. Some nutritional value is provided in watermelon fruit, but not very much. Watermelon seeds are good sources of carbohydrate, protein, and fat, however, consumption as snack food suggests that the total nutritional contribution is small.

Watermelon may be sold as U.S. Fancy, U.S. No. 1, or U.S. No. 2 largely according to external appearance as outlined in the U.S. Standards for Grades of Watermelon. In practice, watermelons are rarely graded to these standards, but many, if not all, of the criteria are included in the decision to market or to cull the fruit. The strength of the market determines the absolute quality necessary to market watermelons. Accordingly, quality may be somewhat lower on a strong market than on a weak market. In other words, the market is more charitable towards mediocre watermelons when they are in short supply. This system tends to provide a temporary reward but in the long run may have a detrimental effect on consumption. The ideal situation is to ship only watermelons of the highest quality. Practically, this is difficult to achieve.

Sweetness, one of the prime quality factors in watermelon fruit is related to total soluble solids (TSS), as measured by °Brix with a refractometer. The U.S. Standards for Grades of Watermelons indicates watermelons may be labeled as having good internal quality with 8% TSS as determined in a random sample by an approved refractometer. Likewise, fruit may be labeled as having very good internal quality with TSS of 10% or greater. Having personally sampled thousands of watermelon fruit, it is my contention that fruit with 8% TSS are in fact not very good and those with 10% TSS are barely enjoyable. Most people would thoroughly enjoy fruit with 11%–12% TSS.

TSS is a measure of the concentration of the reducing sugars fructose and glucose and the nonreducing sugar sucrose. The relative concentration of these sugars is influenced by variety and stage of maturity. Glucose and fructose concentrations generally increase up to 24 days after pollination (DAP) and decline thereafter. Sucrose is first detectable at 20 DAP and increases thereafter. The relative concentration of these sugars is important since they vary in perceived sweetness with sucrose having a value at 1.0, glucose 0.60–0.75, and fructose 1.40–1.75. Accordingly, varieties or maturity resulting in high fructose concentrations is a desirable feature.

Until recently, the pigment lycopene was thought to be important only as it contributed to flesh color. Watermelon flesh has an average of 4100 µg/ 100 g (range 2300–7200) lycopene compared to 3100 µg/100 g (range 879–4900) in raw tomato, 3362 µg/100 g in pink grapefruit, and 5400 µg/ 100 g (range 5340–5500) in raw guava. Processed tomato products have two or three times greater lycopene concentrations than raw tomatoes because of water depletion in those products. Lycopene is one of the major carotenoids in Western diets and accounts for about 50% of the carotenoids in human serum. Among the common dietary carotenoids lycopene has the highest singlet oxygen quenching capacity in vitro. Other outstanding features are its high concentrations in testes, adrenal gland, and prostate. In contrast to other carotenoids its serum values are not regularly reduced by smoking or alcohol consumption, but is reduced by increasing age. Remarkable inverse relationships between lycopene intake or serum values have been observed in particular for cancers of the prostate, pancreas, and to a certain extent of the stomach. In some studies, lycopene was the only carotenoid associated with risk reduction. Accordingly, although watermelon consumption may help reduce risk of certain cancers, tomato has a larger role in risk reduction because of greater per capita consumption, 165 lb, compared to 17 lb for watermelons. Watermelon not only tastes good but is good for you, a combination hard to beat.

General References

Allred, A.J. and G. Lucier. 1990. The U.S. watermelon industry. Commodity Econ. Div., Econ. Res. Serv., U.S. Dept. Agr. Staff Rpt. AGES 9015.

Clinton, S.K. and E. Giovannucci. 1998. Diet, nutrition, and prostate cancer. Annu. Rev. Nutr. 18:413–440.

Elmstrom, G.W. and P.L. Davis. 1981. Sugars in developing and mature fruits of several watermelon cultivars. J. Amer. Soc. Hort. Sci. 106:330–333.

Food and Agricultural Organization. 1998. F.A.O. production yearbook. vol. 51. Food Agr. Org. United Nations, Rome.

Lucier, G. 1998. U.S. watermelon industry. http://usda.mannlib.cornell.edu.

Maynard, D. and D.N. Maynard. 2000. Cucumber, melon, watermelon, p. 298–313. In: Kenneth F. Kiple and Kriemhild Conee Ornelas (eds.). The Cambridge world history of food. vol. 1. Cambridge Univ. Press. New York.

Mohr, H.C. 1986. Watermelon breeding, p. 37–66. In M.J. Bassett (ed.). Breeding vegetable crops. AVI Publ. Co., Westport, Conn.

Robinson, R.W. and D.S. Decker-Walters. 1997. Cucurbits. Crop production science in horticulture 6. CAB Intl., New York.

Rubatzky, V.R. and M. Yamaguchi. 1997. World vegetables. Principles, production, and nutritive values. 2nd ed. Chapman & Hall, New York.

U.S. Department of Agriculture. 1978. United States standards for grades of watermelon. Agr. Mktg. Serv., U.S. Dept. Agr., Wash., D.C.

U.S. Department of Agriculture. 1999. Vegetables, 1998 summary. U.S. Dept. Agr. Vg 1–2, Wash., D.C.

Whitaker, T.W. and G.N. Davis. 1962. Cucurbits: Botany, cultivation, and utilization. Interscience Publ., New York.

CHAPTER 2

ORIGIN, DISTRIBUTION, AND USES

V.E. Rubatzky

Watermelon, like most common cultivated plants, has a long and interesting history from wild types to today's sweet and succulent fruits. As watermelons were disseminated along trade or emigration routes, they were readily accepted because of their distinctive appearance, refreshing qualities, crisp texture and delicious taste.

ORIGIN

Considerable evidence suggests that the watermelon is indigenous to the drier open areas of tropical and subtropical Africa. Early explorers in central Africa, such as David Livingstone, in 1857 reported finding wild watermelon vines covering large areas, especially in years with unusually heavy rains. Both sweet and bitter forms were found growing together in the wild which were consumed by humans and animals. South Central Africa near the Kalahari desert is a region where wild forms are still found (Fig. 2.1), some of which do not have bitter fruit. It is logically presumed that the inedible bitter fruit achieved reproduction mostly in situ whereas animals and humans were responsible for a greater and wider dispersal of seeds from sweet fruit. Whereas evidence is strong that India was a secondary center of diversification, the view that India was the center of origin is not supported.

Watermelons were originally domesticated in central and southern Africa where they are an important part of African agriculture

Figure 2.1. Watermelon fruit are scattered over the landscape in rural Botswana. (Source: D.N. Maynard, from video International Watermelon Summit'94 in Daiei.)

Figure 2.2. A woman places watermelon fruit slices on branches to dry. The dried fruit will be later ground to make a coarse flour. (Source: D.N. Maynard, from video International Watermelon Summit'94 in Daiei.)

(Fig. 2.2) adapted to savanna zones as not only a food plant, but also as a vital source of water in arid regions. They have been referred to as botanical canteens.

One theory of origin proposes that watermelon was derived from a perennial relative, *Citrullus colocynthis* which is endemic to Africa and can hybridize with watermelon. Colocynth seeds have been found in early archaeological sites preceding the finding of watermelon remnants. Interestingly, *C. colocynthis* is reported to also grow wild in India.

Another theory is that watermelon was domesticated in Africa from putative wild forms of *Citrullus lanatus*. Wild populations of *C. lanatus* var. *citroides*, which are common in central Africa, are suggested to have given rise to the domesticated var. *lanatus*. A related species, *Citrullus lanatus* var. *citroides*, known as citron appears to have a similar origin. However, some botanists regard citrons as varieties of watermelon and not progenitors.

Large variation occurs within *Citrullus lanatus* (Fig. 2.3), ranging from small, hard, bitter, and inedible fruit to the large, succulent, sweet fruits that make watermelon popular throughout the world. Obviously varieties grown today have little resemblance to ancient African forms.

DISTRIBUTION

The watermelon was known to the ancient Egyptians and based on archeological evidence such as wall paintings,

Figure 2.3. Variation among feral watermelon fruit in Botswana. (Source: D.N. Maynard, from video International Watermelon Summit'94 in Daiei.)

Figure 2.4. Roasted 'Malali' watermelon seeds are a popular snack food in Israel. (Source: D.N. Maynard.)

seeds, and plant remnants found in Egyptian tombs appears to have been cultivated in the Nile valley before 2000 BC. It is also very likely that watermelons were widely grown in prehistoric times by agricultural people of sub-Saharan Africa resulting in the development of many landraces varying in fruit size, shape, and color of seeds, flesh, and rinds.

Watermelons were cultivated for centuries by peoples bordering the Mediterranean Basin. The Berbers of North Africa, early Egyptians, and Spanish all have names for the plant which attests that watermelons were long known in these cultures. The Sanskrit name testifies to its early introduction into the Asian subcontinent. From Africa, watermelons were introduced to India about 800 AD, and China about 1100 AD. From India and China, cultivation spread to Southeast Asia in the 15th century, and reached Japan in the 16th century.

The Moors introduced watermelon to Europe during their conquest of Spain. Cultivation spread into other parts of Europe, although slowly due to a less favorable growing climate. Nevertheless, watermelons were mentioned in European herbal writings in the 1500s, and by 1625 were widely planted as a minor crop in European gardens. The first recorded appearance of watermelon in England dates to 1597.

The watermelon was transported and introduced to the Americas in post-Columbian times by the early European colonists and with the importation of African slaves. Spanish colonists were growing watermelons in Florida by 1576, and before 1600 in Panama, Colombia, and Peru. By the middle 1600s, watermelons were commonly grown in Latin America, Brazil, and in British and Dutch colonies of the New World. Watermelons were reported to be grown in the Massachusetts colony as early as 1629. Watermelon was readily accepted and disseminated by native Americans, especially in the Mississippi Valley and the southwestern United States.

In the cultural history of the United States, Thomas Jefferson was an enthusiastic grower of watermelons at Monticello as first noted in his Garden

Book in 1774. Henry David Thoreau proudly grew large and juicy watermelons in Concord, Mass., and Mark Twain wrote in *Puddn'head Wilson* that: "the true southern watermelon is a boon apart and not to be mentioned with commoner things. It is chief of this world's luxuries, king by the grace of God over all the fruits of the earth. When one has tasted it, he knows what the angels eat." Watermelons have an important role in American popular culture in numerous areas including folk art, literature, advertising, and merchandising. There are many annual summer watermelon festivals throughout the country with parades, watermelon-eating contests, seed spitting contests, watermelon queens, sports events, and plenty of food and music.

Growing and exhibiting large watermelons is an active pastime in some rural areas of southern United States. Closely guarded family secrets for producing large watermelons and seeds from previous large fruit are carefully maintained. According to The Guinness Book of Records, the largest recorded watermelon in the United States was grown by B. Carson of Arrington, Tenn., in 1990 and weighed a phenomenal 262 lb. The Guinness seed spitting record is 75 ft, 2 inches, established in 1975 by Jason Schayot in DeLeon, Texas.

USES

Watermelons are grown for their fleshy, juicy, and sweet fruit. Mostly eaten fresh, they provide a delicious and refreshing dessert especially in hot weather. Esthetically the fruit can present a bright color to meal preparations. Occasionally immature fruit are used like summer squash, a fairly popular practice in parts of Africa. Some watermelons are used for feeding livestock.

In some situations the fruit can serve as a source of potable water, especially in drought areas or where drinking water is contaminated. The juice can be extracted, boiled down to a heavy sweet syrup, and also fermented to produce a beer-like alcoholic beverage.

All parts of the fruit are edible. The rind is pickled, typically in a sweet brine or candied, but also in a sour preparation. The rind can be used as a condiment or finely chopped and added for texture, bulk and moisture retention to fruit cakes or muffins. However, citron often is preferred because of its stronger flavor and firmer texture.

In China and many Asian countries, large-seeded varieties are grown expressly for their oil and protein rich seeds. Commercial production of black watermelon seed has been ongoing in northwestern China for more than 200 years. The seeds are eaten after drying or roasting primarily as a popular snack food. It has been noted that many Chinese adults have grooves in their incisor teeth from opening watermelon seeds since childhood. Furthermore, it has been suggested that examination of skulls may provide clues to the antiquity of watermelon in China, and to the time when consumption of seeds became popular. The two most common types of edible-seed watermelons produce large black seeds or red seeds. The black seed types have a black edge and white center while the red seed varieties are completely red, and are narrower than black seed. Seeds occur in other colors, i.e., green, white, and some have multiple colors, as well as different sizes.

In Israel, the local variety 'Malali' has been used for seed consumption because of its large white seeds which are popular with consumers (Fig. 2.4) Consumer preference is given to the largest, widest, and thickest seeds.

The flesh of most watermelons grown for their edible seed is poor with soluble solids concentrations about 4%–5%. Some varieties with dual seed and flesh usage have soluble solids in the range of 6%–7%, whereas high quality dessert fruit achieve sugar content of 10%–12%, and some even as high as 16%.

Some use is made of the edible oil expressed from seed for cooking in India and China. In India, dried seeds are ground into powder and baked like bread. Ground seeds are used for porridge in south tropical Africa, and in west Africa roasted seeds are used as a coffee substitute.

During its domestication and long history of cultivation, the watermelon has acquired diverse medicinal uses in both Old and New World cultures. It has been implied that cucurbitacins, the principle compound responsible for the bitter taste of the fruit may have curative properties for kidney and urethral problems. For example, the flesh is used as a diuretic, and juice as well as leaf extracts are used as a tonic for various kinds of discomfort. Dried ground seeds boiled or steeped in water were used for urinary discomfort. Native Americans used preparations made from seeds for treatment of urinary problems. A leaf extraction is used as antimalarial medication in Mexico.

Quality can be ascertained in the field or in the market by plugging, the practice of making a small triangular or round hole to sample the flesh. A triangular cut is easier to make than a circular opening. After sampling, the fruit is either harvested or left on the vine if not ripe or bitter. This practice possibly developed to avoid discovery of bitter fruit after carrying the bulky and heavy watermelon home. Sometimes, plugging is necessary in direct marketing situations to demonstrate quality to prospective buyers. Replacement of the plug does not avoid contamination and secondary disease organisms soon infect and cause fruit decay.

Bright red or yellow flesh color offers consumers the initial perception that the watermelon is sweet, but this is not always true. Ultimately, a combination of sweetness, texture and color contribute to watermelon quality.

There is little agreement about fruit shape preferences, and regional differences are common and unexplainable. Size preferences are more easily understood and generally are influenced by consumption habits and intended usage. Family size and frequency of consumption generally determines which fruit size is preferred. The market presentation of cut pieces of watermelon is now very common and this has made the consumption of large fruit more feasible.

Major fruit forms are long cylindrical and round, although many varieties are intermediates of these forms. For maximum edible use, the shape of a long fruit should be a cylinder with blocky, well filled ends. For a round melon a slight flatten surface at the stem and blossom end is preferred.

Most consumers prefer seedless fruit, especially since recently introduced varieties are of excellent quality. Rapid acceptance of seedless fruit may be restricted by the higher cost of seedless relative to seeded fruit. Nonetheless, the demand for seedless fruit is on the increase.

General References

Ficklen, Ellen. 1984. Watermelon. Amer. Folklore Ctr., Library of Congr., Wash., D.C.

Harlen, J.R. 1992. Crops and man, 2nd ed. Amer. Soc. Agron.–Crop Sci. Soc. Amer., Madison, Wis.

Harlen, J.R., J.M.J. DeWet, and A.B.L. Steinler. 1976. Origins of African plant domestication. Mouton Publishers, The Hague.

Hedrick, U.P. (ed.). 1919. Sturtevant's notes on edible plants. Rpt. N.Y. Agr. Expt. Sta. 1919.

Maynard, D. and D.N. Maynard. 2000. Cucumber, melon, watermelon, p. 298–313. In: K.F. Kiple and K. Conee Ornelas (eds.). The Cambridge world history of food. vol. 1. Cambridge Univ. Press. New York.

Nerson, H., Y. Burger, and R. Berdugo. 1994. High plant density and irrigation increase watermelon yield grown for seed consumption. Adv. Hort. Sci. 8:101–105.

Robinson, R.W., and D.S. Decker-Walters. 1997. Cucurbits. Crop Prod. Sci. Hort. 6. CAB Intl., Wallingford, United Kingdom.

Rubatzky, V.E., and M. Yamaguchi. 2nd ed. 1997. World vegetables—Principles, production, and nutritive values. Chapman & Hall, New York.

Sauer, J.D. 1993. Historical geography of crop plants: A select roster. CRC Press, Boca Raton, Fla.

Valder, P. 1999. The garden plants of China. Timber Press, Portland, Ore.

Whitaker, T.W. and G.N. Davis. 1962. Cucurbits—Botany, cultivation, and utilization. Interscience Publ., New York.

Zhang, J. 1996. Breeding and production of watermelon for edible seed in China. Cucurbit Genet. Coop. Rpt. 19:66–67.

CHAPTER 3

BREEDING AND SEED PRODUCTION

T.C. Wehner, N.V. Shetty, and G.W. Elmstrom

Watermelon has been cultivated in Africa and the Middle East for thousands of years and in China since at least 900 AD. Watermelon was brought to the New World in the 1500s. In the United States, watermelon is a major vegetable crop that is grown primarily in the southern states. The major watermelon producing states are Florida, California, Texas, Georgia, and Arizona.

Watermelon has been improved by domestication and formal plant breeding from a late maturing vine with small fruit having hard, white flesh and bland or bitter taste, into an early maturing, more compact plant with large fruit having edible, sweet flesh. In the last century, plant breeders working in public or private programs in the United States and around the world have released varieties having disease resistance, dwarf vines, larger fruit, higher sugar content, higher lycopene content, seedlessness, and new flesh colors, such as dark red, orange, and yellow. Recent advances in the breeding of seedless triploid hybrids have resulted in renewed popularity of watermelons, and per capita consumption has increased 37% since 1980.

BOTANY
Taxonomy

Watermelon (*Citrullus lanatus*) has 22 chromosomes (2n=22, x=11). The genus *Citrullus* belongs to the subtribe Benincasinae. Similar genera in the Cucurbitaceae are *Acanthosicyos* and *Eureiandra*. Other members of the Cucurbitaceae with 22 chromosomes include *Gymnopetalum*, *Lagenaria*, *Momordica*, *Trichosanthes*, and *Melothria*. None appear to be closely related to watermelon. In 1924, four species (*C. lanatus*, *C. colocynthis*, *C. ecirrhosus*, and *C. naudinianus*) were listed based on their distribution in Africa.

The authors are grateful for the assistance of W.R. Henderson, professor emeritus, North Carolina State University, and F. McCuistion, Seminis Seeds, for information on germplasm and pollination methods.

Figure 3.1. Lobed (l) vs. non-lobed (r) leaf. (Source: G.W. Elmstrom.)

In 1930, L.H. Bailey proposed dividing cultivated watermelon *C. vulgaris*, into botanical variety *lanatus* and botanical variety *citroides*. The variety citroides includes the citron or preserving melon, which produces fruit with hard, inedible flesh, and green or tan seeds. The species could be classified based on the cucurbitacin or bitter principle content. One group of closely related species (*C. lanatus*, *C. colocynthis*, and *C. ecirrhosus*) had cucurbitacin E as the bitter substance, while the other group (*C. naudinianus*) had cucurbitacin B and E (and their derivatives). Morphological and cytogenetic studies have revealed that the four species are cross compatible with each other. The maintenance of identity of the different species was attributed to geographical isolation, differences in flowering habit, genetic differences, and structural changes in chromosomes.

The genus *Citrullus* has now been revised to include *C. lanatus* (syn. *C. vulgaris*), *C. ecirrhosus*, *C. colocynthis*, and *C. rehmii*. *Citrullus ecirrhosus* is more closely related to *C. lanatus* than either is to *C. colocynthis*. There are two other closely related species: *Praecitrullus fistulosus* from India and Pakistan, and *Acanthosicyos naudinianus* from southern Africa.

Morphology and physiology

Watermelon is a warm-season crop. It is not chilling resistant and requires a long growing season. Flowering and fruit development are promoted by high light intensity and high temperature. Watermelon is the only economically important cucurbit with pinnatifid (lobed) leaves; all of the other species have whole (nonlobed) leaves. The leaves are pinnately divided into three or four pairs of lobes, except for an entire-leaf (nonlobed) gene mutant controlled by the *nl* (nonlobed) gene (Fig. 3.1). Watermelon growth habit is a trailing vine. The stems are thin, hairy, angular, grooved, and have branched tendrils at each node. The stems are highly branched and up to 30 ft long, although there are dwarf types (*dw-1* and *dw-2* genes) with shorter, less-branched stems. Roots are extensive but shallow, with a taproot and many lateral roots.

Watermelon has small flowers that are less showy than other cucurbits. Flowering begins about 8 weeks after seeding. Flowers of watermelon are staminate (male), perfect (hermaphroditic), or pistillate (female), usually borne in that order on the plant as it grows. Monoecious types are most common, but there are andromonoecious (staminate and perfect) types, mainly the older varieties or accessions collected from the wild. The pistillate flowers have an inferior ovary, and the size and shape of the ovary is correlated with final fruit size and shape. In many varieties, the pistillate or perfect flowers are borne at every seventh node, with staminate flowers at the intervening nodes. The flower ratio of typical watermelon varieties is 7 staminate : 1 pistillate, but the ratio ranges from 4:1 to 15:1.

The fruit of watermelon are round to cylindrical, up to 24 inches long and have a rind 0.4–1.5 inches thick. The edible part of the fruit is the endocarp (placenta). That contrasts with melon (*Cucumis melo*), where the edible part of the fruit is the mesocarp. Fruit as large as 262 lb have been recorded, but usually they weigh 8–35 lb. In Asia, even smaller watermelon fruit in the range of 2–8 lb are popular. Fruit rind varies from thin to thick, and brittle to tough.

Seeds continue to mature as the fruit ripens and the rind lightens in color. Seeds will be easier to extract from the fruit if the fruit is held in storage (in the shade or in the seed processing room) for a few days after removing them from the vine. If seeds are left too long in the fruit they will germinate in situ. There is no dormancy in watermelon seeds, so they can be harvested on one day, cleaned, dried, and planted on the next day. Seeds germinate in 2 days to 2 weeks depending on temperature and moisture conditions. Seeds will not germinate below 60 °F. The optimum germination temperature is 85 to 90 °F, especially for triploid seeds. For germination of triploid hybrid seeds, temperature and moisture are more critical, and it is especially important to avoid excess moisture.

Horticultural types

CITRON. The preserving melon is *C. lanatus* var. *citroides*. Its rind is used to make pickles, and the fruit are fed to livestock. The flesh of the citron is white or green, and may vary from bland to bitter tasting. Citron grows wild in the United States where it causes problems as a weed in crop production areas of the south, especially in Florida, Georgia, and Texas. Watermelon seed production fields should be isolated from weedy areas of citron since plants of these two botanical varieties cross readily.

EGUSI. Egusi melon from Africa is *Citrullus colocynthis*. Egusi is a confectionery type, used for its edible seeds, which are roasted and eaten directly, or ground into flour. The seeds are also used in oil production, with the residue made into protein balls.

STANDARD. Standard varieties are available in many fruit sizes, shapes, and rind patterns (Table 3.1, Fig. 3.2). Fruit size of the edible flesh type can be ice box, small, medium, large, or giant. Fruit size is inherited in polygenic fashion. Fruit shape can be round/oval or blocky/elongate. Rind pattern can be solid dark green, solid medium green, solid light green, gray (speckled light green), wide stripe, medium stripe, or narrow stripe. The stripes can be

Table 3.1. Classification of watermelon varieties by shape and rind pattern.

Shape	Rind pattern		Varieties
Round/Oval	Solid	Light	Ice Cream, King and Queen
		Dark	Black Diamond, Cannonball, Sugar Baby
	Gray	Gray	Mickylee, Minilee, New Hampshire Midget
	Striped	Narrow	Boston (3x), Dixielee, Queen of Hearts (3x), Scarlet Trio (3x), Sugarlee, Tiger Baby
		Medium	AU-Producer, Crimson Sweet, Crimson Trio (3x), Millionaire (3x), Petite Sweet, Super Sweet, Tri-X-313 (3x)
		Wide	---
Blocky/elongate	Solid	Light	---
		Dark	Congo, Picnic, Peacock, Smokeylee
	Gray	Gray	Calhoun Gray, Charlee, Charleston Gray, Fairfax, Prince Charles, Sun shade, Sweet Charlie, Sweet Princess
	Striped	Narrow	Freedom (3x), Georgia Rattlesnake, Jubilation, Jubilee, Jubilee II, Juliett, Klondike Striped Blue Ribbon, Royal Jubilee
		Medium	Lady, Revolution (3x), Royal Sweet, Starbrite, Star Gazer
		Wide	Allsweet, Banner (3x), Calsweet, Dumara, Fiesta, Mardi Gras, Piñata, Royal Flush, Royal Majesty, Sangria, Summer Flavor 800, Sunsugar

Figure 3.2. Watermelon fruit types, showing elongate with medium stripe (left row), blocky with medium stripe (row 2), blocky with narrow stripe (row 3), round with narrow stripe (rows 4 and 5), round with solid dark (rows 6 and 7), round with medium stripe (row 8). (Source: G.W. Elmstrom.)

over a light or medium green background. For example, 'Dixielee' has narrow stripes on a light green background, whereas 'Florida Favorite' has narrow stripes on a medium green background.

HORTICULTURAL TRAITS

VINES. Vine length of watermelon varies from dwarf to long. For example, 'Charleston Gray' and 'Jubilee', large-fruited varieties, have vines up to 30 feet long. Short or medium length vines are well suited to varieties with small or medium sized fruit. For example, 'Sugar Baby', 'New Hampshire Midget', and 'Petite Sweet' are short vined, and 'Crimson Sweet' has intermediate vine length.

Dwarf mutants have been discovered in watermelon. Two genes cause dwarfing when they are in homozygous recessive condition: *dw-1* and *dw-2*. 'Kengarden' has the genotype *dw-1 dw-1*. Another gene mutant (Japanese Dwarf, *dw-2 dw-2*) has increased branching from the crown. Dwarf plants having both sets of genes (*dw-1 dw-1* and *dw-2 dw-2*) have hypocotyls 50% the length of normal vining plants, so can be selected in the seedling stage (Table 3.2).

SEX EXPRESSION. Most modern varieties are monoecious, and that appears to be the preferred type of sex expression for commercial seed production of inbred lines and hybrid varieties. Andromonoecy (*aa*) is recessive to monoecy.

Most varieties have a ratio of 7 staminate : 1 perfect or pistillate flower. There are some varieties with a ratio of 4 staminate : 1 pistillate flower. It may be possible to breed for gynoecious sex expression by selecting for increased proportion of pistillate nodes in a segregating population. There is no advantage to andromonoecious sex expression, since the perfect flowers must be pollinated by bees to set fruit. Thus, they are no more likely to set

Table 3.2. Gene list of morphological characters and disease and insect resistance for watermelons.

Gene	Previous	Character
a	---	Andromonoecious. Recessive to monoecious.
Af	---	*Aulacophora faveicollis* resistance. Resistance to the red pumpkin beetle. Dominant to susceptibility.
Ar-1	B, Gc	Anthracnose resistance to race 1 of *Glomerella cingulata* var. *orbiculare*.
Ar-2[1]	-	Anthracnose resistance to race 2 of *Colletotrichum lagenarium* derived from PI 299379 and PI 189225. Resistance in *Citrullus colocynthis* is due to other dominant factors.
bl	*tl*	Branchless. Meristems for tendrils and branches are ultimately replaced by floral meristems.
C	---	Canary yellow flesh. Dominant to pink; *ii* inhibitory to *CC*, resulting in red flesh. In the absence of *ii*, *CC* is epistatic to *YY*.
d	---	Dotted seedcoat. Black dotted seeds when dominant for *r*, *t*, and *w*.
db	---	Resistance to gummy stem blight caused by *Didymella bryoniae* from PI 189225. Recessive to susceptibility.
dg	---	Delayed green. Cotyledons and young leaves are initially pale green but later develop chlorophyll. First reported to be hypostatic to *I-dg*. More recent evidence (submitted for publication) indicate simple recessiveness.
dw-1	---	Dwarf-1. Short internodes, due to fewer, shorter cells than normal. Allelic to *dw-1^s*.
dw-1^s	---	Short vine. Allelic to dw-1. Vine length intermediate between normal and dwarf. Hypocotyl somewhat longer than normal vine and considerably longer than dwarf. *dw-1^s* recessive to normal.
dw-2	---	Dwarf-2. Short internodes, due to fewer cells.
e	*t*	Explosive rind. Thin, tender rind, bursting when cut.
f	---	Furrowed fruit surface. Recessive to smooth.
Fo-1	---	Dominant gene for resistance to race 1 of *Fusarium oxysporum* f. sp. *niveum*.
For-1	---	Fructose 1,6 diphosphatase-1
Fwr	---	Fruit fly resistance in watermelon. Dominant to susceptibility to *Dacus cucurbitae*.

Table 3.2. Continued.

g	*d*	Light green skin. Light green fruit recessive to dark green (*D*) and striped green (*d^s*)
g^s	*d^s*	Striped green skin. Recessive to dark green but dominant to light green skin.
gf	---	Green flower color.
gms	*ms$_g$*	Glabrous male sterile. Foliage lacking trichomes; male sterile—caused by chromosome desynapsis.
go	*c*	Golden. Yellow color of older leaves and mature fruit.
I-dg	---	Inhibitor of delayed green. Epistatic to *dg*: *dg dg I-dg I-dg* and *dg dg I-dg i-dg* plants are pale green; and *dg dg i-dg i-dg* plants are normal. This gene was not present in more advanced germplasm.
i-C	---	Inhibitor of canary yellow, resulting in red flesh.
ja	---	Juvenile albino. Chlorophyll reduced by short days in seedlings, leaf margins, rind.
l	---	Long seed. Long recessive to medium length of seed; interacts with *s*.
m	---	Mottled skin. Greenish white mottling of fruit skin.
ms	---	Male sterile.
ms^{dw}	---	Male sterile, dwarf
nl	---	Nonlobed leaves. Leaves lack lobing; dominance incomplete.
O	---	Elongate fruit. Incompletely dominant to spherical.
p	---	Pencilled lines on skin. Inconspicuous; recessive to netted fruit.
w	---	White seedcoat. Interacts with *r* and *t*.
Wf	*W*	White flesh. *Wf* is epistatic to the second gene *b* (or *C*?) which conditions yellow (Canary yellow?) and red flesh. *Wf_B_* and *Wf_bb* are white fleshed, *wf wf B_* is yellow fleshed, and *wf wf b b* is red fleshed.
y	*r*	Yellow flesh ('Golden Honey' type). Recessive to *Y* (red flesh).
y^o	---	Orange flesh (from 'Tendersweet Orange Flesh'). Allelic to *y*. *Y* (red flesh) is dominant to *y^o* (orange flesh) and *y* (yellow flesh); *y^o* (orange flesh) is dominant to *y* (yellow flesh).
Yl	---	Yellow leaf (from 'Yellow Skin'). Incompletely dominant to green leaf.

Figure 3.3. Chinese male sterile (l) vs. male fertile (r) flower. (Source: G.W. Elmstrom.)

without bees or to be self-pollinated, than monoecious varieties.

Male sterility is useful for the production of hybrid seeds without the requirement for expensive hand pollination. The glabrous male sterile (*gms*) mutant provides male sterility, but the plants are less vigorous, have poor seed set, and are susceptible to cucumber beetles because they lack hairs. A second male sterile mutant, the Chinese male sterile (*cms*), has been more useful for hybrid production (Fig. 3.3).

Fruit can be set parthenocarpically. Although there are no gene mutants that make plants parthenocarpic, fruit set may be achieved without pollination by applying growth regulators to the plants. Thus, commercial production of seedless watermelon may be possible in areas where bees have been excluded by applying growth regulators at a particular growth stage to diploid pistillate flowers that would otherwise produce seeded fruit.

YIELD. Yield varies among watermelon accessions and current varieties. Growers want high weight per acre of marketable size fruit, with a low percentage of culls. The yield goal expressed by many growers is at least one load (45,000 lb) per acre. Most watermelon breeders are selecting for yield in their programs, but it is not clear whether significant progress has been achieved.

In the production of triploid hybrids, up to one third of the field must be planted to a diploid seeded variety. Therefore, higher yield of seedless watermelon per acre could be obtained by using a more efficient pollenizer that would allow more than two thirds of the field to be planted to the triploid variety. Alternatively, parthenocarpic fruit set (genetic or hormone-induced) to stimulate fruit set would permit the entire field to be planted to the triploid variety.

EARLINESS. Early maturity is desirable because prices for watermelon usually are best at the beginning of the local season. However, late maturity is associated with varieties that have large fruit size and high yield. Thus, it may be necessary to sacrifice some earliness to obtain high yield or large fruit.

Time from pollination to fruit harvest ranges from 26 days for early maturing, small-fruited varieties such as 'Petite Sweet' to 45 days for large-fruited varieties such as 'Super Sweet'.

The selection process for early maturity should involve both days from seeding or transplanting to first fruit set, and days from first fruit set to fruit harvest. Days to fruit harvest should be based on fruit having fully developed sugars as verified by a hand-held refractometer or by taste evaluation.

FRUIT SIZE, SHAPE, AND RIND PATTERN. Fruit size is an important consideration in a breeding program since there are different market requirements for particular groups of shippers and consumers. The general categories are: icebox (<12 lb), small, sometimes called pee-wee (12–18 lb), medium (18–24 lb), large (24–32 lb), and giant (>32 lb). Fruit size is inherited in polygenic fashion, with an estimated 25 genes involved. Shippers in the United States work with particular weight categories, such as 18–24 lb for seeded and 14–18 lb for seedless.

Old varieties tend to have larger fruit size than current varieties, because one of the things growers were interested in was winning competitions for fruit weight. Competitions are still being held to grow the largest fruit, but commercial production concentrates on high quality. Another reason for larger fruit in the past is that they are more efficient for hand harvest and shipping; large fruit handled individually permit more weight to be moved per unit. Also, there was demand for large fruit to be sold or served by the slice for restaurants and cafeterias. Today, most supermarkets request fruit that weigh 18–24 lb.

Small- or medium-fruited types were the result of adapting watermelon to the northern areas of the United States. Varieties developed for the northern United States were bred from early maturing Asian varieties brought from Japan and Russia. A.F. Yeager produced the early varieties 'White Mountain' and 'New Hampshire Midget' from sources, which have 2–4 lb fruit with a 65-day maturity. The early variety 'Petite Sweet' has 5–10 lb fruit.

Even though icebox varieties with 4–11 lb fruit have been developed to fit easily in a small refrigerator, most of the demand in the marketplace for small fruit has been met using sections cut from a large fruit. A large watermelon fruit cut into quarters has the same weight as an icebox melon, but it has a different shape, and consumers can see what they are buying. 'Sugar Baby', a small-fruited variety popular in some parts of the world, was selected in Oklahoma by M. Hardin in 1956.

Fruit shape is also an important part of market type. The general categories are round, oval, blocky, or elongate. There is one gene involved in round vs. elongate, with the F_1 being intermediate (blocky). In some cases, fruit shape is related to cotyledon shape at the seedling stage. Plants with elongate fruit have elongate cotyledons, and plants with round fruit have round cotyledons. However, others have concluded that selection for fruit shape at the seedling stage is ineffective. Among old varieties with elongate-shaped fruit, there was greater susceptibility to production of gourd-neck or bottle-neck fruit, which are culls. Old varieties with round fruit were more susceptible to hollowheart. Thus, some of the first hybrids were made between elongate and round inbreds to reduce the incidence of these defects. Recently, genetic resistance to those defects has been incorporated into new varieties, and has made fruit shape less important to consider.

The third area of importance in market type is rind pattern, which can be gray, striped, or solid. Stripes on the rind can be narrow, medium, or wide where the stripes are the dark green areas. The striped pattern can be on light green or medium green background. Solid rind color can be light or dark green. Solid dark green is dominant to gray rind pattern. Solid dark green is dominant to striped, and striped is dominant to solid light green rind pattern. However, the striped pattern can be seen on a solid dark green fruit after the color has been bleached by the sun.

In addition to the common rind patterns, there is furrowed vs. smooth rind, controlled by the recessive gene, f (Table 3.2). Most current varieties have smooth rind. Another interesting mutant is golden rind, which is controlled by the recessive gene, *go*. Its usefulness as an indicator of fruit ripeness is limited because the change in fruit color at fruit maturity is accompanied by chlorosis of the leaves. Furthermore, it does not appear to be a reliable indicator of ripeness, and may be disadvantageous for yield, especially if the grower is using a multiple harvest system.

We propose that watermelon varieties be categorized by fruit size, shape, and rind pattern as follows: Fruit size = icebox (<12 lb), small (12–18 lb), medium (18–24 lb), large (24–32 lb), or giant (>32 lb). Fruit shape = round, oval, blocky, or elongate. Rind pattern = gray, solid light, solid medium, solid dark, or narrow, medium, or wide striped on a light green or medium green background (Table 3.1, Fig. 3.2). Using these categories, we would classify 'Allsweet' as large, elongate, with wide stripes on a light green background. 'Crimson Sweet' would be classified as medium size, round, with medium stripes on a light green background. 'Charleston Gray' would be large, elongate, with gray rind.

EXTERNAL FRUIT QUALITY. Rind durability is important on varieties that are to be shipped to market. On large-fruited varieties, the rind should be thick and tough; whereas on small-fruited varieties, the rind should be thin and tough. Rind thickness should be a small percentage of flesh diameters to keep it in a balanced proportion for best appearance. Large-fruited varieties look better with a thicker rind, and need the extra protection for postharvest handling and shipping. The rind can be tough and hard as in 'Peacock' or tough and soft as in 'Calhoun Gray'. Brittle rind as in 'New Hampshire Midget' is not useful for varieties that are to be shipped to market.

Rind flexibility can be tested by cutting a 1/16 to 1/8 inch × 3 inch piece of rind from a fruit and bending the rind into an arc. If the rind bends into a tight arc, it is flexible and tough. If it breaks early in the attempt, it is tender and explosive.

Rind toughness can be measured by driving a spring-loaded punch into the rind. A tough rind would require more force to punch through, whereas a tender or brittle rind requires less force. Watermelon breeders often use faster methods to test for rind toughness, however. One method is to drop the fruit onto the ground from a particular height (for example, knee height) to see whether it breaks open or not. The drop height would depend on the soil type of the field being used. Another method is the thumb test, where the breeder presses on the rind at a particular location on each fruit. If the rind breaks when only a small amount of force is applied, then it has a tender rind; otherwise it should be resistant to shipping damage.

INTERNAL FRUIT QUALITY. Flesh color is one of the primary traits consumers look for in a watermelon fruit. Color can be dark red, light red, orange, canary yellow, salmon yellow (golden), or white. Light red (YY) is dominant to orange ($y^o y^o$), which is dominant to salmon yellow (yy). Canary yellow (CC) is dominant to noncanary yellow (cc), and epistatic to (overcomes) the y locus for red-orange-salmon yellow. Light red is recessive to the white flesh color, which is found in citron (Table 3.2). Dark red color from 'Peacock' has been used to develop many new varieties because of its attractive color. However, the inheritance of the dark red flesh color is unknown. Varieties with dark red flesh include 'Dixielee', 'AU-Sweet Scarlet', 'Red-N-Sweet', and 'Sangria'.

Sugar content is a major component of flavor. Breeders select for high sugar content as indicated by taste and refractometer readings. Refractometer readings are easily made in the field using a handheld unit, and provide data on percentage of soluble solids (°Brix). These translate to sugar content, which should be a minimum of 10%. Newer varieties have Brix as high as 14%. Some varieties have higher levels of fructose, which tastes sweeter than sucrose. The difference in taste is not measured by a refractometer.

Selection should be made for good watermelon flavor, independent of sweetness (sugar content). Flavor should include freedom from bitterness, which is controlled by a single dominant gene, and may be introduced in crosses with *C. colocynthis* accessions. Another component is caramel flavor as in 'Sugar Baby' fruit, which some taste testers find unpleasant. The flavor is sometimes associated with dark red flesh color. Its inheritance is not known, but caramel flavor does respond to selection. Thus, breeders should select lines with mild (not bitter) taste, high sugar content (°Brix), freedom from caramel flavor, and excellent watermelon taste. It is important that varieties with excellent taste be included as checks in all selection blocks to provide a comparison for the plant breeder. Examples of varieties with good quality that are commonly used include 'Allsweet', 'Crimson Sweet', and 'Sweet Princess'.

Flesh texture is an important part of internal quality. Watermelon fruit can have flesh that is soft or firm, and fibrous or nonfibrous. The objectives for plant breeders should be to develop varieties with flesh that is firm and nonfibrous. The genes controlling those traits are not known, but they are heritable.

SEEDS AND SEEDLESSNESS. Seed color can be white, tan, brown, black, red, green, or mottled. White seed color usually is not preferred since it suggests that the fruit is immature, and can make it difficult to distinguish mature from immature seeds. On the other hand, white seeds may be a useful objective for the development of near-seedless varieties that have few, small, and inconspicuous seeds. Black seed color is attractive with red or canary yellow flesh color. Black, brown, or tan seeds look good with orange flesh color.

Seed size should be large for confectionery (edible seeded) type, and small or medium sized for the standard (edible flesh) type (Fig. 3.4). A new seed size mutant discovered recently is called tomato seed. The seed size is about half that of the small watermelon seed size, and is controlled by a single recessive gene, *tss*.

Seed number should be high for the confectionery type, but should be low or medium for the edible flesh type. Seed number should be lower in small-fruited varieties so that the seeds will not appear to include more than the usual percentage of the fruit volume. Seed number should be high enough to make seed production economical, but low enough to make the flesh easy to eat.

In theory, seedless triploid hybrids should provide higher yield than diploid hybrids because no energy is used in seed production. However, in practice this may not be the case. Fruit production in triploids is limited by the availability of viable pollen to induce fruit set.

During the development of tetraploid inbreds, seed yield is often low in early generations, so selection for fertility is essential. Some tetraploids are

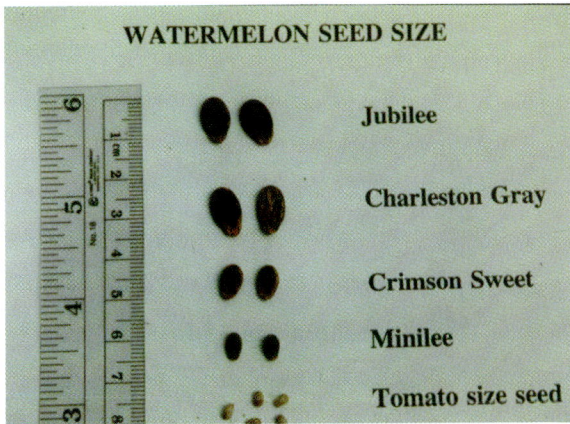

Figure 3.4. Watermelon seed sizes (top to bottom) showing large, large (different variety), medium, small, and tomato seed. (Source: G.W. Elmstrom.)

more fertile than others, and should be selected to keep seed costs low for triploid hybrid production, since the hybrid seeds are produced on the tetraploid parent line.

Triploid hybrids are generally seedless, but occasionally hard seedcoats form in the fruit. The presence of objectionable seedcoats is affected by environment, but can also be selected against in the development of the inbred parents of the hybrid. Inbred parents that do not develop objectionable seedcoats in the fruit in different production environments should be selected for triploid hybrids.

DISEASE, INSECT, AND STRESS RESISTANCE
Disease

SEEDLING TESTS. Disease resistance is an important objective of most breeding programs. Screening for resistance to several important diseases using greenhouse seedling tests is useful, and provides several advantages. Plants that are found to be resistant to the diseases being tested can be transplanted from the test flats to soil or other growth medium in bags or pots where they can be grown and self-pollinated, or crossed with other lines. Greenhouse tests can be run at a time when plants cannot be grown outside, permitting more generations of testing each year, and the disease testing greenhouses can be isolated from other watermelon research to keep the diseases from spreading. At North Carolina State University, gummy stem blight tests are isolated in one area, and virus tests in another area so that the diseases do not spread to a third area where the other breeding work is located.

For some diseases such as anthracnose, it is useful to have a humidity chamber to incubate the disease after inoculation. A humidity chamber can be built on a greenhouse bench using one humidifier for each 24 ft² of bench area. An air conditioner can be used to keep the temperature cool, since some diseases do best in cool and humid conditions. The greenhouse temperature is usually kept between 75° and 95°F for optimum plant growth, and the humidity chamber is usually kept between 65° and 75°F for optimum disease development. A less expensive option for disease chambers is to build a frame on a greenhouse bench and cover it with polyethylene film on the top and sides. Humidifiers placed inside the chamber several hours before disease inoculation should be able to raise the relative humidity above 95%.

FUSARIUM WILT. Fusarium wilt is caused by *Fusarium oxysporum* f. sp. *niveum* (see Figs. 7.13, 7.14). The disease was first reported in 1889 in Mississippi, and was widespread throughout the southern parts of the United States by 1900. Three types of pathogen spores are commonly observed: small, colorless, oval, nonseptate microconidia; large, sickle shaped, septate macroconidia; and thick walled circular chlamydospores. There are three races known: 0, 1, and 2. Most current varieties are resistant to race 0, and some also are resistant to race 1. Race 2 was discovered more recently, and occurs mainly in the south central production areas such as Texas and Oklahoma, but it also has been found in Florida.

Race 0 causes wilt in older, susceptible varieties such as 'Florida Giant', 'Black Diamond', and 'Sugar Baby'. Race 1 is more virulent than race 0 and affects more plants within susceptible varieties, but does not affect resistant 'Calhoun Gray'. Race 2 is highly virulent and can affect otherwise resistant varieties such as 'Calhoun Gray', 'Summit', 'Smokylee', and 'Charleston Gray'. Races of fusarium can be identified using differentials. 'Sugar Baby' and 'Black Diamond' are susceptible to all the three races; 'Quetzali', 'Mickylee', 'Charleston Gray', and 'Crimson Sweet' are susceptible to races 1 and 2, while 'Calhoun Gray' is susceptible to only race 2. Resistance to race 2 is available in PI 296341 and PI 271769.

Fusarium wilt race			
0	**1**	**2**	**Variety or accession**
S	S	S	Black Diamond (or Sugar Baby)
R	S	S	Quetzali (or Mickylee)
R	M	S	Charleston Gray (or Crimson Sweet)
R	R	S	Calhoun Gray
R	R	R	PI 296341 (or PI 271769)

Fusarium can survive in soil as a saprophyte. The pathogen is spread locally by moving soil, compost, manure, water, tools, and machinery from one field to another, as well as by humans and animals moving between fields. The pathogen can also persist on infested seeds for more than 2 years.

Fusarium enters plants through root tips and openings in roots where lateral roots emerge. Presence of root-knot nematodes is also thought to increase the incidence of the disease. After penetration, the fungus grows into the xylem where it accumulates materials that plug the xylem and cause wilting. Watermelon is attacked at all growth stages by the pathogen. At the seedling stage there is damping-off, and cotyledon wilt results in slower growth and stunting. The vascular tissue inside wilted stems may be discolored. A white or pink colored fungus growth usually appears on the surface of dead stems in wet weather conditions. The ideal temperature for infection and disease development is 80 °F. However, seedling rot occurs at soil temperatures of 61–65°F, while seedling wilt is severe between 77–82°F. The disease is also promoted by high soil organic matter.

The first fusarium wilt resistant variety 'Conqueror' was released in 1908. It was developed by W.A. Orton of the USDA using a wilt-resistant citron accession crossed with 'Eden'. 'Conqueror' did not have high fruit quality, so was not grown much after its release. However, varieties developed using resistance from 'Conqueror' such as 'Iowa Belle' and 'Iowa King' had improved fruit quality, so were used commercially. More recent varieties such as 'Calhoun Gray', 'Smokylee', and 'Dixielee' have resistance, as well as improved horticultural performance.

Two types of fusarium wilt resistance are known, having different patterns of inheritance. Resistance to race 1 in 'Calhoun Gray' is controlled by a single dominant gene, with some modifier genes, and provides a high level of resistance that is easy to transfer into new breeding lines. There is also a source of resistance to race 1, which is controlled by several recessive genes. That source of resistance has been difficult to fix at a high level in stable, inbred lines. Varieties resistant at high inoculum levels are 'Dixielee' and 'Smokylee'. In wild species, resistance to fusarium has been reported to be polygenic. Resistance to race 2 has been reported in PI 296341, and the selection PI 296341-FR is resistant to all three races of fusarium. Also, PI 271769 was reported to be highly resistant to race 2.

ANTHRACNOSE. Anthracnose caused by *Colletotrichum lagenarium* is an important disease of watermelon in the United States (see Figs. 7.2–7.4). Symptoms caused by this pathogen may occur on leaves, stems, and fruit. Lesions on leaves are irregular shaped, limited by the leaf vein, and brown to black in color. Lesions on the stem are oval shaped and tan colored with a brown margin. Lesions similar to those found on stems and leaves also appear on the fruit. Older fruit show small water-soaked lesions with greasy, yellowish centers that are somewhat elevated.

Seven races of the anthracnose pathogen have been reported. Races 4, 5, and 6 are virulent in watermelon, but races 1 and 3 are most important. Many varieties are resistant to races 1 and 3, and resistance to race 2 will be needed in the near future.

The first source of resistance to anthracnose was identified in an accession, Africa 8, sent to D.V. Layton of the USDA by R.F. Wagner in Umtali, South Africa. Layton developed anthracnose resistant 'Congo', 'Fairfax', and 'Charleston Gray' from that source. Resistance was later found to be inherited as a single dominant gene, *Ar-1*. The gene provides resistance to races 1 and 3, but not to race 2. 'Crimson Sweet' and many other current varieties have that source of resistance. Several genes were found to be responsible for resistance to Race 2.

PI 189225, PI 271775, PI 299379, and PI 271778 have been reported to carry resistance to complex *Colletotrichum* species. Some of the other sources of resistance to anthracnose reported in the literature are PI 203551, PI 270550, PI 326515, PI 271775, PI 271779, and PI 203551. 'R 143' was reported to be resistant to race 2 of the pathogen. PI 512385 had the highest resistance to race 2 of the pathogen from a screening test involving 76 plant introductions.

GUMMY STEM BLIGHT. Watermelon is one of the most susceptible of the cucurbit species to gummy stem blight, caused by *Didymella bryoniae* (see Figs. 7.15–7.17). The disease occurs throughout the southern United States, particularly the southeast. Field and greenhouse tests are available, but the results are variable, and it can be difficult to get reproducible results.

The USDA collection of plant introduction accessions has been screened for gummy stem blight resistance by several teams of researchers. Some accessions have resistance to the disease, including PI 189225 and PI 271778.

POWDERY MILDEW. Watermelon is one of the most resistant cucurbit species to powdery mildew (*Sphaerotheca fuliginea*) (see Figs. 7.20, 7.21). However, there are a few regions of the world where powdery mildew is a problem on watermelon. For example, watermelons grown in southern India are affected with the disease, but not in northern India. In southern India, 'Arka Manik' is resistant to powdery mildew. The *pm* gene causes susceptibility to the disease, but most varieties have the resistance allele. Powdery mildew is becoming more of a problem in the United States, especially in the western states, and has been reported in the southeastern states as well.

YELLOW VINE. Yellow vine is a relatively new disease of watermelon, caused by an unknown, phloem-limited bacterium. Evidence indicates that leafhoppers vector the disease. The disease was first observed in central Texas and Oklahoma in 1991 and has caused severe losses in early-planted watermelon in some years. In 1998, the disease was detected in watermelon and pumpkin in Tennessee. Production areas of Georgia, Florida, and other parts of southeastern United States may be at risk in the future. Low levels of resistance or tolerance have been identified in a few open-pollinated and hybrid varieties, although the mechanism of resistance is unknown. Research is needed to identify good sources of resistance.

BACTERIAL FRUIT BLOTCH. Bacterial fruit blotch of watermelon is a serious disease of seedlings and fruit caused by *Acidovorax avenae* subsp. *citrulli* (see Figs. 7.6–7.9). Disease incidence increases under high humidity or where overhead irrigation is used. The disease was first reported to occur in commercial watermelon production areas in the United States in 1989. Early-season outbreaks can result in total loss of fruit by harvest time. Bacterial fruit blotch is also reported to attack cantaloupe fruit in the field, as well as other cucurbits. Bacterial fruit blotch epidemics during 1994 in certain states in the United States resulted in litigation, and had a devastating effect on the watermelon industry. Currently, most seed companies require growers to sign waiver forms to reduce the possibility of litigation. Some companies have restricted seed sales in certain states where the risk of disease is high. Seed costs have increased due to the changes in the seed handling, packaging and testing required for reducing the incidence of disease.

The characteristic symptoms of bacterial fruit blotch are the appearance of a dark olive green stain, or blotch, on the upper surface of infected fruit. Apart from attacking the fruit, the pathogen is also reported to attack the leaves and seedlings, and can be seed transmitted. D.L. Hopkins and coworkers reported that fermentation of seeds for 24–48 h followed by 1% hydrochloric acid or 1% calcium hypochlorite treatment for 15 min before washing and drying were the most effective treatments for bacterial contaminated watermelon seeds. This treatment is for diploids; triploid seed germination is drastically reduced by fermentation. However, an effective, cost efficient, and environmentally safe method for disease control would be development of resistant varieties.

A seedling test for early screening of watermelon fruit blotch was developed in 1992, and research on a few watermelon lines using this test has been reported. There has been some research to identify genetic resistance in the watermelon germplasm collection. Based on seedling tests, PI 295843 and PI 299378 were reported to be resistant to the pathogen. In 1993, D.L. Hopkins and coworkers conducted a study of 22 varieties and 2 PI accessions for resistance to fruit blotch of watermelon and reported that none were immune to the pathogen. Research is underway to find sources of resistance in the germplasm collection.

Fruit resistance to the pathogen appears to be related to rind color and ploidy, with diploid varieties having light rind color being most susceptible and triploid varieties with dark rind color being less susceptible. Fruit with stripes appeared to be intermediate in their resistance. Detached leaf tests have been developed that are effective in screening plants for resistance in a breeding program.

BACTERIAL RIND NECROSIS. Bacterial rind necrosis is caused by *Erwinia* species. However, some other bacterial species (*Pseudomonas*, *Enterobacter*, and *Bacillus*) are also known to cause similar symptoms. Typical symptoms of bacterial rind necrosis on watermelon fruit are characterized by a light brown, dry, hard area of discoloration interspersed with light areas generally limited to the rind (see Fig 7.5). The disease was first reported in Texas in 1968. The most resistant varieties in studies conducted in Florida over a 3-year period were 'Sweet Princess' and 'Jubilee', while the most susceptible were 'Klondike Blue Ribbon' and 'Louisiana Queen'.

ROOT-KNOT NEMATODES. Watermelon is susceptible to root-knot nematodes caused by *Meloidogyne* sp. (see Figs. 6.1–6.3). The USDA collection of plant introduction accessions is being screened for resistance. Root-knot resistance may be an important future breeding objective if resistant accessions are identified.

VIRUS DISEASES. The main virus problems in watermelon production in the United States are papaya ringspot virus-watermelon strain (PRSV-W, formerly watermelon mosaic virus-1), watermelon mosaic virus-2 (WMV-2) (see Figs. 7.23, 7.24), and zucchini yellow mosaic virus (ZYMV). The watermelon germplasm collection has been screened for resistance to some virus diseases. Accessions reported to be resistant to WMV-2 are PI 244018 and PI 244019. Resistance to ZYMV is found in PI 482299, PI 482261, PI 595203, and PI 255137. Research is in progress to identify sources of resistance to PRSV-W as well. Multiple virus resistance will be an important breeding objective for new varieties in a few years.

OTHER DISEASES. Verticillium wilt is an increasing problem in the western United States, but little is known about sources of resistance. Resistance to alternaria leaf spot (see Fig. 7.1) has been identified in varieties such as 'Sugar Baby', 'Fairfax', and 'Calhoun Gray'.

PHYSIOLOGICAL DISEASES. Many of the watermelon fruit defects have a genetic component. Breeders should select lines to be free of defects under conditions conducive to the problem. Fruit defects include hollowheart (see Fig. 7.25), rind necrosis (see Fig. 7.5), blossom-end rot (see Fig. 7.26), and cross stitch (see Fig. 7.29). Hollowheart is a separation of the tissue within the endocarp caused by rapid fruit growth and weak tissue. More research is needed to identify sources of defect resistance, and environmental conditions that help reduce their frequency.

Insect resistance traits

Little research has been done on insect resistance in watermelon. This may be due to the fact that most insect pests can be controlled with insecticides. The major insect and arachnid (arthropod) pests of watermelon are aphids (see Figs. 8.1–8.3), pickleworm, spider mite (see Fig. 8.14), and spotted, striped (see Figs. 8.12, 8.13), and banded cucumber beetles.

PI 299563 is resistant to melon aphid (*Aphis gossypii*). 'Congo' and 'Giza 1' were the most resistant of five accessions evaluated for resistance to spider mite. Several genes were found to control nonpreference type resistance to spotted cucumber beetle in 'Hawkesbury' x a resistant accession. Resistance to spotted and banded cucumber beetles was due a single recessive gene.

A single dominant gene, *Fwr*, was responsible for resistance to the melon fruit fly (*Dacus cucurbitae*) in the watermelon line JI8-1. 'Afghan' is reported to have resistance to red pumpkin beetle (*Aulacophora foveicollis*), and 'Blue Ribbon' and 'Crimson Sweet' are resistant to pickleworm.

Stress

Little research has been done on stress resistance in watermelon. Water stress is an important cause of reduced yield in watermelon. It may be that some genotypes are more efficient in water use than others, but it probably will be difficult to develop highly efficient varieties since watermelon fruit have very high water content. In Israel, deep-rooted varieties are used in unirrigated desert areas.

Pollination problems are responsible for improper fruit development. It is necessary for all three lobes of the stigma to be fully pollinated if the fruit is to develop fully, and without curvature. Proper fruit development requires adequate numbers of honeybees or bumblebees during flowering, along with weather that is conducive to pollination. Bumblebees can be more effective pollinators than honeybees. Cold, rainy weather leads to poor pollen shed, and hot weather often leads to reduced bee activity. In the case of triploid hybrids, it is necessary to have up to one third of the field planted to a diploid pollenizer to assure adequate fruit development in the triploids which are male sterile.

Growers plant early in the season, often using transplants and plastic mulch (with row covers in some cases) when there is a danger of frost. Cucurbits are susceptible to chilling injury at air temperatures below 42 °F. Chilling injury is a concern in watermelon because of the value of early harvested fruit. There might be chilling resistance in the watermelon germplasm collection that could be incorporated into new varieties as has been done in other cucurbits. Watermelon appears to be more chilling resistant than melon and cucumber. Symptoms of chilling are white areas on the cotyledons and white or light brown margins on the fully expanded leaves.

Chilling injury is increased by a longer duration of chilling, lower temperature, high intensity of light during chilling, high wind speed during chilling, or a higher growth temperature before chilling occurs. Watermelon is thermophilic, meaning that plants have a high optimum growth temperature. Although the optimum is probably 80–90 °F, temperatures above 90 °F reduce growth rate, and can reduce fruit yield. Above 105 °F, plants can be injured, and young leaves will be light green with yellow margins.

Measles is a condition where green-brown spots develop on the fruit surface, covering a small area or even the entire surface, and starting out as minute watersoaked areas. The spots become tan, slightly raised areas with necrotic centers. The symptoms occur when excessive guttation is encouraged by periods of high humidity or during the early fall production season when the humidity is high and the nights are cool. The fruit symptoms become evident 21–25 days after the conducive environmental conditions occur. There is usually no economic loss from the stress, and it might be controlled by reducing the amount of irrigation in the fall production season.

GERMPLASM RESOURCES
Centers of origin

Watermelon is thought to have originated in southern Africa because it is found growing wild throughout the area, and reaches maximum diversity there. It has been cultivated in Africa for over 4,000 years. In 1857, David Livingstone reported watermelon growing profusely in the Kalahari Desert (Namibia and Botswana) after unusually heavy rainfall. The natives there knew of sweet as well as bitter forms growing throughout southern Africa. De Candolle, in 1882, considered the evidence sufficient to prove that watermelon was indigenous to tropical Africa, more specifically the southern parts of Africa.

Citrullus colocynthis is considered to be a wild ancestor of watermelon, and is now found native in north and west Africa. Fruit are small, with a maximum diameter of 3 inches. The flesh is bitter and the seeds are small and brown. Crosses of *C. lanatus* with *C. colocynthis* produced F_1 hybrids with nearly regular meiosis. The pollen was 30%–40% fertile, and 35% of the seeds were fertile.

Although *Citrullus* species grow wild in southern and central Africa, *C. colocynthis* also grows wild in India. India and China may be considered secondary centers of diversity for the genus. Cultivation of watermelon began in ancient Egypt and India, and is thought to have spread from those countries through the Mediterranean area, Near East, and Asia. The crop has been grown in the United States since 1629.

Germplasm is the foundation of breeding programs, so germplasm collection and evaluation are important aspects of breeding. Priorities for collection of *Citrullus* germplasm include India, especially the Indo-Gangetic plains and areas in the northwest parts of the country; Africa including the south and southwest (Kalahari Region); southern areas of the former USSR and Iran; and tropical Africa.

Recent work in germplasm collection and exchange has provided the USDA germplasm system with a total of 51 *Citrullus* accessions that were collected during a scientist exchange visit with the People's Republic of China led by Wehner in 1993. Later, in 1996, a team of four researchers led by Wehner collected germplasm of *Citrullus* in the Republic of South Africa.

Centers of diversity

The primary center of diversity for watermelon is southern Africa, with wild relatives also found in west Africa. The secondary center is China, and related species can be found in India. Areas of the middle east as well as countries near the Mediterranean Sea may also be good places to collect old land races and wild accessions of *Citrullus*.

T.W. Whitaker considered *C. colocynthoides* to be the likely ancestor of watermelon. It is morphologically similar to *C. lanatus*, but with bitter fruit and small seeds. However, the bitter forms of *C. lanatus* were considered the probable ancestor of watermelon by others. That theory was supported based on the fact that they had the same number of chromosomes as *C. lanatus*, were freely intercrossable, and were found in the same areas of Africa and Asia. Citron was considered to be an intermediate stage between the primitive, bitter form of *C. lanatus* and the cultivated form of today.

Germplasm repositories

Several germplasm collections, along with current varieties marketed by seed companies, represent the major sources of germplasm for watermelon breeders interested in the United States market. The USDA collection is stored at the Regional Plant Introduction Station, Griffin, Ga., with the backup collection at the National Seed Storage Laboratory (NSSL), Fort Collins, Colo. There are 1644 accessions in the collection, with about 85% currently available to researchers, and the rest needing to be regenerated to increase seed quantity or germination percentage. The collection includes representatives of all *Citrullus* species and botanical varieties. In addition, about 300 heirloom varieties are kept at NSSL.

The Cucurbit Genetics Cooperative has curators who volunteer to collect and maintain seeds of gene mutants published for many of the cultivated cucurbit species. Some gene mutants are no longer available, but small amounts of seeds of some of the gene mutants can be obtained from the curator for that species, T.C. Wehner.

Additional collections are kept by seed savers and other groups interested in heirloom varieties, and by watermelon breeders around the United States. There are also watermelon germplasm collections in other countries that are being kept for national researchers in those countries.

Important varieties

Watermelon varieties have been described in the vegetable variety lists maintained by the American Society for Horticultural Science. Also, a complete set of descriptions for all vegetable crops from lists 1–25 has been collected into a book to be produced by ASHS Press. Seeds are available for many of the open pollinated and inbred varieties on the list, but there are a significant number of varieties that are no longer available. Watermelon breeders should obtain and evaluate a sample of the varieties available to become familiar with the diversity of germplasm. It is also useful to observe the improvement in horticultural traits that has been made in varieties developed over time.

A breeding program usually is started by intercrossing the best varieties currently available, or by crossing the best varieties with accessions having one or more useful traits missing from the elite varieties. Thus, in the beginning a watermelon breeder will need to obtain seeds of the best varieties, a set of varieties developed at different times in the past, a set of accessions from germplasm repositories, and lines with useful or interesting gene mutants.

A survey of popular varieties in the ten major watermelon-producing states in the United States by D.N. Maynard in 2000 indicated that popular varieties for commercial production were almost all hybrids, with few open-pollinated varieties being used commercially. Popular diploid (seeded) open-pollinated varieties ('Allsweet', 'Black Diamond', 'Calsweet', 'Crimson Sweet', 'Jubilee II', and 'Legacy') were grown mostly in one state each, suggesting regional adaptation or local demand. Hybrids generally were grown in several states, suggesting they have wider adaptation. The 'Allsweet' type, generally considered to be of high quality, was represented by more than half of the listed varieties (three of the open-pollinated and 11 of the hybrids). The most popular diploid (seeded) varieties were 'Sangria' and 'Royal Sweet' (seven states), 'Fiesta' (six states), and 'Mardi Gras' and 'Regency' (five states). For triploid (seedless) varieties, almost half of the varieties were 'Tri-X-313' type. The most popular triploid varieties were 'Tri-X-313' (ten states), 'Summer Sweet 5244' (nine states), 'Millionaire' (eight states), 'Genesis' (five states), and 'Tri-X-Shadow' (four states).

To develop improved varieties for an industry in a particular region of the world, the watermelon breeder will need to have seeds of varieties, breeding lines, populations, plant introduction accessions, and gene mutants that express the traits of interest at a high level. The breeder should identify a source that has the highest level of expression. That would be true whether the trait is quantitatively inherited (fruit yield, earliness, size, sweetness) or qualitatively inherited (dwarfness, anthracnose resistance, flesh color). If there is a choice of accession for a particular trait (for example, white flesh), it is better to use an adapted accession with the best genetic background. Thus, 'Cream of Saskatchewan' would be a better choice to use in the development of white flesh varieties for use in the United States, than a wild-type, white-fleshed citron having large vines, late maturity, hard flesh, bitter flavor, large green seeds, and seed dormancy.

GENETICS
Qualitative traits

The inheritance of watermelon traits has been studied extensively, and single genes have been identified that are of value to plant breeding programs. Examples include *A* for monoecious vs. andromonoecious sex expression, *Ar-1* and *Ar-2* for resistance to anthracnose races 1 and 2, *C* for canary yellow flesh color, *dw-1* and *dw-2* for dwarf vines, *E* for nonexplosive rind, *F* for nonfurrowed fruit surface, *Fo-1* for fusarium wilt resistance, *g^s* for striped green rind pattern, *Go* for nongolden rind at maturity, *M* for nonmottled fruit skin, *O* for elongate rather than oval fruit shape, *Pm* for resistance to powdery mildew, *s* and *l* for short seeds, *y^o* for orange flesh, and *Υ* for red flesh (Table 3.2).

Nonlobed leaves are a mutant expressed beginning in the seedling stage that is controlled by a single recessive gene. The single-gene trait can be useful for indication of hybrid plants. Hybrid seeds can be produced on one inbred line used as the female parent and having nonlobed leaves. If it is pollinated using bee pollination in an isolation block, and the male parent has normal, lobed leaves, then it will be possible to distinguish hybrid from nonhybrid at the seedling stage in the commercial seed lot. The hybrid seeds can then be planted in excess in grower fields and the nonlobed seedlings (produced by self- or sib-pollination) can be removed to leave just hybrid plants. Alternatively, nonhybrid seedlings can be removed from the flats during transplant production.

Inbreeding depression and heterosis

Watermelon is monoecious, and is naturally cross-pollinated like maize. However, there is not as much inbreeding depression or heterosis as one might expect. This is similar to other cucurbits such as cucumber and melon. It has been suggested that the lack of inbreeding depression is due to the small population size used by farmers during the domestication of the species. Watermelon plants are large, so only a few plants probably were grown in each area. Therefore, even with monoecious sex expression and insect-pollinated flowers, there would have been considerable inbreeding among the few plants representing the population. Since there is little inbreeding depression in watermelon, inbred lines are developed using self-pollination with little loss of vigor from the parental population.

In studies of heterosis in watermelon, some estimates have shown a 10% advantage of the hybrid over the high parent, but only for some parental combinations. The small amount of heterosis observed in watermelon hybrids makes hybrids unnecessary for high yielding commercial varieties since inbreds should perform as well. However, hybrid varieties are useful for combining traits inherited in a dominant fashion from the two parents. Examples of such traits include red or canary yellow flesh, resistance to fusarium wilt and anthracnose, and lack of susceptibility to powdery mildew. Hybrids are necessary for protecting proprietary breeding lines from unauthorized use. However, one of the most important uses of hybrids is the production of seedless varieties. The primary method for production of seedless watermelons involves the cross of a tetraploid female parent with a diploid male parent to produce a triploid, which will be sterile, and therefore, seedless. Currently, triploid hybrids are the most practical method for production of seedless watermelons.

BREEDING
Pollination

Watermelon is a cross-pollinated species with monoecious or andro-monoecious flowering habit. There is a popular myth that watermelon should not be grown close to other cucurbits such as cucumber, cantaloupe, or squash because of an adverse effect on horticultural traits such as flavor. However, watermelon will not cross with any other cucurbits except for species within the genus *Citrullus*. Furthermore, there is no effect of foreign pollen on fruit development (xenia) in watermelon.

GREENHOUSE. Controlled pollinations can be made easily in a greenhouse or screenhouse since there is no need to cover individual flowers the previous afternoon to protect them from pollinating insects such as bees. The greenhouse or screenhouse should be well sealed to prevent insects from getting in. In those structures, pollinations should be made in the morning, and plant maintenance work should be left for the afternoon. Computer controlled heating and cooling, and automated irrigation and fertilization make it possible to operate the greenhouse with fewer labor inputs.

Greenhouse plants can be grown in ground beds, plastic bags or pots containing the growth medium, or in various liquid media such as ebb and flow benches or nutrient film technique. If pots or bags are used, different container sizes should be evaluated to obtain the proper plant size. A minimum pot size for proper growth of watermelon plants in our greenhouses in North Carolina is 8 inches in diameter. Plants grown in 10- or 12-inch-diameter pots will have longer vines that are more difficult to train and prune, larger fruit, and more seeds per pollination.

In the greenhouse, plants are usually trained vertically onto supports such as strings held by overhead wires. This saves floor space and makes better use of available light. The overhead wire should be 6.5 ft above the walkway to permit most workers to reach the trellis without standing on a ladder, while being able to walk under it without ducking. Plants should be pruned to one main stem, usually with no branches. Because of their weight, fruit must be supported in a sling. Stem length of most watermelons usually requires that plants be trained up the string to the trellis wire, and back down again. Plants should be given sufficient floor space in the greenhouse to grow and flower. For elite varieties and breeding lines, each plant should have 2 ft² or more. It may be necessary to give wild accessions more space, perhaps 4 ft² per plant or more.

In some latitudes, it may be necessary to provide supplemental lighting for plant growth. We find it difficult to grow plants in Raleigh, N.C., in the winter without extra lighting. However, plants grow well and produce flowers, fruit, and seeds properly when grown in the spring (February through June) and fall (July through November) seasons.

FIELD. Natural pollination of watermelons in the field is usually by honeybees that visit the flower to collect pollen and nectar. Bumblebees also are effective pollinators. Hand pollination of watermelon flowers is usually less effective than bee pollination. It is necessary to protect flowers from bee visits before and after making controlled pollinations. Flowers open shortly after sunrise and remain open for 1 day. Usually a pistillate flower and the staminate flower below it (proximal to it) opens on the same day, making self-pollination possible. Many breeders have found that hand pollination is more effective from 6–9 AM than later in the day.

The two main methods for protecting controlled pollinations from insect pollination in the field are to begin pollinating before bees become active in the morning, or to cover the flowers the previous afternoon. For the first method, pollinations can be made on newly opened flowers (Fig. 3.5),

Figure 3.5. Pollination of pistillate flower (on vine) by staminate flower (in hand). (Source: T.C. Wehner.)

which are then covered to keep bees away. This method requires less time per pollination, but care must be taken to stop pollinating when bees are observed in the field. Staminate and pistillate flowers can be covered with gelatin capsules (size OO), cotton wool, plastics caps, or paper rolled into a cylinder (often, holding a pencil inside as the paper is rolled) and closed at one end by folding. It is also possible to use inverted styrofoam or plastic cups (6–12 oz size) held over the flower (and onto the soil surface) with a J-shaped wire (about 10 gauge thickness) stuck through the cup, or by a wooden stake glued to the cup. Breeders have also made flower covers using mesh or cloth bags (Fig. 3.6), which in some cases are supported by a wire frame that can be stuck into the ground over the flowers to be protected.

The second method requires that flowers predicted to open the next morning be capped the previous afternoon. These flowers will be one or two nodes above the flowers (toward the shoot apex) that are newly opened, and should have some yellow color in the petals. Flowers more than three nodes above the newly opened ones that are completely green will probably not open the next day. Capping of flowers is most useful if done on sunny days, since the pollen does not shed freely after rainy or cloudy days. The following morning, the caps are removed, flowers pollinated, and the caps replaced to keep bees away. This method permits the pollination crew to keep working longer as bees begin to work the field.

Figure 3.6. Protection of pistillate flower from bee pollination with net bag. (Source: G.W. Elmstrom.)

In a large field pollination nursery, workers often prefer to mark the flowers that have been capped in the afternoon with a flag (for example, white), which is then exchanged with a flag of a different color (for example, blue) after the pollination has been made. Thus, it is easy to go to the white flags in the morning to make the pollinations, and to go to the blue flags in the afternoon to check whether the pollinations from previous mornings are developing properly. The setting of one fruit inhibits other fruit on the same plant from setting, so it is useful to remove pistillate flowers that have not been used for controlled pollinations as the pollinating crew moves through the field in the afternoon.

Andromonoecious plants have perfect flowers as well as staminate ones. Unfortunately, perfect flowers will not set fruit without being hand pollinated, or visited by a pollinating insect, so they are no more likely to be self-pollinated than pistillate flowers. After pollinating a pistillate flower, a tag is placed on the peduncle or on the stem just below the peduncle. Placing the tag on the stem causes less damage to the pollinated flower and developing fruit. The tag usually has the plot number of the female and male parents and the date the pollination was made. It can also have the initials of the person making the pollination, and the name of the study involved.

Controlled pollinations are made by removing a recently opened staminate flower from the plant to be used as the male parent. The petals of the staminate flower are bent back until they break. The flower can then be used like a paintbrush to pollinate a recently opened pistillate flower on the plant to be used as the female parent.

A nursery for field pollination should be designed to make it easy to make controlled pollinations, and care for the plants. Direct seeding or transplants can be used. For direct seeding, the seeds should be treated with a registered fungicide before planting. Use of herbicides will significantly reduce the need for hand weeding. For transplants, plastic mulch and drip irrigation will help with weed control. Drip irrigation, or other low-level system (furrow, subirrigation) is superior to overhead irrigation to keep the plants dry, so hand pollinations can be made without having to wait for the watering to be completed, and to avoid having pollination caps washed off the flowers.

Pollinations are made easier by planting the lines to be crossed together in one area. Lines to be self-pollinated can be planted together in a second area. It is useful to plant each pair of lines to be crossed in adjacent rows or tiers.

If it is difficult to make self-pollinations in the field on a particular set of lines (perhaps selections from a trial), one or more cuttings can be taken from each of the plants to be selected. The cuttings can be rooted in moist sand in a greenhouse by burying the bottom (proximal) internode, with two to five nodes of leaves above. The resulting plants can be transplanted from the rooting bench to the greenhouse for trellising and self- or cross-pollination of the selections to produce seeds for the next generation.

Breeding objectives

Major objectives for watermelon breeding include proper fruit type, early maturity, high fruit yield, high sugar content, tough flexible rind, and proper seed type. It is important to determine breeding objectives carefully before starting variety development. For example, seed type changes significantly for different market classes. Parental lines for seedless hybrids should have small seeds, whereas confectionery seed types should have large seeds. For commercial varieties, black seeds are preferred because of their contrast with red, yellow, or orange flesh. Also, white seeds indicate immaturity to buyers, so white mature seed color can be a confusing trait for them. Most of the old varieties are diploid, open-pollinated or inbred lines, but hybrid diploid and hybrid triploid varieties are taking over the commercial market in the United States.

After determining the breeding objectives, methods for measurement of the traits of interest should be developed, selection methods should be determined (specifying the operations to be carried out for each generation), and parents with high expression of the traits of interest should be chosen. Vine type should be long for commercial production and dwarf (bush) for home garden. It may also be possible to use the dwarf plant type for once-over harvest in commercial production. Sex expression should be monoecious, with a ratio of 7 staminate : 1 pistillate flowers, or better (preferably 4:1). Andromonoecious sex expression and ratios of 15:1 are more typical of older varieties.

For production in most areas of the United States, watermelon must have resistance to fusarium wilt. Races 0 and 1 are common, and race 2 is becoming important, especially in Texas and Oklahoma where plastic mulch culture and fumigation are less common. Production areas in the southern United States usually have anthracnose race 1 and may also have problems with race 2. Gummy stem blight is a disease for which resistance is needed in most southern production areas. Powdery mildew is becoming a problem, especially in the western United States (possibly because of a new race), and should be a breeding objective for new varieties. Bacterial fruit blotch was a problem in the 1990s, and resistant accessions have been identified. The disease can be effectively controlled by genetic resistance and by large-scale seed testing followed by destruction of contaminated seed lots. Protection from viruses in the United States production areas should include resistance to papaya ringspot virus-watermelon strain (formerly watermelon mosaic virus-1), watermelon mosaic virus (formerly watermelon mosaic virus-2), and zucchini yellow mosaic virus.

Finally, breeding objectives should emphasize early maturity, high fruit yield, durability for shipping, high internal quality, freedom from internal defects (hollowheart and rind necrosis), and proper seed type in a diploid (seeded) or triploid (seedless) hybrid. Internal quality traits include dark red flesh, high sugar content, proper sugar to acid ratio, excellent flavor, high nutritional value (vitamins and lycopene), firm (not soft) and nonfibrous texture. Seeds should be black color, medium size (or small for inbreds to be made into tetraploids), and few to medium quantity per fruit (few for consumers, but medium to keep seed costs down). Flesh color should be dark red (Y gene with modifier genes) with uniform color throughout the fruit. For specialty types, flesh color could be bright orange (y^o gene), canary yellow (C gene), or white (Wf gene). Other colors such as salmon yellow (y gene) exist (Table 3.2), but are not preferred because the flesh looks overmature. Older varieties have light red flesh, but dark red is becoming the preferred type. Diploid inbreds should be made into tetraploid inbreds and tested for fertility, seed yield, and ability to set fruit using controlled pollination. Tetraploid lines for use in triploid seedless hybrid production can be induced with colchine. Finally, triploid hybrids should be tested for absence of seedcoats in the fruit within a range of production environments.

Variety development

There were no defined varieties of watermelon before the 1820s. Early varieties include 'Black Spanish' (imported to United States from Portugal in 1827), 'Carolina' (available at least since 1827), and 'Imperial', 'Mountain Sprout', 'Seminole', and 'Mountain Sweet' (introduced by southern growers from 1840 to 1850). Other heirloom varieties include 'Bradford', 'Clarendon', 'Odell', 'Ravenscroft', and 'Souter' (originating in South Carolina before 1850). Classic watermelon varieties include 'Peerless' or 'Ice Cream' (1860), 'Phinney Early' (1870), and 'Georgia Rattlesnake' developed by M.W. Johnson in Atlanta, Ga., about 1870.

Planned variety development programs began in the United States in 1880 to 1900. Important varieties developed for the southern United States included 'Cuban Queen' developed and marketed by Burpee in 1881, 'Round Light Icing' (1885), 'Kolb Gem' developed by Reuben Kolb of Alabama in 1885 and marketed by D.M. Ferry, 'Florida Favorite' selected from the cross of 'Pierson' x 'Georgia Rattlesnake' by Girardeau in Monticello, Florida in 1887, 'Dark Icing' developed in 1888 by D.M. Ferry, and 'Dixie' selected from the cross of 'Kolb Gem' x 'Cuban Queen' or 'Mountain Sweet' by George Collins in North Carolina and marketed by Johnson and Stokes. Important varieties developed for the western United States included 'Chilean' (black or white seeded) brought from the west coast of South America and introduced to California in 1900, 'Angeleno' developed by Johnson and Musser in Los Angeles, Calif., in 1908, and 'Klondike Solid' and 'Klondike Striped' of unknown origin developed about 1900. Important varieties developed for shipping include 'Tom Watson' developed by Alexander Seed Co. in Augusta, Ga., in 1906, and 'Stone Mountain' developed by Hastings Co. in Atlanta in 1924.

Important varieties developed in the latter part of last century have built on past accomplishments. 'Charleston Gray' (USDA, Charleston, 1954), 'Crimson Sweet' (Kansas State University, 1963), 'Calhoun Gray' (Louisiana State University, 1965), and 'Dixielee' (1979), 'Jubilee' (1963), and 'Smokylee' (1971) (all from the University of Florida) have high resistance to fusarium wilt. 'Dixlee' (University of Florida, 1979) and 'Sangria' F_1 (Syngenta, 1985) have dark red flesh. 'Millionaire' F_1 3x (Harris Moran, 1992) and 'Royal Jubilee' F_1 (Seminis) have consistently high yields. 'Crimson Sweet' (Kansas State University, 1963) and 'Sugarlee' (University of Florida, 1981) have high soluble solids. 'Kengarden' (University of Kentucky, 1975) has dwarf vines. 'Tri-X-313' F_1 3x (Syngenta, 1962) is seedless. 'Minilee' and 'Mickylee' (University of Florida, 1986), 'New Hampshire Midget' (University of New Hampshire, 1951), 'Sugar Baby' (M. Hardin, Oklahoma, 1955), and 'Tiger Baby' (Seminis) are icebox size. 'Yellow Doll' (Seminis, 1977) has canary yellow flesh.

BREEDING PLAN. Once the breeder has determined the objectives of the program, the choice of parental materials is one of the most important aspects of a breeding program. Using knowledge of the crop and predicting the traits consumers will be interested in having in future varieties, the breeder gathers parental lines for crossing. The breeder should know which parent will contribute the traits of interest, and which methods will be used to evaluate the progeny for those traits. Thus, it is often necessary to collect and evaluate large numbers of PI accessions, varieties, and breeding lines for the traits of interest to identify appropriate parents to use in the program. This work often continues in parallel with the main part of the breeding program.

The next step is to determine the breeding method to use for each part of the program. It is important for the breeder to consider the advantages and disadvantages of particular breeding methods, and how they can be incorporated into the overall breeding plan. Also, it is common to use more than one breeding method at a time to accomplish several sets of objectives. For example, one part of the program might be to use recurrent selection to develop a base population with general adaptation and the proper fruit type that also has high yield and early maturity. A second part of the program might be to use pedigree selection on the cross of two lines to develop in-bred lines with the high yield, early maturity, and proper fruit type of one parent, and the dark red flesh color, high sugar content, and firm crisp flesh texture of the other parent. A third part of the program might be to use backcross breeding to make a canary yellow flesh version of an elite red-fleshed hybrid with top performance.

RECURRENT SELECTION. Although watermelon is a cross-pollinated crop, population improvement methods popular in some cross-pollinated crops have not been used. The main reason for that appears to be the large size of the plants, and the low rate of natural outcrossing that occurs. Also, because there are few plant breeders working on watermelon, and because of the requirement for many qualitative traits to be present in the new varieties being tested for release, it is expensive to spend additional years in population improvement for quantitative traits.

It may be possible to improve quantitative traits such as yield in watermelon using recurrent selection, i.e., repeated selection and massing of selected plants, but the populations should probably be developed initially to have the necessary qualitative genes in them. Those would include proper flesh color, fruit size, and disease resistance. Due to large plant size and a 5-month generation time, recurrent selection methods should be those that have few generations per cycle, and few plants per family (or single-plant selection).

One approach would be to develop an elite population by intercrossing two to four of the best red fleshed hybrids available, trying to choose a set that was genetically unrelated. A population with a wide genetic base could also be developed by intercrossing 20 or more elite varieties by hand for two or more generations, and using bees in an isolation block for two or more generations before beginning a mild selection pressure for important quantitative traits such as yield. Simple recurrent selection (Fig. 3.7) could be used for selection among single-plant hills for a set of highly heritable traits. A more complex method such as reciprocal recurrent selection would permit simultaneous improvement of two populations for combining ability for yield (Fig. 3.8). This would be an expensive program to run, but would produce two populations that could be used to develop inbreds to be used as the female and male parents (respectively) of elite hybrids.

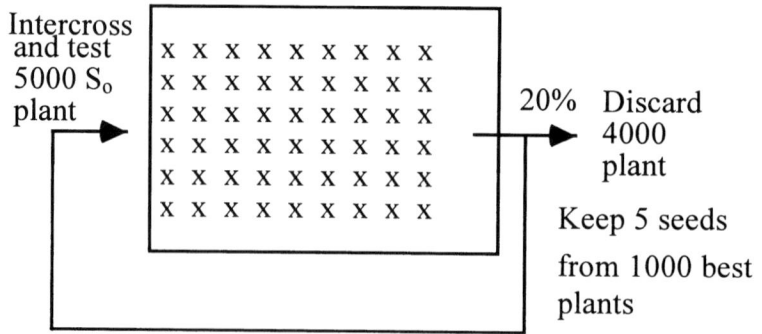

Figure 3.7. Diagram for simple recurrent selection in watermelon; selection intensity could be higher for faster progress but reduced genetic variation in the population (for example, keep 5 seeds of best 1000 plants).

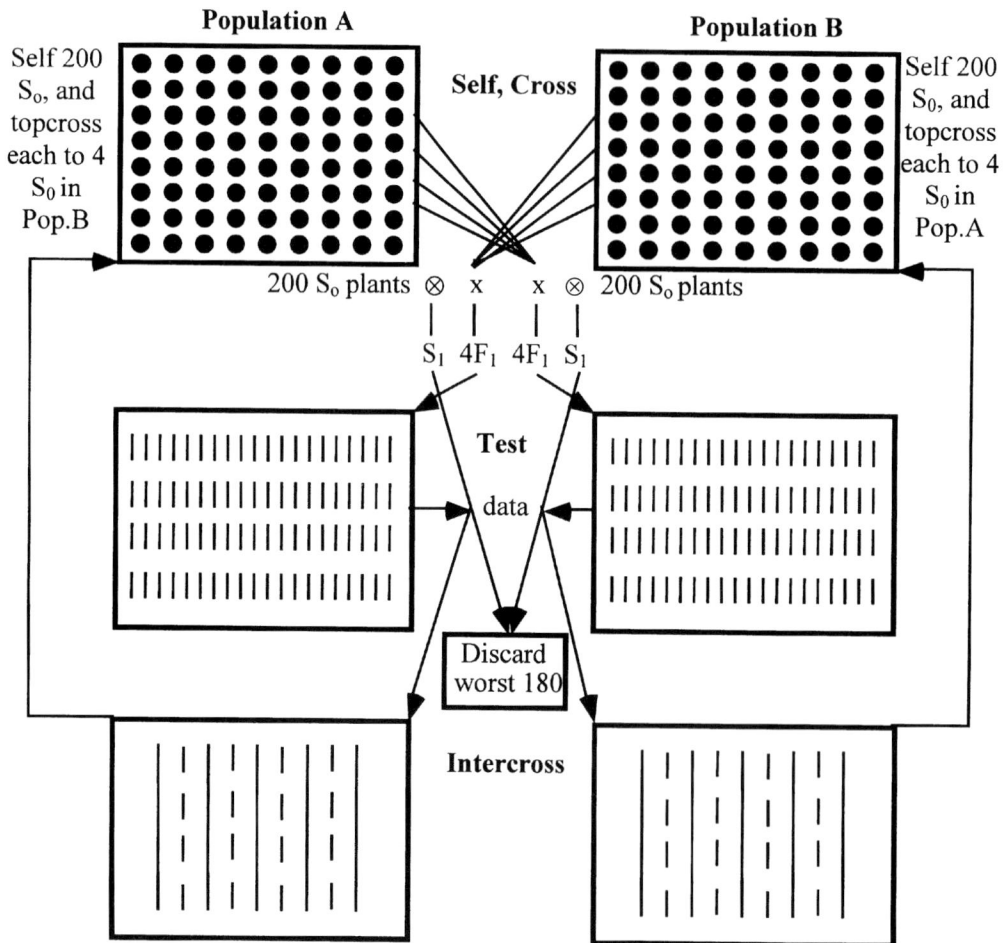

Figure 3.8. Diagram for reciprocal recurrent HS selection.

During population development, it would be necessary to identify methods for yield testing that were efficient for use in large yield trials. The usual guidelines for recurrent selection are to test at least 200 individuals (or progenies of individuals) per population, and to select at least 20 to intercross for the next cycle of selection. A yield trial involving 200 replicated families would require more resources than many breeding programs could afford if the trial were done using current methods.

Recurrent selection could be used to improve quantitative traits, such as yield, which are difficult to improve using qualitative methods such as pedigree and backcross breeding. Each year, the improved population would be used to begin the development of inbred lines to feed into other parts of the breeding program.

PEDIGREE BREEDING. Probably the most common method for watermelon breeding is pedigree. In pedigree breeding, the breeder begins by choosing two or more adapted parents, which complement each other in their traits. For example, one parent might be good for yield, earliness, and type but have disease susceptibility and the other might be good for yield, earliness, and type but have poor fruit quality. The objective would be to produce new lines with high yield, early maturity, proper type, high fruit quality, and good disease resistance. The varieties or breeding lines are crossed to form the hybrid (F_1) generation, which is then self- or sib-pollinated to form a segregating (F_2) population (Fig. 3.9). The F_2 is self- or sib-pollinated while selecting for traits having high heritability to form the F_3 generation. If multiple plants are tested from each selected F_2 plant, then the

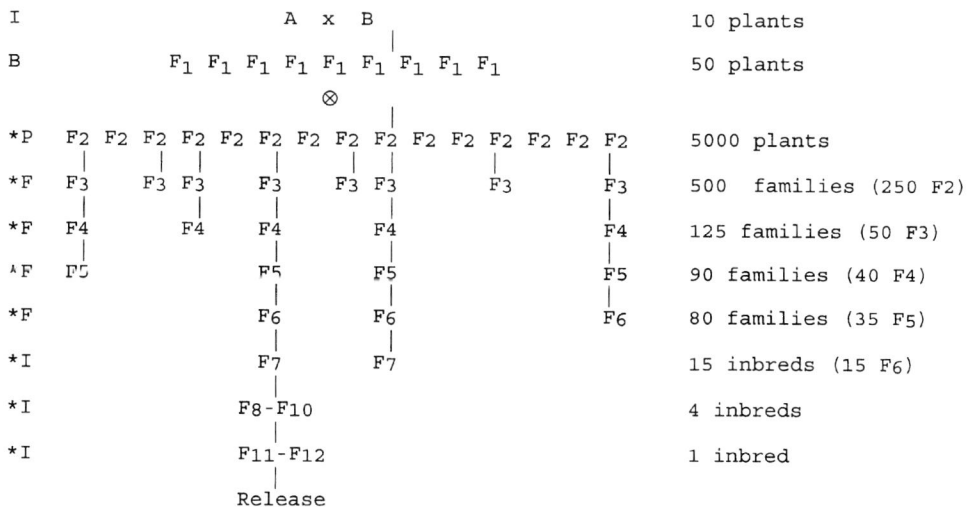

```
I                          A  x  B                    10 plants
                              |
B                F1 F1 F1 F1 F1 F1 F1 F1 F1           50 plants
                           ⊗
                              |
*P   F2 F2 F2 F2 F2 F2 F2 F2 F2 F2 F2 F2 F2 F2        5000 plants
     |       |  |       |       |  |       |    |
*F   F3      F3 F3       F3      F3 F3      F3   F3    500   families (250 F2)
     |          |        |          |           |
*F   F4         F4       F4         F4          F4    125 families (50 F3)
     |                   |          |           |
ᴬF   F5                  F5         F5          F5    90 families (40 F4)
     |                   |          |           |
*F                       F6         F6          F6    80 families (35 F5)
                         |          |
*I                       F7         F7               15 inbreds (15 F6)
                         |
*I                     F8-F10                        4 inbreds
                         |
*I                     F11-F12                       1 inbred
                         |
                       Release
```

Figure 3.9. Diagram for pedigree breeding in watermelon (I = inbred lines, B = bulk, P = single plant hills, F = families)

breeder concentrates on selecting the best plants in each of the best F_3 families. This might include selection in the seedling stage in the greenhouse in the F_2 and F_3 generations for disease resistance such as fusarium wilt races 0, 1, and 2 and anthracnose races 1 and 2.

Beginning at the F_4 generation, selection would begin to emphasize family-row performance for quantitative traits. Plants within family rows that have excellent performance for qualitative traits should be selected for the next generation. As the families reach six generations of self-pollination (S_6 or F_5), they become more uniform, and can then be handled as inbred lines. This could include selection using eight-plant plots for early flowering, number of pistillate flowers, and fruit number. The number handled might decrease from 54 F_2 plants of a cross to 36 F_3 families, 24 F_4 families, and 18 F_5 lines.

Single-seed-descent is a modification of pedigree breeding in which inbred lines are developed rapidly by self-pollination in greenhouses and winter nurseries, and selection is not practiced until later generations, such as S_3 to S_6. This method requires less record keeping and works better where the main objective is to improve quantitative traits such as yield and earliness, rather than qualitative traits such as flesh color and disease resistance. However, traditional pedigree breeding is probably the more useful method for watermelon since there are many qualitative traits that can be selected in early generations. In that way, plants or families having unsuitable traits that are simply inherited (such as poor fruit flesh color) can be eliminated in early generations. Otherwise, they would be carried along until the S_3 to S_6 generation when field-testing would be practiced in the single-seed-descent breeding method.

BACKCROSS BREEDING. Backcross breeding is used to transfer one qualitative (highly heritable) trait into an otherwise superior inbred. The superior inbred is referred to as the recurrent parent. Often, six generations of selection and backcrossing to the recurrent parent are used to recover the genotype of the recurrent parent (except for the addition of the new trait) without the other undesirable traits from the nonrecurrent (donor) parent. Two versions of the backcross method are used depending on whether the gene of interest is recessive or dominant.

For the transfer of a trait controlled by a recessive gene, the recurrent parent is crossed with the donor parent, and the F_1 backcrossed to the recurrent parent (Fig. 3.10). In one scheme, the F_1 is self-pollinated to produce the F_2, which will segregate for the trait of interest. Individuals having the trait can then be backcrossed to the recurrent parent to produce the BC_1. The BC_1 generation is then tested for the trait, and individuals having it are

```
P                    aa x AA
                       |
F1                    Aa ⊗
                     / / \
F2               AA+Aa + aa  x AA
                   |         |
                Discard      |

BC1                         Aa ⊗
                           / / \
BC1S1                  AA+Aa + aa x AA
                         |       |
                      Discard   etc. (for BC2,3,4,5)
                                 |

BC5                             Aa ⊗
                               / / \
BC5S1                      AA+Aa + aa ⊗
                             |       |
                          Discard    |
BC5S2                             New variety
```

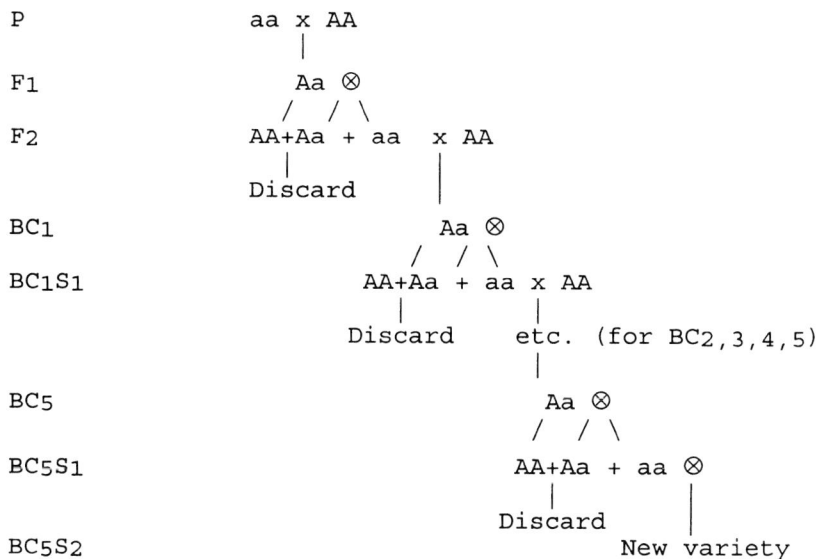

Figure 3.10. Diagram for backcross breeding in watermelon for transferring a recessive trait.

self-pollinated once again to produce a segregating generation for selection and backcrossing to the recurrent parent. The process is repeated until the BC_6 generation when the best individuals are self-pollinated and selected for the trait to produce the improved inbred. The inbred does not need to be tested extensively in trials, because it will be identical to the original inbred, but with one new trait.

For the transfer of a trait controlled by a dominant gene, the recurrent parent is crossed with the donor parent, and the F_1 backcrossed to the recurrent parent. The BC_1 generation is then tested for the trait, and individuals having it are backcrossed to the recurrent parent. The process is repeated until the BC_6 generation when the best individuals are self-pollinated and selected for homozygous expression of the trait using progeny testing.

INBRED DEVELOPMENT. The best selections from the recurrent selection program should be self-pollinated each cycle to begin inbred development. Pedigree selection, and backcross breeding result in the production of elite inbred lines. Each year, those inbred lines that are produced from the different parts of the breeding program should be increased by self-pollination, tested for useful horticultural traits, and used in the production of tetraploid inbred lines, as well as directly for the production of diploid hybrids based on the traits they have, and what is needed by the market.

Isolation blocks or screen cages can be used to make large seed increases of the inbreds if that is needed. Isolation blocks should be away from other watermelon fields, requiring a separation of at least 1 mile. Bees should be provided in the isolation block or cage by bringing in one strong hive, unless there are sufficient numbers of wild bees.

HYBRID TESTING. The final stage of breeding is to produce hybrids for testing. Hybrids are usually made between two monoecious inbreds. For triploid hybrid production, the seed parent should have a distinctive rind pattern that has recessive inheritance. For hybrid production with less labor input, the seed parent could be male sterile. The seed increase of the male sterile inbred would be accomplished by pollinating male sterile plants with the heterozygote (*Ms ms*) as the pollen parent. For seedless hybrid production, the seed parent would be a tetraploid inbred.

Once they have been developed, all inbreds can be crossed in all possible combinations. However, that might produce too many entries to evaluate properly. For example, 20 inbreds could produce $(20 \times 19)/2 = 190$ different hybrids, without including reciprocals. Thus, it may make more sense to make hybrids only from pairs of inbreds having complementing traits of the proper type.

Testing of experimental hybrids should progress in stages, with fewer hybrids to test in later stages where more effort is spent on each hybrid. The first year trials might have two replications in each of two locations. In the second year, the best hybrids could be evaluated in 8–12 locations using the conditions available at each (grower fields, state university experiment stations). In the third year, the hybrids would be sent to grower trials throughout the production regions of interest for trials involving 0.25–1.0 acre using a total of 5–10 lb of seeds for all trials. Seeds should be screened for bacterial fruit blotch before sending to growers. One can usually get good data from at least 10 of the 50 trials. Information from the 3 years of trialing should lead to the release of the best one or two hybrids in the fourth year.

Although there is not much advantage of hybrids over open-pollinated varieties for most traits, it is thought that the former are more uniform. Thus, it may be possible to get the same yield in fewer harvests because of more uniform growth and a more concentrated fruit set. Hybrids offer several advantages over open-pollinated varieties. A major advantage is the production of seedless triploids, which are produced by crossing a tetraploid female inbred with a diploid male inbred. Hybrids also can express heterosis, with the hybrid performing slightly better than the best parent in some cases. The amount of heterosis in watermelon is around 10%. Another advantage is the ability to get an intermediate fruit shape by crossing an elongate-fruited inbred with a round-fruited one. Inbreds can be used to combine dominant genes for resistance from each parent into a hybrid that has more dominant genes expressed than either parent. A hybrid that has large seeds for the grower to plant and small seeds in the fruit sold to the consumer can be produced by crossing a large-seeded female inbred with a small-seeded male inbred. Finally, hybrids provide a way for the seed company to protect their proprietary inbreds from theft.

The disadvantages of hybrids are that they add an extra step to the breeding process, and increase the cost of seeds since they are produced by hand pollination rather than by bee pollination. Use of male sterile inbreds for seed production should help reduce the cost of hybrid seeds in the future.

Seedless variety development

TETRAPLOID PRODUCTION. Use of triploid hybrids has provided a method for production of seedless fruit. The tetraploid method for seedless watermelon production was invented by H. Kihara. He began development of tetraploids in 1939, and had commercial triploid hybrids available 12 years later. The development of triploid varieties adds several problems to the process of watermelon breeding: extra time for the development of tetraploids; additional selection against sterility and fruit abnormalities in tetraploid lines; choice of parents for low incidence of hard seedcoats in the hybrids; the reduction in seed yield per acre; reduced seed vigor for the grower; and the necessity for the diploid pollenizer to use up to one-third of the grower's production field.

Seedless varieties are produced by crossing a tetraploid ($2n = 4x = 44$) inbred line as the female parent with a diploid ($2n = 2x = 22$) inbred line as the male parent of the hybrid. The reciprocal cross (diploid female parent) does not produce seeds. The resulting hybrid is a triploid ($2n = 3x = 33$). Triploid plants have three sets of chromosomes, and three sets cannot be divided evenly during meiosis (the cell division process that produces the gametes). This results in nonfunctional female and male gametes although the flowers appear normal. Since the triploid hybrid is female sterile, the fruit induced by pollination tend to be seedless. Unfortunately, the triploid has no viable pollen, so it is necessary to plant a diploid variety in the production field to provide the pollen that stimulates fruit to form. Usually, one third of the plants in the field are diploid and two thirds are triploid, although successful production has been observed with as little as 20% diploids. Varieties should be chosen that could be distinguished easily so the seeded diploid fruit can be separated from the seedless triploid fruit for harvesting and marketing.

Breeders interested in the production of seedless triploid hybrids need to develop tetraploid inbred lines to be used as the female parent in a cross with a diploid male parent. One of the major limiting steps in breeding seedless watermelons is the small number of tetraploid inbreds available. Development of seedless hybrids will be discussed in the following stages: 1) choice of diploid lines, 2) production of tetraploid plants, 3) tetraploid line development, and 4) hybrid production and testing.

Stage 1 involves choice of diploid lines to use in tetraploid production. Most of the tetraploid lines being used by the seed industry have gray rind so that, when crossed with a diploid line with striped rind, it will be easy to separate self-pollinated progeny (which will be seeded fruit from the female parent line) from cross-pollinated progeny (which will be seedless fruit from the triploid hybrid). The grower should discard the gray fruit so they are not marketed as seedless watermelons by mistake.

Stage 2 is the production of tetraploid plants. Many methods have been used effectively in other crops to produce polyploids, including tissue culture regeneration, temperature shock, and X-rays. In watermelon, tetraploids can be produced routinely using plants regenerated from tissue culture or using the herbicide oryzalin. Colchicine ($C_{22}H_{25}O_6N$), a poisonous alkaloid used in the treatment of gout, from the seeds and bulbs of *Colchicum autumnale* is a widely used method in watermelon for tetraploid production. Colchicine inhibits spindle formation, and prevents separation of chromosomes at anaphase. Of all the methods of colchicine application, shoot apex treatment at the seedling stage was found most effective.

For the seedling treatment method, the diploid line of interest is planted in the greenhouse in flats (8 × 16 cells is a popular size) on heating pads that keep the soil medium at 85 °F for rapid and uniform germination. When the cotyledons first emerge from the soil, the growing point is treated with colchicine to stop chromosome division and produce a tetraploid shoot with four sets of chromosomes rather than two. The colchicine solution is used at a concentration of 0.1% for small-seed size varieties ('Minilee', 'Mickylee', 'Sweet Princess'), 0.15%–0.2% for medium-seed size varieties ('Allsweet', 'Crimson Sweet', 'Peacock Striped', 'Sugar Baby'), and 0.2%–0.5% for large-seed size varieties ('Black Diamond', 'Charleston Gray', 'Congo', 'Dixielee', 'Klondike Striped Blue Ribbon', 'Northern Sweet'). Colchicine is applied to the seedling growing point in the morning and evening for 3 consecutive days, using 1 drop on small- or medium-seed size plants and 2 drops on large-seed size varieties. The treatment produces plants that are diploid, tetraploid, or aneuploid, so it is necessary to identify and select the tetraploids in later stages. Treatment of the T_o diploids with colchicine results in about 1% of the seedlings (referred to as T_1 generation tetraploids) being tetraploids. Some diploid varieties and breeding lines produce a higher percentage of tetraploids than others. For example, 'Early Canada' produces many tetraploids and 'Sweet Princess' does not.

Tetraploids can be detected by the direct method of counting chromosomes of cells under the microscope, or by comparing stem, leaf, flower, and pollen size with diploid controls. A popular method involves counting the number of chloroplasts in stomatal guard cells using a leaf peel under the microscope. Tetraploids have about 10–14 chloroplasts in each guard cell (20–28 total on both sides of the stomate), whereas diploids have only 5–6 in each guard cell (10–12 total). The method is useful for screening many plants for ploidy level in the seedling stage before transplanting to the main part of the greenhouse or field nursery for self-pollination. Usually, multiple methods are used, identifying tetraploid seedlings using their phenotype in flats before transplanting, the chloroplast number in the stomatal guard cells of the true leaves in seedling flats and greenhouse pots, and by the appearance of the fruit and seeds at harvest after self-pollination in the greenhouse. Tetraploids usually have thicker leaves, slower growth, and shorter stems than diploids.

Stage 3 involves tetraploid line development. Tetraploid plants are selected (using methods such as leaf guard cell chloroplast number) in the T_0 generation (plants from colchicine treated diploids) from the greenhouse flats where they were treated with colchicine. It is then necessary to plant the T_1 generation in flats to verify that the plants are tetraploids in that next generation, and transplant the selections to greenhouse pots for self-pollination. Seeds from those selections (T_2) can then be increased in larger plantings such as field isolation blocks to get sufficient numbers of seeds per tetraploid line to use in triploid hybrid production.

The fertility and seed yield of tetraploid lines will increase over generations of self- or sib-pollination, probably because plants with chromosome anomalies are eliminated, resulting in a tetraploid line with balanced chromosome number and regular formation of 11 quadrivalents. Seed yield of tetraploid lines in early generations is often only 50–100 seeds per fruit and sometimes as low as 0–5 seeds compared to 200–800 seeds for diploids. Another problem with early generation tetraploids is poor seed germination, making it difficult to establish uniform field plantings. It may require as much as 10 years of self-pollination before sufficient seeds of tetraploid lines can be produced for commercial production of triploid hybrids. Advanced generations of tetraploid lines usually have improved fertility, seed yield, and germination rate compared to the original lines. Some companies require more than 100 lbs of seed of a tetraploid inbred to be available before beginning commercial production of the triploid hybrid variety. About 110 tetraploid plants are required for production of each pound of triploid seeds.

Stage 4 is the evaluation of tetraploids (usually T_3 generation or later) as parents of triploid hybrids. The tetraploids should be evaluated directly for rind pattern, high seed yield, and other traits such as male sterility for reduced hand labor in hybrid seed production. The major test for tetraploids however, is as female parents in triploid hybrid seed production after making controlled crosses using diploid male parents. The resulting hybrids are tested in yield trials with two rows of triploid plots alternating with one row of diploid plots to assure adequate pollen for fruit set in the triploid hybrids. Useful tetraploid inbreds should produce triploid hybrids with excellent yield and quality for the market type and production area of interest.

TRIPLOID EVALUATION. Evaluation of triploid hybrids is similar to evaluation of diploid varieties already discussed. There are a few special considerations, however. Triploids are not inherently superior to diploids, so triploid hybrids can be better or worse than their diploid parental lines. Therefore, as in the case of diploid hybrids, many combinations of parental lines should be evaluated in triploid yield trials to identify the ones producing hybrids with the best performance. In general, diploid inbred parents that have poor horticultural performance will produce triploid hybrids having poor performance.

One problem affecting triploid hybrids is empty seedcoats (colored or white) in the fruit. Under some environmental conditions, fruit are produced with large obvious seedcoats that are objectionable to consumers. Triploid fruit should be evaluated for seedcoat problems during trialing. Some selection should also be done on the parents before triploid production. Seedcoats will be large in the hybrids if the parents have large seeds. Seed size is genetically controlled, with at least three genes involved: *l*, *s*, and *tss*. Use of tetraploid lines with small or tomato-size seeds may help solve the problem. Besides genetic effects, certain unknown environmental conditions seem to increase the number of hard seedcoats in poor performing triploid hybrids.

Commercial production of elite triploid hybrid seed is done by hand in locations where labor is inexpensive, or by bee pollination in isolation blocks. The tetraploid and diploid inbreds are planted together in alternating rows, or in alternating hills within each row. Where labor is abundant, the staminate flowers can be collected from the male (diploid) parent and used to pollinate the pistillate flowers on the female (tetraploid) parent. Pollinated flowers should be capped the previous day to keep bees out, then covered after pollination to prevent self or sib-pollination after the cross has been made. The flowers should be tagged with the date so that the fruit can be harvested 35–50 days later.

A method that requires less hand labor is to plant the pollen and seed parents in alternating rows, and to remove all pistillate flowers from the seed parent rows during flowering time, usually a period lasting several weeks. Pistillate flowers on the female parent are tagged on the day they open with the date to assure that the fruit are mature when harvested, and to harvest only fruit that were pollinated during the time staminate flowers were removed from the female parent. Seeds that are harvested can also be sorted mechanically for size, weight or density to separate triploid seeds (resulting from cross pollination) from tetraploid seeds (resulting from self- and sib-pollination).

When seed production is by bee pollination in isolation blocks, the tetraploid flowers are sib- or cross-pollinated 84% of the time, producing 3x and 4x seeds (progeny). If the 2x and 4x parents of the 3x hybrid have different rind patterns, each of the three-ploidy levels can be distinguished at harvest. For safety, the pollen parent plants should be destroyed after fruit are set on the seed parent plants. A useful combination is for the tetraploid parent to have fruit with a gray rind pattern, and the diploid parent to have fruit with wide stripes, so the resulting triploid hybrid will have striped fruit, easily distinguished from the gray fruited tetraploids that result from self- or sib-pollination of the female parent.

Mechanization

The job of watermelon breeding can be made easier and more efficient if mechanization is used for as many steps in the process as possible. Small plot equipment can be used for fieldwork to permit more germplasm to be tested with fewer workers and at a lower cost. Small-plot seeders can be used to plant seeds in the field with optimum seed spacing and planting depth using fewer workers than if seeds are planted by hand. If transplants are used to plant the test plots, machine transplanters can be used to punch the hole before the workers on the machine set the seedling into the hole, and follow up with water and fertilizer after the worker has pressed soil around the seedling, all while riding down the field row. Seeds can be packeted using a seed counter, and plot size can be optimized to gain the maximum information for the lowest cost. Research indicates that optimum plot shape is rectangular and block (replication) shape is square. It is difficult to mechanize harvest since it is done by hand, and each fruit is counted and weighed. However, some efficiency can be gained by using portable computers to collect and analyze data. In the advanced trials, it is useful to estimate flesh sweetness (fruit soluble solids content) using a refractometer, and rind toughness using a spring-loaded punch or penetrometer.

If a greenhouse generation is used to expedite inbred development or hybridization, automation systems are useful for handling the many plants to be grown for self- or cross-pollination. Such systems include automatic heating and cooling, drip irrigation with fertilizer and/or other chemicals injected into the water, trellis support for easy vertical training of the plants, automatic overhead curtains to keep the greenhouse from overheating during the day in the summer, and to keep the greenhouse warmer at night in the winter. Computer systems can provide efficient control of the greenhouse equipment and help provide optimum conditions for plant growth.

For seed harvesting and handling, it is useful to have a bulk seed extractor, washing screens, a seed sluice, and seed dryers. Seed companies have used such machines for years, and it is useful for the plant breeder to build smaller versions that match the size of the plant breeding program (Fig. 3.11). Watermelon breeding is a labor-intensive job, but mechanization can help make the most of the available workers, funds, and time.

SEED PRODUCTION

Early watermelon varieties were mostly inbred lines produced commercially by open pollination of bulk-increased or hand-pollinated breeder seeds. In the 1970s, large-scale production of diploid hybrid seed began. Diploid hybrids have now taken over most of the commercial production in North America, Western Europe, and Japan.

Hybrid production

Hybrid seeds are produced in the seed parent by pollination from staminate flowers in the male parent. Hybrid production can be by hand pollination using inbred lines grown in adjacent rows in the field, or by planting the two parental lines in an insect-proof cage. Pollinations are marked for later seed harvest using

Figure 3.11. Small-scale seed extractor for use in breeding programs. (Source: G.W. Elmstrom.)

tags or bags after pollination. Each fruit will have 200–800 seeds, and fewer than 4000 seeds are needed per acre of commercial production.

A less expensive alternative to hand pollination is to plant the two parental inbreds in an isolation block. Staminate flowers are then removed daily from the plants in the seed parent rows to avoid self- and sib-pollination. All pistillate flowers in the seed parent row that are pollinated during the days of staminate flower removal are tagged for hybrid seed harvest. Another solution would be to incorporate a recessive seedling marker such as nonlobed leaf or the glabrous gene into the seed parent. Seedlings resulting from self- or sib-pollinations would have the marker and could be removed from the planted field or removed from the transplant flats to get 100% hybrid seedlings. Conversion of the seed parent to a near-isogenic male sterile line offers the possibility of hybrid seed production without the work associated with the above three methods. However, genetic male sterility requires that male fertile plants be rogued out of the seed parent rows in the hybrid production block.

Seeds can be sorted after the seed cleaning operation by size, weight, or density to increase the proportion of hybrid seed in the lot. Diploid open-pollinated seed yields should be higher than 251 lb/acre (average for United States in 1976–77). Very good seed yields would be 400 lb/acre. Triploid seed yields average about 20–40 lb/acre (about 10% what diploids would produce).

Commercial systems

Most commercial watermelon seed production is located in arid or semi-arid areas of the world such as western China, Chile, Mexico, Thailand, and the United States (California and Colorado). Arid conditions favor the production of high quality, disease-free seeds. With the outbreak of bacterial fruit blotch of watermelon in the late 1980s, seed production in areas of low humidity and no rainfall has become even more desirable to produce disease-free seed.

Sanitation is important at all stages of production. Workers should wash their hands with antibacterial soap or rinse them with 70% isopropyl alcohol before handling plants or fruit and between seed lots. All equipment should be cleaned and all soil and plant material removed before use in production areas. Clean and disinfect harvesting tools and equipment with alcohol or 0.5% NaOCl or $Ca(OCl)_2$ between seed lots. Sanitation, harvest, and control procedures for production of foundation and stock (parent) seed should be at least as stringent as that for commercial seed.

The process of growing watermelon seed crops is similar to that for growing market crops except that site selection is more critical. Choose a field that has not had any cucurbits (watermelon, cantaloupe, honeydew, cucumber, summer or winter squash, pumpkin, or gourd) in it for at least 2, but preferably 4 years. A field that has a history of fusarium wilt or anthracnose should be avoided. Fields for open-pollinated watermelon seed production should be isolated by at least 1 mile from other watermelon fields to prevent contamination by outcrossing. Isolation also prevents disease spread from fields containing watermelon and cantaloupe crops of unknown origin or planted with seeds that have not been tested for seedborne disease. The production site should be as far as possible from fields where bacterial fruit blotch occurred the previous year to reduce contamination from leftover debris. Wild cucurbits, such as citron and volunteer watermelons, must be removed from a 1-mile radius surrounding the production field to eliminate outcrossing and disease contamination.

Selection of parental seed from elite or foundation seed is the first critical element of seed production. Use seed that was produced in dry climates and has been tested to be free of the pathogens causing gummy stem blight, watermelon fruit blotch, anthracnose, and squash mosaic. Direct-seeded plantings reduce the risk of seedling contamination in greenhouses. If transplants are used, they should be produced in a greenhouse that does not contain other cucurbits. Irrigation of transplants in the greenhouse preferably should be from an ebb and flow or a float system. Overhead irrigation of seedlings in the greenhouse should be avoided. Greenhouses for transplant production should have good air circulation and low relative humidity.

Drip or furrow irrigation should be used in the production field instead of overhead irrigation to reduce leaf wetting and disease spread. Roguing of off-type and diseased plants within the field should be done throughout the growing season. There are four useful stages for roguing. The first is before flowering when vegetative characters are checked. The second stage is at early flowering when morphology of undeveloped fruit is checked. The third stage is when the developing fruit are checked for trueness to type, and the final roguing is confirming the external morphological characters of the fruit to be harvested. Roguing for off-types is not effective after pollination in a field for open-pollinated seed production. It is only effective when fruit have been self or cross-pollinated and the male has no off-types. Inspectors should be trained to recognize variations in watermelon fruit blotch symptoms.

Preventative applications of copper fungicide can also help in reducing fruit blotch contamination of seed. The first spray should be 2 weeks before flowering. Application of registered fungicides will reduce gummy stem blight seed contamination. Seed should not be harvested from fields where there is confirmation of fruit blotch or until the possibility of fruit blotch is eliminated. Seeds harvested from fields in which fruit blotch is confirmed or which were adjacent to contaminated fields should not be used.

All fruit should be inspected by trained technicians for symptoms that are suspected to be fruit blotch. All fruit suspected of having fruit blotch must be discarded. No fruit should be harvested from vines that have anthracnose or gummy stem blight symptoms. When seeds of open-pollinated fruit, and in some cases, hybrid fruit, are mature the fruit are windrowed by machine. Windrowed fruit are picked up by self-propelled vine seed harvesters that crush the fruit and separate the seeds and pulp from the rind. For some hybrid seed production, fruit are harvested by hand and various sized seed extractors are used (Fig. 3.12). In either case, the diploid seed slurry is transferred to bins where it is allowed to ferment for 24–48 h. During this time the sugars and gelatinous material surrounding the seeds are degraded.

Fermentation plus acid washing (1% hydrochloric acid) can reduce the chance of seed transmission of fruit blotch. Fermentation and acid treatment of triploid seed reduces seed viability, so is not recommended. Seeds extracted from tetraploid fruit for triploid seed production should be washed immediately. Seeds are separated from pulp and juice by washing in a rotary washer or flume system (Fig. 3.13). Some seed lots are dried by heat from the sun. However, higher quality seeds are produced using forced air warmed by propane heaters. Seeds are placed on flat drying beds or in large rotary dryers. Dry seeds are run through a mill containing sizing screens that separates large seeds from trash and small seeds.

All seed lots should be assayed for the presence of the fruit blotch bacterium, squash mosaic virus, and gummy stem blight pathogen by the best methods available. In Asia, cucumber green mottle virus is a problem and is seed transmitted. For fruit blotch, seedling grow-outs of at least 10,000 seeds per lot are currently used, but polymerase chain reaction (PCR) techniques may provide more effi-

Figure 3.12. Workers harvesting watermelon fruit with seed extraction in a tractor-pulled unit. (Source: G.W. Elmstrom.)

Figure 3.13. Seed sluice for washing watermelon seeds after fruit have been run through the seed extractor and the seeds have been fermented 1 day. (Source: D.N. Maynard.)

cient and sensitive methods. Coupling seedling grow-outs with PCR may be necessary for some situations. Squash mosaic virus can be screened with grow-outs. For gummy stem blight, seedling grow-outs or blotter tests using a minimum of 1,000 seeds per lot are recommended. However, PCR techniques may provide better methods in the future. Commercial seeds should be treated with a registered protectant such as Captan and Thiram before sealing them into cans, bags, or packets. Seeds should be stored in hermetically sealed containers at 6.5% moisture content, and no greater than 10% moisture. Under favorable storage conditions, seeds should last 4 years. To be salable, germination of the seed lot must be at least 70%.

General References

Crall, J. 1981. Fifty years of watermelon breeding at ARC Leesburg. Proc. Fla. State Hort. Soc. 94:156–158.

Eigsti, O.J. and P. Dustin. 1955. Colchicine in agriculture, medicine, biology, and chemistry. Iowa State College Press, Ames.

Fehner, T. 1993. Watermelon, *Citrullus lanatus* (Thunb.) Matsum. & Nakai, p. 295–314 In: G. Kallo and B.O. Bergh (eds.). Genetic improvement of vegetable crops. Oxford, Pergamon Press. New York.

Kihara, H. 1951. Triploid watermelons. Proc. Amer. Soc. Hort. Sci. 58:217–230.

Mohr, H.C. 1986. Watermelon breeding, p. 37–66. In: M.J. Bassett (ed.). Breeding vegetable crops. AVI Publ. Co. Westport, Conn.

Orton, W.A. 1907. A study of disease resistance in watermelons. Science 25:288.

Parris, G.K. 1949. Watermelon breeding. Econ. Bot. 3:193–212.

Porter, D.R. 1933. Watermelon breeding. Hilgardia 7:533–552.

Rhodes, B. and F. Dane. 1999. Gene list for watermelon. Cucurbit Genet. Coop. Rpt. 22:61–77.

Rhodes, B. and X. Zhang. 1999. Hybrid seed production in watermelon, p. 69–88. In: A.S. Basra (ed.). Hybrid seed production in vegetables: Rationale and methods in selected crops. Food Products Press, New York.

Robinson, R.W. 2000. Rationale and methods for producing hybrid cucurbit seed, p. 1–47. In: A.S. Basra (ed.). Hybrid seed production in vegetables: Rationale and methods in selected crops. Food Products Press, New York.

Robinson, R.W., H.M. Whitaker, and G.W. Bohn. 1976. Genes of the Cucurbitaceae. HortScience 11:554–568.

Wehner, T.C. 1999. Heterosis in vegetable crops, p. 387–397. In: J.G. Coors and S. Pandey (eds.). Genetics and exploitation of heterosis in crops. Amer. Soc. Agron., Madison, Wis.

Whitaker, T.W. and G.N. Davis. 1962. Cucurbits: botany, cultivation, and utilization. Interscience Publ., New York.

CHAPTER 4

BIOTECHNOLOGY

A. Levi

The term biotechnology refers to old and new technologies that use an organism or a biological product to manipulate living cells and their molecules. Examples of biotechnologies are the use of yeast in baking and *E. coli* bacteria for genetic engineering. Biotechnology has many applications in medicine and agriculture and opens new avenues for crop improvement. Biotechnological applications in the improvement of watermelon are mostly in the field of molecular genetics to study and analyze genes at the molecular (DNA) level. The applications include 1) development of molecular (DNA) markers that can be used by plant breeders to identify and select plants that have valuable genes, e.g., genes that improve fruit quality or genes that confer disease resistance, 2) isolating and sequencing the DNA of valuable genes, 3) incorporating such valuable genes into commercial varieties using genetic engineering methods (genetic transformation). Additional applications include tissue culture for rapid propagation of valuable plants. This chapter outlines examples of current biotechnological approaches in the improvement of watermelon.

TISSUE CULTURE

Tissue culture allows the use of various methodologies to improve watermelon, i.e., genetic transformation and rapid propagation of valuable plants. In recent years, there has been an increasing demand for seedless watermelon varieties. Seedless watermelons are fruits of triploid plants in which each type of chromosome is represented three times (3x) in each cell. Triploid plants arise from seeds obtained by crossing tetraploid (4x) and the normal diploid (2x) plants. Tetraploid plants are usually obtained by treating terminal buds of a diploid plant with the alkaloid colchicine, which stops cell division resulting in polyploid cells (cells with more than two sets of chromosomes such as 3x, 4x, 5x, 6x). These plants undergo further screening to define their ploidy level and to select the tetraploid plants. In a recent study, many tetraploid plants were produced by regeneration from cotyledons of seedlings cultured in vitro. This procedure proved reproducible in giving rise to tetraploid plants for various watermelon varieties, and is an efficient alternative to the colchicine procedure. Tetraploid plants have low fertility and produce low numbers of viable seeds. Tissue culture protocols have been developed to rapidly propagate tetraploid watermelon plants for use as pollinators of diploid plants to mass-produce triploid seeds (Fig. 4.1).

IDENTIFICATION OF PLANTS USING MOLECULAR (DNA) MARKERS

New methodologies have been introduced for genetic analysis and development of DNA markers linked to valuable traits in plants. DNA markers are sequences of DNA used as reference points in mapping genes on a chromosome. DNA markers are also useful for the plant breeder to identify plant varieties (DNA fingerprinting) and to estimate the genetic relatedness of plants within specific breeding populations.

In recent years a technology called polymerase chain reaction (PCR) has revolutionized the molecular biology field, allowing rapid analysis of DNA. During PCR, specific sequences of DNA are quickly reproduced from minute to visual amounts (about 10^7–10^9 times the original amount) by an enzyme called Taq-DNA polymerase. The PCR procedure termed random amplified polymorphic DNA (RAPD) is most widely used for analyses of DNA from plants including watermelon. Additional useful PCR-based procedures are simple sequence repeats (SSR) analysis and amplified fragment length polymorphism (AFLP) analysis.

Over 40 genes have been described in watermelon. Known genes confer pest and disease resistances and control plant traits like flower type, fruit shape, and fruit quality. Efforts are underway to find DNA markers linked to these genes. DNA markers can be highly informative when used to define the identity, purity, and stability of new watermelon varieties and hybrid lines. DNA markers are also helpful in estimating genetic relatedness among watermelon varieties and within breeding populations. In a current study, we are using DNA markers (Fig. 4.2) for DNA fingerprinting of watermelon heirloom varieties. We are also using them to estimate genetic relatedness among the heirloom varieties and among wild accessions [plant introductions (PIs) that have virus or disease resistances].

About 60 DNA sequences of watermelon genes have been published. Some of

Figure 4.1. Tetraploid watermelon plants formed in tissue culture, transplanted to soil. (Source: Dennis Gray, University of Florida.)

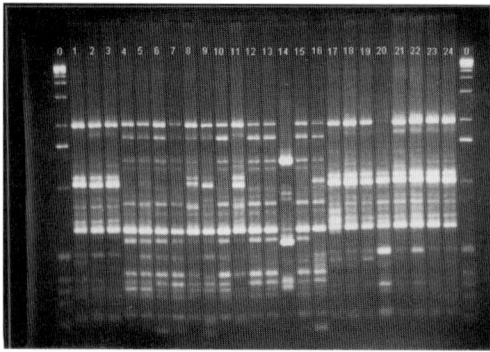

Figure 4.2. PCR-RAPD patterns (on agarose-gel) produced from DNA of watermelon varieties and plant introductions (PIs). Lanes are 0) DNA markers showing molecular size, 1) Summit, 2) Sweet Princess, 3) Tiger Baby, 4) PI 189225, 5) PI 244018, 6) PI 244019, 7) PI 248774, 8) PI 255137, 9) PI 270562, 10) PI 270563, 11) PI 271779, 12) PI 299378, 13) PI 299379, 14) PI 346082, 15) PI 482252, 16) Griff. 14113, 17) PI 162667, 18) PI 165451, 19) PI 169289, 20) PI 169290, 21) PI 185635, 22) PI 185636, 23) PI 186975, 24) PI 189316, 25) PI 189317, 26) PI 192937, 27) PI 203551, 28) PI 248178. (Source: Susan Fox and Amnon Levi, USDA, ARS.)

these sequences are used as markers in the construction of a genetic linkage map for watermelon. Efforts are underway to use molecular markers to identify and select simply inherited traits like anthracnose resistance, dwarf habit, fruit shape, fruit sweetness, rind color, and earliness. DNA markers are also useful to detect pathogens that cause watermelon diseases. Recently, DNA markers were developed for the identification of the pathogenic fungus *Didymella bryoniae* that causes the gummy stem blight disease on watermelon (Fig. 4.3).

GENETIC TRANSFORMATION OF WATERMELON

Genetic transformation provides new opportunities to improve important crop plants. With genetic transformation, single genes can be inserted into a plant while genetic barriers are avoided, and the plant genotype is not significantly altered as in conventional breeding. The soilborne bacterium *Agrobacterium tumefaciens* (the pathogen that causes crown gall disease) is often used as a vehicle to transfer genes into plants. *Agrobacterium*-mediated transformation involves a DNA segment termed transfer or T-DNA. Following infection with *Agrobacterium*, the T-DNA (which carries the transforming gene) is inserted into the plant cell, and is incorporated into the plant genome resulting in stable genetic transformation. The range of plant species that can be transformed using *Agrobacterium* is limited. However, physical methods to directly transfer T-DNA into plant cells have proved successful in experiments with various crop plants. Among these physical methods, the microparticle-bombardment procedure is the most widely used. This procedure involves coating the T-DNA on tungsten or gold microparticles and projection of the coated microparticles into target cells using a gun powered with helium. This technique allows effective penetration by the T-DNA carrying the transforming gene through the cell wall, resulting in genetic transformation. There are at least three reports of genetic transformation in watermelon using either *Agrobacterium* or microparticle bombard-

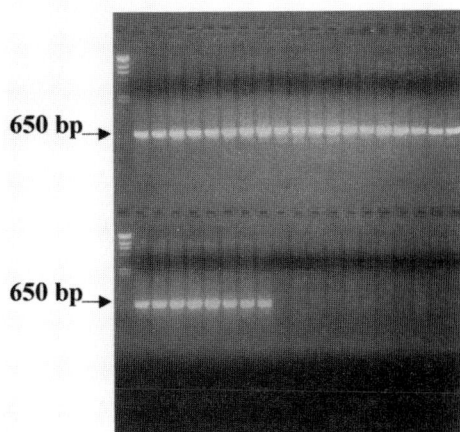

Figure 4.3. A 650-base pair DNA marker of the pathogenic fungus *Didymella bryoniae* amplified with a specific PCR primer. Lanes that do not show the marker contain a nonpathogenic *Phoma* species. (Source: by Anthony Keinath and Benesh Somai, Clemson University, South Carolina.)

650 bp→

650 bp→

ment. The primary focus of these efforts is the introduction of single genes that confer fungal, bacterial, or virus resistance in watermelon. Additional goals are improving fruit quality and tolerance to environmental stress. As with other crop species, genetic transformation of watermelon requires in vitro sterile conditions and tissue culture procedures.

Virus diseases in watermelon are caused by squash mosaic virus (SQMV), cucumber mosaic virus (CMV), papaya ring spot virus-watermelon strain (PRSV-W), zucchini yellow mosaic virus (ZYMV), and watermelon mosaic virus (WMV). The last three viruses are the most widespread in watermelon. Genetic transformation may offer a short cut in the development of watermelon varieties with virus resistance. In a preliminary study, watermelon plants were transformed with a ZYMV gene that may disrupt virus penetration into the plant cell, and thus confer virus resistance.

CONCLUSIONS

Biotechnology provides new opportunities for improving watermelon. There is a great interest in the development of molecular markers and genetic linkage maps. There is also much interest in the isolation and characterization of disease resistance genes, and the incorporation of these genes into the watermelon genome using genetic transformation methods. Future studies are required to optimize genetic transformation methods and obtain stable transgenic watermelon plants. Genetically engineered watermelon varieties may be commercially available in the future.

General References

Lee, S.J., J.S. Shin, K.W. Park, and Y.P. Hong. 1996. Detection of genetic diversity using RAPD-PCR and sugar analysis in watermelon [*Citrullus lanatus* (Thunb.) Mansf.] germplasm. Theor. Appl. Genet. 92:719–725.

Compton M.E., D.J. Gray, and G.W. Elmstrom. 1993. A simple protocol for micropropagating diploid and tetraploid watermelon using shoot-tip explants. Plant Cell, Tissue Organ Cult. 33:211–217.

Compton M.E., D.J. Gray, and G.W. Elmstrom. 1996. Identification of tetraploid regenerants from cotyledons of diploid watermelon cultured in vitro. Euphytica 87:165–172.

Srivastava D.R., V.M. Andrianov, and E.S. Piruzian. 1989. Tissue culture and plant regeneration of watermelon (*Citrullus vulgaris* Scrad. Cv. Melitopolski). Plant Cell Rpt. 8:300–302.

CHAPTER 5

CULTURAL MANAGEMENT

G.J. Hochmuth, E. Kee, T.K. Hartz, F.J. Dainello, and J.E. Motes

Successful watermelon production depends on attention to various cultural practices. This involves soil management practices with special attention to proper fertilization, use of plastic mulch, crop establishment with appropriate spacing, the introduction of bees for pollination, and suitable pollenizers for seedless watermelon, irrigation, and pest management. Harvesting and handling will be discussed in chapter 10.

SOIL MANAGEMENT

Watermelon performs best on sandy loam soils (Fig. 5.1), which are nonsaline, well-drained and slightly acidic. Sandy soils are especially important in humid growing regions because water drains from them easily. Sandy soils warm faster in the spring, which helps speed early crop development in cooler growing areas.

ROTATION. Many insect, disease organisms, weed, and nematode pests negatively impact watermelon growth. Crop rotation can play an important role in reducing the impact of these problems. Most rotation recommendations are for withholding watermelon production in fields that have had watermelons planted within the previous 4–8 years. This rotation is particularly important for varieties of watermelon susceptible to the disease organism that causes fusarium wilt. Rotation with vegetables unrelated to watermelon, or rotation with grain crops or pasture grasses would minimize some of the pest problems facing successful watermelon culture in most production areas in the United States.

Figure 5.1. Watermelons growing on sandy loam soil in northern Florida. (Source: G.J. Hochmuth.)

When available land for rotation is scarce, growers should follow strict sanitation practices. Old watermelon plant residue can harbor insects, nematodes, and disease organisms. Therefore, this season's crop residue should be thoroughly incorporated in the soil to decompose before planting watermelon in a neighboring field. Careful planning must be given to a rotation scheme to maximize the benefit.

SOIL TESTING. Lime requirements and fertilizer needs for watermelon are determined by calibrated soil tests. Not all soil testing labs can provide proper lime or fertilizer recommendations for any one soil sample. Growers should seek assistance from the local extension service for recommendations for a suitable private or public lab to test the soil samples. Soil samples should be representative of the production field or management unit in a large field. Depending on previous cropping practices or history of the field, native soil fertility or pH may vary considerably across the field. Careful sampling will detect differences in native fertility and lead to maximum efficiency in lime and fertilizer use. Most soil testing labs recommend sampling units of 10–20 acres with about 20 soil cores taken from the upper 6 inches of soil in each unit. Most labs will provide sampling and mailing bags and instructions on proper soil sampling. Soil testing is particularly important for watermelon, compared to other vegetables, when long rotations with unfertilized pastures are practiced.

SOIL REACTION (pH). Watermelon can be successfully produced on soils varying in reaction from 5.5–7.5. Most University soil testing specialists recommend a soil pH of 6.0–6.5 for watermelon production. Watermelon tolerance of slightly acidic soils was recognized by early watermelon producers in the southeastern United States when watermelon was often the first crop to be produced on newly cleared land. Unless otherwise stated, most text references to pH are for pH measured in a mixture of soil and water. This water pH measurement is usually not sufficient alone to determine the amount of lime needed. Most labs will conduct a buffer-pH test for lime requirement. A calibrated lime requirement test should be used to evaluate the soil's pH and determine the amount of lime to use, if needed. Dolomite or calcite lime can be used to increase the soil pH. Dolomite would be the choice if an increase in magnesium (Mg) is needed as determined by the soil test. Lime requires time to fully counteract the soil acidity. However, if lime is needed and timely application well before planting is not possible, it is better to apply it closer to planting than not to apply it at all.

LIME AND CALCIUM. Often the calcium (Ca) concentration in the soil is confused with soil pH. Low soil pH does not always mean low Ca concentration. Growers should be concerned about the soil's Ca status, independent of pH, since Ca deficiency can lead to increased blossom-end-rot in watermelon (see Fig. 7.26). Liming of an acidic soil to correct the pH usually provides ample Ca.

However, soils in the slightly acidic, but acceptable pH range might not need Ca. For example, soils in Florida of pH (water) 6.0 and testing above 300 ppm Mehlich-1 Ca would not require lime or Ca fertilizer. A soil with less than 300 ppm Ca may require Ca fertilization. Seeded and seedless watermelons have similar soil pH and Ca requirements.

FERTILIZER. Optimum fertility management begins with the calibrated soil test. The term calibration refers to the process of determining the best soil test procedure and then field-testing the fertilizer recommendations made with that test. Therefore, the soil test procedure used in the lab is calibrated to give the proper fertilizer recommendations for a particular growing region and soil. A soil test procedure calibrated for the high-pH soils of the southwestern United States would not likely be calibrated for the sandy, acidic soils of the humid, southeastern United States. Soil testing and fertilizer recommendations can be greatly influenced by the particular soil test methodology and fertilization philosophy employed by a particular lab. Watermelon growers should carefully investigate the soil testing lab's procedures and recommendations, using guidance from the local extension service. The fertilizer recommendations presented in this chapter (Table 5.1) are only to document watermelon fertilizer recommendations from various regions in the country and should not be construed as generally applicable.

The following discussion on fertilizer management for watermelon presents general guidelines used in many states, however it is not meant to be a specific recommendation. The reader is encouraged to learn more about the details of fertilizer management pertaining to specific production areas from the local extension service.

Most labs test soil for phosphorus (P), potassium (K), Mg, Ca, and several micronutrients, including manganese (Mn), copper (Cu), zinc (Zn), and boron (B). The test results are interpreted in most labs in categories such as "very high," "high," "medium," "low," and "very low." These categories refer to the current fertility status of the soil for a particular nutrient in question. For example, a "very high" test interpretation for P would mean the soil is very high in P and fertilization with P would not be expected to return an economic benefit in terms of increased yield, earliness, or fruit quality. If the soil test is calibrated, then growers should be confident that refraining from applying fertilizer to a "very high" soil would not cause reductions in crop yield or quality. Most universities in the country would recommend 100–150 lb/acre P_2O_5 and a similar amount of K for the season for soils testing very low in these nutrients. These rates are calculated for watermelons planted in rows or beds with 8 ft between the center of one row or bed to the center of the adjacent row or bed.

Nitrogen (N) can leach in most agricultural soils; therefore, most soil testing

Table 5.1. Maximum recommended fertilizer amounts for selected watermelon-growing regions in the United States.

Producing region	Fertilizer recommendation (lb N–P_2O_5–K_2O/acre)[z]
Florida	150–150–150[y]
Maryland/Delaware	150–30–100[x]
Oklahoma	100–100–250
Texas	120–80–80[x]
Central California	150–100–0[w]

[z]Rates adjusted downward depending on soil test results.
[y]Rates calculated based on crop planted in rows on 8-ft centers.
[x]Typical fertilizer needs for most farms.
[w]K added if soil test indicates a need.

labs do not employ soil testing to determine N fertilizer needs for watermelon. Some labs in more arid climates occasionally use a soil NO_3-N test to help predict sidedress N fertilizer needs. Nitrogen recommendations usually consist of a total amount of N required by the crop and guidelines on how to manage the N during the season. Most recommendations are for 100–150 lb of N per acre. Excessive N, particularly in cool growing regions or seasons, can increase hollowheart incidence.

Placement and time of application of fertilizer depends largely on the soil type and cultural practices to be employed for watermelon production. For example, for watermelons produced on very sandy soils, split applications of the mobile nutrients, such as N and K are important to avoid losses of these nutrients to leaching. On finer-textured soils, K is less subject to leaching and, under this situation, one application of K might be suitable.

In most production situations, banding the P and micronutrients and a portion of the K near the row is recommended. An alternative practice, especially with polyethylene mulch culture, is to incorporate the fertilizer in the bed area. This modified broadcast method places the fertilizer in the root zone under the mulch and not in the area between the rows where the fertilizer might be subject to leaching or would be available only to weeds. In unmulched cultural systems, a general recommendation would be to apply all P and micronutrients, and a portion of the K and N either banded or by the modified broadcast method. Typically, only a portion of the K and N is applied in the bed at or before planting because high rates of fertilizer may damage young seedlings or transplants. In addition, N and K are the nutrients most likely to leach, especially from sandy soils, and hence, reserving a portion of this fertilizer for application later in the

Figure 5.2. Black polyethylene mulched beds provide protection of fertilizer from leaching. (Source: G.J. Hochmuth.)

season, saves resources and money.

The remaining fertilizer is applied to the sides of the plants in one or two applications as the crop develops, usually at the four- to five-leaf stage, and again when early runners are forming. On sandy soils, additional N and K might be needed to replace leached N or K after heavy rainfall.

FERTILIZATION WITH POLYETHYLENE MULCH CULTURE. Many watermelon producers have been turning to the polyethylene mulch cultural system for production of their crop (Fig. 5.2). With mulch culture, the fertilizer can be protected from leaching. All the fertilizer can be placed under the mulch if soluble fertilizer burn is not a concern, as might be the case on heavier soils. With the mulch system, fertilizer can still be applied in split-applications by drip irrigation or by a liquid injection wheel. The injection wheel is an implement that pierces the mulch film and injects fertilizer into the soil. With mulch culture, typically all of the P and micronutrients, and a portion of the N and K are applied in the bed by banding or modified broadcast and the remaining N and K would be applied by drip irrigation or the injection wheel.

Table 5.2. Injection schedule for N and K for drip-irrigated watermelon production in Florida on soils low in K.

Crop development stage[y]	Stage (weeks)	Injection (lb per acre per day)[z]	
		N	K_2O
1	2	1.0	1.0
2	2	1.5	1.5
3	4	2.5	2.5
4	3	1.5	1.5
5	2	1.0	1.0

[z]All nutrients injected. Actual amounts may be lower depending on amount of N and K placed in the bed and on the soil test result.
[y]Starting from date of seedling emergence or transplanting. First 2 weeks worth of injecting can be omitted if 25% of total N and K was placed in the bed preplant.

Many watermelon growers using polyethylene mulch are also using drip irrigation to supply the fertilizer. In the drip system liquid fertilizer is injected into the irrigation system, referred to as fertigation. Typically, injections consist of N and K only and can be scheduled according to the crop growth pattern (Table 5.2).

Foliar application with N, P, and K has not been proven to be effective. Watermelon plants have unusually effective and extensive root systems for absorbing nutrients. Proper timing of application of nutrients or fertigating with drip irrigation will supply enough nutrients at the correct time for normal watermelon crop development. Sometimes, watermelon crops might benefit from foliar application of micronutrients. Some micronutrients might not be readily available to the plant in very high pH soils so foliar application of zinc or manganese might be beneficial.

Likewise, foliar application of purported plant growth stimulant chemicals has not been shown to be consistently beneficial for watermelon yield or fruit quality. In most crops where the fertilizer and irrigation programs are being well

Table 5.3. Plant tissue analysis (dry weight basis) of most-recently-matured leaves of watermelon at several growth stages.

Growth stage status	N (%)	P (%)	K (%)	Ca (%)	Mg (%)	S (%)	Fe (ppm)	Mn (ppm)	Zn (ppm)	B (ppm)	Cu (ppm)
Last cultivation											
Deficient	<3.0	0.25	3.0	1.0	0.25	0.20	30	20	20	20	5
Adequate	3.0	0.25	3.0	1.0	0.25	0.20	30	20	20	20	5
Range	4.0	0.50	4.0	2.0	0.50	0.40	100	100	40	40	10
High	>4.0	0.50	4.0	2.0	0.50	0.40	100	100	40	40	10
First flower											
Deficient	<2.5	0.25	2.7	1.0	0.25	0.20	30	20	20	20	5
Adequate	2.5	0.25	2.7	1.0	0.25	0.20	30	20	20	20	5
Range	3.5	0.50	3.5	2.0	0.50	0.40	100	100	40	40	10
High	>3.5	0.50	3.5	2.0	0.50	0.40	100	100	40	40	10
First fruit											
Deficient	<2.0	0.25	2.3	1.0	0.25	0.20	30	20	20	20	5
Adequate	2.0	0.25	2.3	1.0	0.25	0.20	30	20	20	20	5
Range	3.0	0.50	3.5	2.0	0.50	0.40	100	100	40	40	10
High	>3.0	0.50	3.5	2.0	0.50	0.40	100	100	40	40	10
Harvest period											
Deficient	<2.0	0.25	2.0	1.0	0.25	0.20	30	20	20	20	3
Adequate	2.0	0.25	2.0	1.0	0.25	0.20	30	20	20	20	3
Range	3.0	0.50	3.0	2.0	0.50	0.40	100	100	40	40	10
High	>3.0	0.50	3.0	2.0	0.50	0.40	100	100	40	40	10

managed, there is no need for additional nutrient or growth stimulant application.

Fertilizer requirements of most watermelon varieties are similar. Round and oblong-fruited varieties require similar amounts of fertilizer. Likewise, seedless varieties have not been shown to require different amounts of fertilizer, compared to seeded varieties. Fruit flesh color is influenced more by the variety and by the growing conditions than by fertilization. Extra fertilizer, applied at a certain time in the season, will not influence fruit color or firmness, as long as the normal fertilizer program is optimal and is being managed well.

PLANT TISSUE TESTING. Nutritional status of the crop can be monitored by leaf testing or by petiole sap testing. For leaf testing, the most-recently-matured whole leaf (plus petiole) should be collected from representative plants in the field. Leaves should be sent rapidly to a reputable laboratory for analysis of their nutrient content. The analytical results are compared with standard normal nutrient ranges for the crop at the particular growth stage in question. Sufficiency ranges used in Florida are presented in Table 5.3.

Petiole sap testing (Fig. 5.3) is a suitable alternative to leaf analysis where a quick answer is needed for making adjustments in the fertilization program, or for routine monitoring of the crop's nutritional status. Currently, sap analysis procedures have been developed for N and K. For sap testing, petioles of most-recently-matured (usually fourth or fifth leaf from the growing tip) leaves are selected from the field and the sap is expressed from the petiole. The nitrate and K concentrations in the sap are determined by a hand-held colorimeter or ion-specific meter, and the results compared against calibrated standard sufficiency ranges, such as those used in Florida (Table 5.4).

SOIL PREPARATION. Watermelon plants have very deep and extensive root systems. Therefore, well-prepared soils usually lead to the most successful crops. Preparation usually consists of plowing and disking to incorporate any plant residue from the cover crop, and perhaps subsoiling to break any

Figure 5.3. Petiole sap testing. Petioles are chopped and the sap pressed out. Nitrate-N or K concentrations in the sap are measured with an ion-specific meter. (Source: G.J. Hochmuth.)

Table 5.4. Sufficiency ranges for petiole sap testing for watermelon.

Growth stage	Fresh petiole sap concn (ppm)	
	NO$_3$-N	K
Vines 6 inches long	1200–1500	4000–5000
Fruits 2 inches long	1000–1200	4000–5000
Fruits one-half mature	800–1000	3500–4000
At first harvest	600–800	3000–3500

tillage hardpans that might impede root development. Most watermelon crops are grown on raised beds. Raised beds (Fig. 5.4) help the soil dry out and warm up in the spring and protect the plants from flooding in wet periods. In southern California, watermelon growers plant on south-sloping beds to take advantage of the warming of the soil by the sun on the sides of the beds. Bedding also is used in the mulch production system. Bedding might not be an advantage on warm, sandy soils not prone to flooding.

Well-prepared soil is a requirement for the polyethylene mulch system where good soil-to-mulch contact is needed to ensure tight fit of the mulch to the bed. In some cases, a rototiller is needed to finish the soil preparation before bed formation and mulch application.

VARIETY SELECTION

Variety selection, often made several months before planting, is one of the most important management decisions made by the watermelon grower. Failure to select the most suitable variety or varieties may lead to loss of yield or market acceptability.

The following characteristics should be considered in selection of watermelon varieties.

YIELD. The variety selected should produce crops equivalent to the best varieties available. Yields vary considerably among production areas and seasons. The interaction of

Figure 5.4. Raising soil into beds helps warm the soil for early planting and helps water drain from the root zone. (Source: G.J. Hochmuth.)

variety, production technology and weather conditions result in the yield of product produced. Harvested yield may be less than potential yield because of market constraints.

DISEASE RESISTANCE. Varieties that combine disease resistance with other desirable horticultural characteristics should be selected when possible. Watermelon varieties selected for use should have resistance to anthracnose-race 1 and fusarium wilt. There is considerable variation among varieties in the degree of fusarium resistance; select varieties with high wilt resistance that have qualities compatible with other requirements.

HORTICULTURE QUALITY. Watermelon fruit size and shape; rind color; thickness and toughness; seed size, color, and number; and flesh color, texture, soluble solids (10% is required for designation as very good internal quality), and freedom from fruit defects are all important characteristics to be considered in selection of watermelon varieties. In addition, triploid varieties should be free of hard seeds and have undeveloped seeds that are small and innocuous. Ability to germinate in cold soils and general plant vigor may be important in certain situations.

ADAPTABILITY. Watermelons require a rather long growing season with warm days and nights for optimum commercial production. Accordingly, not all areas of the United States have the best weather for growing watermelons. The U.S. Department of Agriculture lists only 17 states as being commercial watermelon producers. Nevertheless, watermelons can be grown successfully in home gardens and for local sales in most states by using adapted varieties and various weather-moderating devices such as row covers or tunnels. (see Fig. 1.4)

MARKET ACCEPTABILITY. Watermelon growers must be aware of the needs of the particular market they intend to supply, and grow types and varieties that satisfy the market.

Table 5.5. Planting dates for selected watermelon-producing regions in the United States.

Growing region	Planting periods[z]
North Florida	15 Feb.–15 Apr.
Central Florida	15 Jan.–15 Mar.
South Florida	15 Dec.–1 Mar.
Eastern Shore of Maryland	15 Apr.–1 May
Southern Delaware	15 Apr.–10 May
Oklahoma	Late March–mid-April
Imperial Valley of California	Mid-December–March

[z]Transplanting done after threat of frost is over, is usually nearer the latter dates in the planting period.

Figure 5.5. Using well-grown transplants may result in earlier yields. (Source: D.N. Maynard.)

CROP ESTABLISHMENT

Watermelon crops can be established in the field from seed or from transplants. Transplanting is becoming more common because transplanting usually results in earlier crops then those that are direct seeded. Transplants are used exclusively to establish seedless watermelon plantings.

Watermelons are planted somewhere in the United States in most months of the year (Table 5.5). Planting begins in the winter months in south Florida and extends into May or June in the northern states. Some growers in Florida and Texas plant a fall crop in late July or August.

TRANSPLANT PRODUCTION. Diploid and triploid watermelon crops can be established easily with high quality transplants (Fig. 5.5). Transplanting helps achieve rapid, complete plant stands, especially where seed costs make direct-seeding risky and expensive, as would be the case with seedless watermelons. Transplanting also often results in the earliest crops, an important factor in achieving production under more favorable early-season prices. Most watermelon growers purchase plants from plant growing experts (Fig. 5.6) who may arrange for transport to the field location (Fig. 5.7).

Containerized production of triploid watermelon transplants is essential because of the special conditions required for seed germination, emergence, and early plant development not found in open-field situations. Furthermore, the extra cost of seedling production is justified because triploid watermelon seeds costs are about six times greater than those of diploid hybrid seeds

Figure 5.6. Commercial production of watermelon transplants. (Source: D.N. Maynard.)

and 60 times greater than open-pollinated diploid watermelon seeds. One seed per cell should be planted 1 inch deep with the radicle (pointed end) up to reduce seedcoat adherence to the cotyledons. Transplants have been successfully produced with peat pellets or in trays containing sterile media with 1–2 inch cell size. The tray is watered lightly to bring the seed and mix in contact. Stacked trays are placed in a germination chamber at 85–90 °F for 2 days or until radicles are visible in the cell drainage holes. The trays are then arranged in a greenhouse with day temperature 70–80 °F and night temperature 65–70 °F where temperature control can be achieved. Plants are fertilized every 3 days with a solution containing 50 ppm N from $Ca(NO_3)_2$ and KNO_3 from cotyledon expansion until the first true leaf is fully expanded, then with a 200 ppm N solution applied every other day until the second true leaf is fully expanded, finally the fertilizer is reduced for several days before transplanting to the field. Plants are ready for transplanting when the roots are sufficiently developed to permit removal from the cell with the entire growing mix volume intact. This will require 4 to 6 weeks depending on cell size and growing conditions.

TRANSPLANTING. Transplanting is done with machines or mechanical planting aides employing people to place the plant in the soil (Fig. 5.8). Small-acreage producers might place the transplants in the field manually. Under cool soil conditions in the spring, transplant establishment usually benefits from fertilization of the plant as it is placed in the soil. Starter fertilizer solution, consisting mostly of N and P can be placed in the planting hole with the transplant mechanically or manually.

Figure 5.8. Transplanting watermelons in the field. The person walking behind is responsible for setting skipped or improperly set plants. (Source: D.N. Maynard.)

FIELD SEEDING. Watermelon seeds should be planted 1/2–2 inches deep using about 1–2 lb of seed per acre. The shallow depth should be used for heavier, cooler soils. The seeding rate will vary depending on the plant spacing desired and the row spacing employed. Use of modern planters that can place single seeds at desired spacing results in efficient seed use (0.25–0.5 lb of seed per acre), especially with the more expensive modern hybrid varieties. Seeds germinate poorly at soil temperatures below 60 °F, and are subject to attack from soilborne disease organisms, resulting in reduced plant stands that may require replanting of the crop.

CROP PRODUCTION

FIELD ARRANGEMENT FOR TRIPLOID PRODUCTION. Watermelon fruit set and enlargement is dependent upon growth regulators from the pollen grains and from embryos in developing seeds within the fruit. Inadequate pollination results in triploid watermelon fruit that are triangular in shape and of poor quality. Inadequate pollination may increase the incidence of hollowheart. Triploid watermelon flowers do not produce sufficient viable pollen to induce fruit set and development. Therefore, pollen from a normal diploid seeded watermelon variety must be provided. Fields should be interplanted with pollenizer, diploid watermelon plants to provide additional pollen. Planting the pollenizer variety in the outside row and then every third row is one recommendation. As an alternative, the pollenizer variety may be planted every third plant in a row but this makes harvesting difficult. Regardless of the planting arrangement, it is necessary to have an adequate bee population for transfer of the pollen (more information on pollination is provided later in this chapter).

It is important to use a pollenizer variety that is marketable because up to one-third of all watermelons produced in the field will be of this variety. The rind pattern and/or shape of the seeded pollenizer fruit should be distinguished easily from that of the triploid fruit to reduce confusion at harvest. Selection of a pollenizer variety should also take into account market demand, plant vigor, pollen production, disease resistance, and environmental conditions.

It is important that pollen from the diploid pollenizer variety is available when female blossoms on the triploid plants are open and ready for pollination. As a general rule, direct field seeding of the pollenizer variety should be done on the same day the triploid seed is planted in the greenhouse. If transplants are used for pollenizers, they can be seeded a few days before triploid transplants are scheduled to be seeded. Small fruited, icebox varieties usually flower earlier than standard watermelon varieties. If icebox varieties are to be used as the pollenizer, then direct seeding should be delayed a week to 10 days. The diploid pollenizer variety will frequently set fruit and stop producing male blossoms while the

Figure 5.9. Small grain (winter wheat) between each bed serves as a windbreak in Jefferson County, Okla. (Source: J.E. Motes.)

triploid variety is still producing many female blossoms. Growers may make a second planting of a pollenizer 2–3 weeks after the initial planting to provide pollen for the late-developing female blossoms. There are no consistent differences among any standard or icebox types in effectiveness of pollination. Icebox varieties used as pollenizers generally result in high early yields; standard varieties used as pollenizers result in high total yields.

WINDBREAKS. Windbreaks should be included in most watermelon production systems in most producing regions in the United States. Windbreaks commonly consist of winter rye cover crop or other small grain for most watermelon regions (Fig. 5.9). In the southern part of Florida, sugar cane is often used. The winter rye can be sown in broadcast fashion in the fall as a cover crop. Then, in the spring, the areas for the watermelon beds are tilled for the watermelon crop and strips of the rye cover are left as windbreaks. Alternatively, the windbreak crop can be planted in strips in the fall. Most recommendations for windbreaks call for spacing them about 12 ft apart for every foot in height. For example, if the rye windbreak is 4 ft tall, then the strips should be placed about 50 ft apart. Closer spacing might be advantageous, especially where watermelons are produced on very sandy soils in windy, exposed locations. Many researchers and growers report success with strips of rye between every bed, as would be the case if the watermelon beds were prepared in a winter rye cover crop. Some growers plant the windbreaks every five or six rows of watermelons. The windbreaks are then mowed or disked at the end of their useful life to become the drive roads for the sprayer or harvesting vehicles.

PLANT AND ROW SPACING. Watermelon plants develop several vigorous and far-reaching vines, thus requiring large amounts of space for optimum growth and fruit development. Years ago, watermelons were seeded with 6 or 8 ft between plants in rows 12–15 ft apart. This wide spacing reflected the greater availability of land then. Also, the wide spacing provided less interplant competition for water, since irrigation was rarely used at that time. Today, cultural practices such as irrigation and polyethylene mulch have led to the use of higher plant

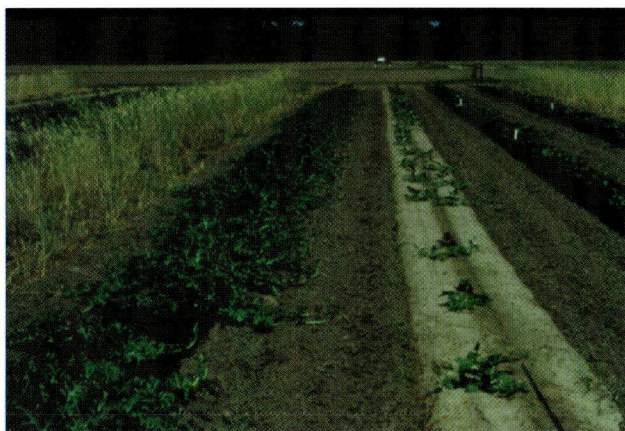

Figure 5.10. Watermelons from transplants on black mulch compared to those from direct seeding on bare ground. (Source: G.J. Hochmuth.)

populations. Row spacing of 6–8 ft apart and plant spacing of 2–4 ft are common. Greater plant populations might lead to smaller average fruit size for some varieties. Often, with close plant spacing, the individual plant sets fewer fruits, which still reach normal size.

MULCHING. Watermelon responds well to mulching the beds with polyethylene film. Mulching has several benefits for watermelon production. Weed growth is reduced in the mulched bed area when opaque mulches, especially black films, are used. Mulch film reduces water evaporation from the soil under the film, thus reducing irrigation requirements. Mulching, especially with clear and black films, promotes warming of the soil, enhancing plant growth rate, and increasing early yields (Fig. 5.10). Earliness is an especially important factor in profitable watermelon production in many areas of the country.

Watermelon growers can choose from several major classes of polyethylene films. Black film (Fig. 5.11) is the most commonly used mulch. This colored film warms the soil (by soil contact) and prevents the growth of most weeds except nutgrass. Black film can be used in most watermelon growing regions of the United States. Clear film (Fig. 5.12) warms the soil more (greenhouse effect) than black film, but clear film does not prevent weed growth; a herbicide or fumigant is needed with clear film for weed control. Clear film finds its widest use in northern growing regions where the extra soil warming is important for earlier harvests. White or white-on-black films are used in grow-

Figure 5.11. Black polyethylene film applied to raised beds in Florida. (Source: G.J. Hochmuth.)

Figure 5.12. Clear polyethylene film for watermelons in Maryland. (Source: G.J. Hochmuth.)

ing regions where heating of the soil is not desired, such as fall production in the southern part of the country. These films reflect radiant energy, thus reducing the buildup of heat in the soil. Specialty films, such as wavelength-selective films and photodegradable films are used in some watermelon production areas. Some wavelength-selective films transmit only parts of the light spectrum, for example excluding the light needed for weed growth. Thus the film behaves like a clear film in warming the soil, but reduces or prevents weed growth under the film since certain light wavelengths needed for plant growth are not transmitted by the film. Photodegradable films become brittle and self-destruct on receipt of a specified amount of radiant energy. These films are promoted on the basis that they degrade in the field and manual removal at the end of the season is not needed. Specialty films should be carefully evaluated in a particular growing region to determine their application for watermelon production in that area.

Mulch films are mechanically applied to the bed area before planting the crop. The beds are prepared by raising well-tilled soil into a bed and then shaping and pressing the soil into a finished bed to which the mulch film is applied. In most watermelon-growing regions, beds 4–6 inches high and 24–40 inches across the top surface are adequate. The edges of the film are buried at the edges of the beds to secure the mulch film against wind. It is important to have a tight fit of the film to the surface of the bed to reduce wind damage of the film and to maximize heat transfer to the soil, especially with black film. If drip irrigation will be used to irrigate or fertigate the crop, the drip tubing would be laid slightly below the soil surface, on the surface of the bed, or in a groove in the surface of the bed before mulch application.

Planting through the film is accomplished by manually punching holes in the film for seeding or transplanting. Mechanical transplanters and seeders, equipped to punch the holes in the mulch at preset plant spacing are available.

Polyethylene film does not biodegrade, therefore it must be removed from the field. Mulch film can be removed by hand. As long as weeds have been controlled, hand removal is not very difficult. Cutting the film down the center

Figure 5.13. Clear polyethylene wire-supported tunnels for crop growth enhancement. (Source: G.J. Hochmuth.)

Figure 5.14. Polypropylene floating row covers for growth enhancement and crop protection. (Source: G.J. Hochmuth.)

Figure 5.15. Styrofoam soup cups used to protect watermelon transplants from frost. (Source: G.J. Hochmuth.)

of the bed makes removal easier. Mulch also can be lifted from the bed mechanically and either hand or mechanically gathered (baled) from the field. Baled mulch is easier to handle for disposal.

GROWTH ENHANCEMENT. Watermelon plants grow most rapidly under warm conditions. Research has documented increased growth rate and earlier crops when watermelons are grown under row tunnels or row covers. Clear, wire-hoop supported polyethylene row tunnels (Fig. 5.13) can be installed over polyethylene mulched beds with transplants. Row tunnels must be removed as flowering begins. Floating row covers (Fig. 5.14) can be laid over the crop to provide growth enhancement or frost protection. Styrofoam plant covers (Fig. 5.15) are an inexpensive means to protect young watermelon plants from frost. The cups can be secured in position in the hole in the mulch film.

IRRIGATION. Irrigation is needed for consistent production of large yields of high-quality fruits. Overhead sprinkler, drip irrigation, furrow, and subsurface irrigation are the most commonly found irrigation systems employed in watermelon production. Irrigation systems vary in capital and operating costs, and in operation efficiency. Therefore, selection of an irrigation system should be made after careful consideration of these

Figure 5.16. Center-pivot system
irrigating watermelons in
Maryland. (Source: G.J.
Hochmuth.)

factors. Sprinkler (Fig. 5.16)
systems (solid-set, side roll,
cable tow, and center pivot)
are common on many veg-
etable farms, some systems
requiring labor to move pipe.
Sprinkler systems wet the
crop leaves, which might promote disease development, and also wet the soil
surface area between watermelon rows, thus promoting weed growth. Furrow
irrigation is inexpensive to use and is applicable to only certain areas of the
country where water can be transmitted down lengths of furrows beside the rows
in the field. Furrow irrigation is not practical in deep, sandy soils. Subsurface
irrigation is used in certain areas, especially Florida, where there is a natural
hardpan below the soil surface on which the irrigator can perch a water table.
Water efficiency is low with this system. Drip irrigation is becoming more standard on many vegetable farms all over the country. Water is applied to the soil in
the bed area only, thus conserving water on the farm. Fertilizers also can be
applied to the crop through the drip tubes.

Irrigation needs of the watermelon crop can be estimated by accounting for
the water needs of the plant, and the water losses by plant transpiration and
evaporation from the soil. The water use in the field is referred to as evapotrans-
piration and irrigation managers need to be able to estimate this value to be able
to efficiently manage water for the watermelon crop (Fig. 5.17). Public or private
advisors can assist growers in managing irrigation systems to maximize efficiency.

Water needs of the
crop are particularly
important at stand estab-
lishment and during fruit
sizing. Water stress at
these times can seriously
reduce crop development

Figure 5.17. Evaporation
pan used to estimate evapo-
transpiration. (Source: G.J.
Hochmuth.)

and fruit yields. Water needs, at certain growth stages, might approach 100% of reference ET, and the irrigation system must be able to deliver the needed amount of water on a timely basis. Tensiometers can be used in the field to monitor soil moisture in the root zone. Tensiometers can help determine irrigation frequency and crop ET estimates can help determine how much water to apply.

Drip irrigation. This is a very efficient system from a water use perspective, but requires time and attention for system management. Drip tubes are laid in or on the soil near the plant row and water application is restricted to the plant root zone. There are many drip tapes available, the expense of which is mostly determined by the thickness of the tape wall and the type of water emitter employed. Tapes come with several options of emitter spacing along the tape. Typically for watermelon, an emitter spacing of 12–24 inches is recommended. The closer spacing is recommended for sandy soils, and the greater spacing for heavier soils.

Drip irrigation systems are operated in short durations during the day or week to apply the needed amounts of water. Since heavy soils can hold more water in the root zone than sandy soils, the duration of irrigation can be longer and the frequency can be less for watermelons grown on loam soils compared to sandy soils. As the crop grows, the crop water needs increase and so must the irrigation amounts. On heavy soils, the length of the irrigation event can be extended. On sandy soils, the best approach is to increase the number of irrigations in the week or day. Since sandy soils hold limited amounts of water in the root zone, extending the irrigation duration too long would result in application of more water than the soil in the root zone could hold. Excess water would then drain deep in the soil, possibly carrying fertilizer nutrients with it. Although drip irrigation can be a powerful tool for water management, it requires careful attention for maximum benefit.

POLLINATION. Watermelon plants usually have separate male and female flowers but sometimes produce perfect flowers. To achieve fruit set, pollen from the male flower must be transferred to a female flower on that plant or another plant in the field. This pollen transfer is accomplished by several naturally occurring insects, but most effectively by the honeybee. The natural populations of honeybees have declined in most watermelon producing areas, so that commercially-supplied honeybees are recommended. Honeybee hives are placed in or near the field at the rate of at least 1 hive per acre. Usually one strong hive of 50 to 60 thousand bees will be sufficient for each acre of watermelons. Placing hives in groups of 8–10 around the edges of fields, rather than in the field, provides for unobstructed access to the fields (Fig. 5.18). Also, the hives are easier to manage and care for during the pollination season. Hives should be placed near the field when female flowers start to appear. Growers will need to contract with reputable beekeepers and usually it is a good

Figure 5.18. Bees are necessary for pollination of watermelon flowers. (Source: D.N. Maynard.)

idea to have a written contract for the services.

Fruit set and fruit size and shape are closely related to the number of visits of the pollinator to each flower. Some research showed that fruit set was significantly reduced when flowers received less than four visits. Poor or ineffective pollination of watermelons results in jug-neck fruits of long-fruited watermelon varieties (see Fig. 7.27). In round-fruited varieties, poorly pollinated fruits can be flat-sided or misshapen.

Honeybees are extremely sensitive to most pesticides used in watermelon fields, and therefore pest control activities must be carefully scheduled to minimize risk to the beehives. Watermelon flowers open in the early morning and remain open through midddle to late afternoon. Honeybees can be observed in the field from early morning until late afternoon or early evening, almost until sunset. This means that pesticide spraying should be delayed until nearly sundown, or death to the pollinating bees might occur.

ANIMAL PESTS. Watermelon crops can be very attractive to several animal pests and the damage can be of economic concern. Most common animal pests of watermelon crops early in the season are rodents, which unearth and eat the seeds. Mowing and brush removal around the edges of fields will help reduce rodent populations. Transplanting might be an alternative to seeding in some fields notorious for rodent damage to seeds.

Deer, coyotes, wild hogs, raccoons (Fig. 5.19), and crows (Fig. 5.20) are particularly attracted to watermelon fruits. Coyotes are becoming serious pests in many watermelon grow-

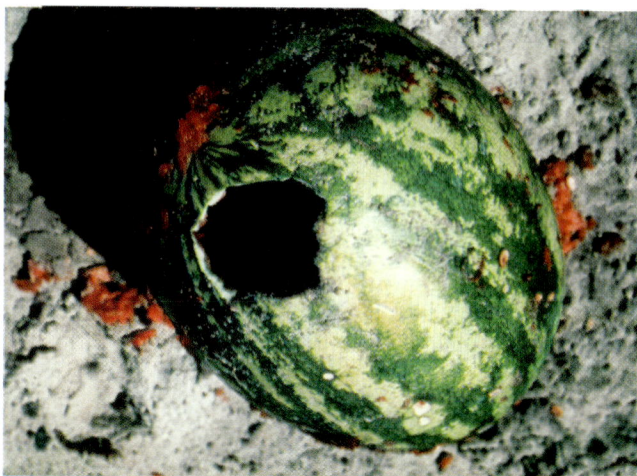

Figure 5.19. Typical raccoon damage to a watermelon fruit. (Source: D.N. Maynard.)

Figure 5.20. Crow damage to a watermelon fruit. (Source: G.J. Hochmuth.)

ing regions of the country. Damage can be severe, just as the fruits are beginning to ripen. Fencing small fields with electric wire sometimes helps reduce the damage from coyote, but is not practical for deer. Propane or carbide noise guns and visual scarecrows or balloons are marginally effective for short periods, until the pests become acquainted with the noise or new sight. Trapping and shooting, where legal or approved, can be effective, but is costly and time consuming. Chemical repellants have been tried with varying amounts of success.

General References

Beste, E., D. Caron, G. Dively, K. Everts, E. Kee, D. Walker, J. Whalen, J. Windsor, and T. Wooten. No date. Watermelon production guide for Delaware and Maryland. Del. Coop. Ext. Serv.

Dainello, F.J. 1996. Texas commercial vegetable production guide. Tex. Agr. Ext. Serv. Hort 6.

Hartz, T. 1999. Watermelon production in California. Web page vric.ucdavis.edu.

Hochmuth, G., D. Maynard, C. Vavrina, and E. Hanlon. 1991. Plant tissue analysis and interpretation for vegetable crops in Florida. Fla. Coop. Ext. Serv. Spec. Ser. Vec. 42.

Maynard, D.N. and S.M. Olson. 2000. Vegetable production guide for Florida. Fla. Coop. Ext. Serv. SP 170.

Maynard, D.N. (ed.). 1992. Watermelon production guide for Florida. Fla. Agr. Ext. Serv. Publ. SP 113.

Motes, J. and G. Cuperus (eds.). 1995. Cucurbit production and pest management. Okla. Coop. Ext. Serv. Circ. E-853.

CHAPTER 6

NEMATODE-INDUCED MALADIES

K.R. Barker and G.J. Holmes

Nematodes are very destructive pathogens on all cultivated cucurbits, including watermelon. Nematodes actually are a very diverse group of organisms that occur worldwide in virtually every environment. There are more species of nematodes than any other group in the animal kingdom, except insects. Nematodes are nonsegmented roundworms with complete digestive, excretory, muscular, nervous and reproductive systems. They range in size from microscopic inhabitants of mushrooms to 27-ft-long parasites of certain whales. Among the thousands of nematodes, some are parasites of plants in natural areas, crop plants, humans, insects, other animals, and many feed on bacteria, fungi, algae, and even other nematodes.

Although less than 5% of nematode species have been studied and identified, some 2500 species are parasitic on plants. Millions of nematodes can be found within a cubic foot of soil, and many of them parasitize plants. Where conditions are favorable for nematodes, populations of plant-parasitic species can increase dramatically and cause extensive damage to the plant. Plant-parasitic nematodes may be divided into two primary groups: endoparasites which feed and reproduce inside plant tissues such as roots, stems, leaves and seeds; and ectoparasites which generally spend their entire lives in the soil and feed periodically on the surface of plant roots. With few exceptions, plant-parasitic nematodes complete part or all of their life cycle in the soil where they live and move in a film of water in pore spaces. They are vulnerable to desiccation and asphyxiation. Nematodes are spread from place to place by water, wind, infested soil, equipment, animals, and on plant parts such as transplants, bulbs and, in some cases, seed.

PRIMARY NEMATODE PARASITES OF WATERMELON

While many species of plant-parasitic nematodes may reproduce on watermelon, three of about 100 species of root-knot (*Meloidogyne*) nematodes result in the most significant losses: *M. arenaria* (peanut root-knot nematode), *M. incognita* (southern root-knot nematode), and *M. javanica* (Javanese root-knot nematode). The fourth most common species, *M. hapla*,

Figure 6.1. Severely galled watermelon root, infected with *Meloidogyne incognita*.

(northern root-knot nematode) usually does not reproduce on watermelon. Worldwide, yield losses of all crops due to nematodes have been estimated to average about 12% of the potential crop per year; and the total economic loss for all major crops amounts to almost 100 billion dollars annually. Yield losses of watermelon due to root-knot nematodes, alone, range from 0%–50%.

Meloidogyne incognita and *M. javanica* are geographically the most widely distributed of the important root-knot species. Their relative importance on watermelon is heavily dependent upon soil texture and climate. In this regard, *M. javanica* has a greater tolerance to drought and high temperature than *M. incognita*. *Meloidogyne arenaria* also is widely distributed, but occurs primarily in temperate and tropical regions, as does *M. javanica*.

SYMPTOMS OF DAMAGE. The characteristic symptoms of root-knot nematode infections are the spotty growth patterns [poor plant growth often in small (few feet) to large (100–200 ft), oval areas of the field], and the associated root galls are diagnostic. Feeding by these nematodes causes root cells to

Figure 6.2. White, pear-shaped females barely visible to the naked eye of *Meloidogyne* in portion of a galled root (Source: J.N. Sasser.)

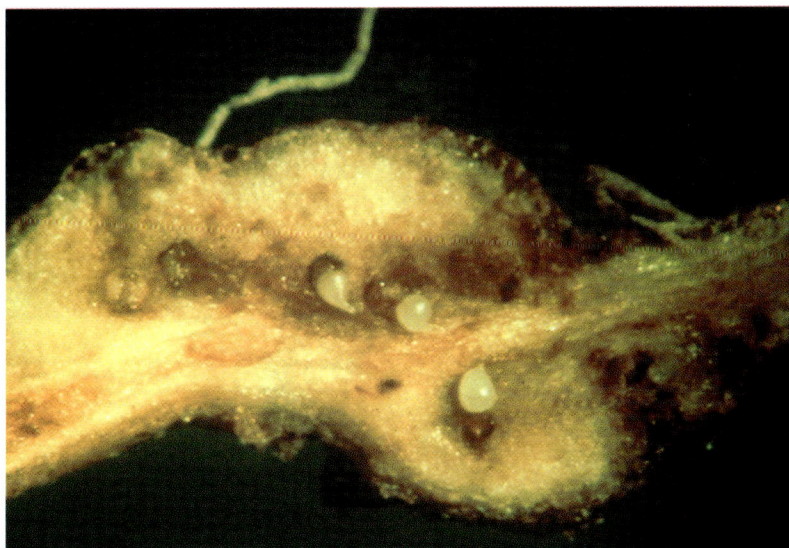

enlarge and multiply, resulting in the formation of galls (Fig. 6.1). Enlarged, pear-shaped females, barely visible to the naked eye, are embedded within galls and can be detected by slicing through the gall tissue with a sharp blade (Fig. 6.2). Many females are often present in a single gall. These galls range from small, individual swellings to severe distortion and restriction of root development. *Meloidogyne incognita* and *M. javanica* typically cause large galls on watermelon which may affect 90%–100% of the root system with the latter causing more extensive gall formation. In contrast, *M. arenaria* induces the formation of bead-like galls which also involves much of the root system. Galled roots often decay due to infections by fungi and bacteria and develop few feeder roots compared to roots of healthy plants.

Above-ground symptoms of infected plants include yellowing of foliage, stunting, fewer leaves and vines, excessive wilting (particularly in dry, hot weather), poor fruit quality and low yields. Heavily infected plants often show nitrogen and/or potassium deficiencies as well as burned/scorched leaf tips and margins. The most severe symptoms, typically occur in a patchy distribution pattern in the field, and this is typical of nematode damage on most crop plants. Although severely damaged plants may die before producing marketable fruit, stunting, wilting, and nutrient deficiencies are more typical. Because of the severe stunting of watermelon plants under heavy nematode infection, weeds are able to grow more readily and become a greater problem than normal. In addition, many weeds, especially broadleaf weeds, are hosts for root-knot nematodes and support reproduction of these pathogens. Thus, the presence of such weeds often increases the severity of root-knot damage on subsequent susceptible crops.

HOST RACES OF *M. incognita* AND *M. arenaria*. Crop-specific or variety-specific forms of some nematode species, including root-knot nematodes, are

Table 6.1. Differential host-test reaction chart for root-knot nematodes.

Meloidogyne species and race	Cotton 'Deltapine 61'	Tobacco 'NC 95'	Pepper 'California Wonder'	Watermelon 'Charleston Gray'	Peanut 'Florunner'	Tomato 'Rutgers'
M. incognita						
race 1		— □ᶻ	— □	+	+	— +
race 2	— □	+	□ +	+	+	— +
race 3	+	□	— □	+	+	— +
race 4	+	□	+ □	+	+	— +
M. javanica	—	+	— □	+	—	+
M. arenaria						
race 1	—	—	++		++	□ +
race 2	—	—	+ —	—	+ —	□ +
M. hapla	— +	+	+	— □	+ □	+

ᶻPlus sign = susceptibility, and minus sign = resistance to *Meloidogyne* species/races. Box indicates key differential host plants. Source: Sasser and Carter, 1985.

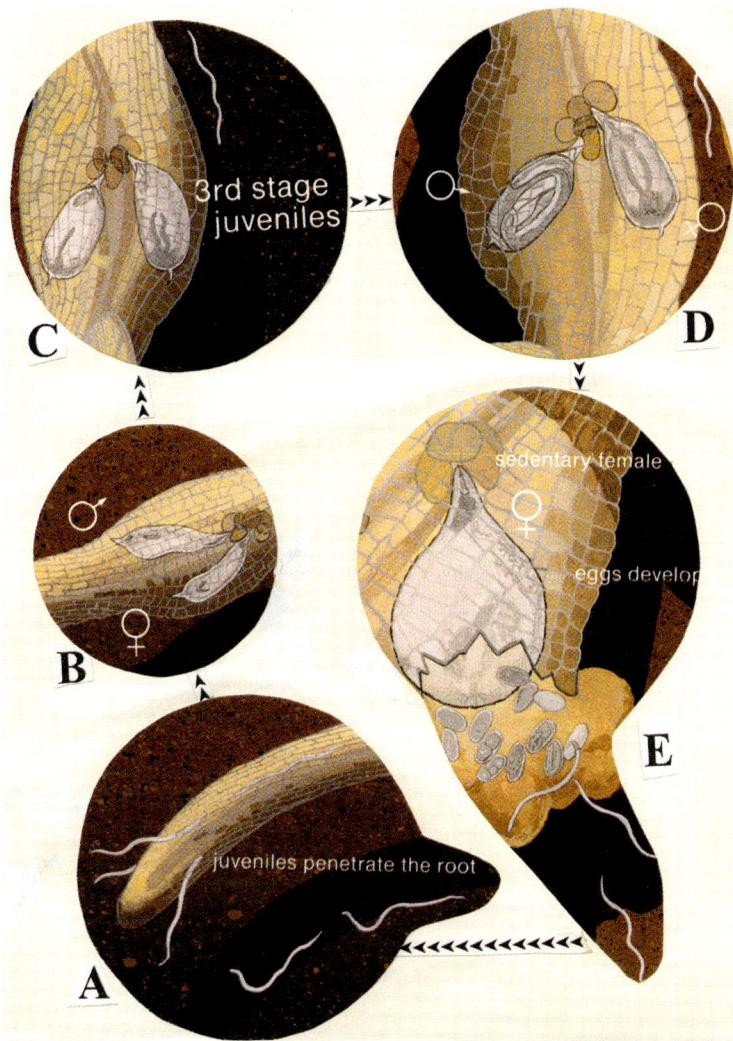

Figure 6.3. Life cycle of *Meloidogyne* species. (A) The second-stage juveniles invading a host root; (B) early development of above juveniles and resulting root gall; (C) next stage (third- stage juveniles) and larger root gall; (D) late fourth stage of nematodes and larger root gall; and (E) mature female with eggs being deposited and juveniles hatching and moving into the soil (portions of a chart drawn by J.D. Eisenback).

called host races. All four of the host races (races 1, 2, 3, and 4) that have been described for *M. incognita* readily attack watermelon. However, knowledge of the host preferences of these races (Table 6.1) can be useful in developing cropping systems that minimize root-knot damage on watermelon. For example race 1 of *M. incognita*, which is the most common form of this nematode in some of the southeastern United States, will not reproduce on cotton or on *M. incognita*-resistant tobacco. In contrast, races 3 and 4 reproduce readily on cotton. Races 2 and 4 attack currently available root-knot resistant tobacco. As with *M. incognita*, the two described host races of *M. arenaria* also attack watermelon. Neither of the *M. arenaria* races reproduce on cotton, whereas only race 1 attacks peanut. Race 2 is the most common race of this nematode, and it attacks a wide range of crops, including all present varieties of tobacco. Although no host races of *M. javanica* have been generally accepted, some forms of this nematode may attack peanut (in Texas), which is not true for most *M. javanica* populations.

BIOLOGY. In the absence of a host, root-knot nematodes exist as eggs and wormlike juveniles (young, threadlike stage) in the soil, mostly in the upper 12 inches of soil. Like all nematodes, *Meloidogyne* species undergo a total of four molts in their life cycle. The first molt occurs inside the egg, and a juvenile emerges. This juvenile is infective and capable of causing infection. Depending on soil conditions, these juveniles may survive for weeks in search of suitable host roots to attack. After infection of host roots such as watermelon, the second-stage juveniles develop rapidly, molting three additional times to become stationary, adult, pear-shaped females or wormlike males (Fig. 6.3). Under optimum conditions (80–100 °F), the life cycle is completed about 3 weeks after infection. Each female produces about 300–1200 eggs. Fertilization by males is not required for reproduction.

POPULATION DYNAMICS. Increases of root-knot nematode populations on watermelon is largely density-dependent (i.e., root-knot population densities peak at different times, depending on the initial levels of infestation). For example, with high initial numbers of nematodes, plant growth is severely limited, thereby decreasing the available feeding sites for subsequent generations. Under these conditions, the population levels will peak before the end of the watermelon-production season and even decline when plants are severely damaged. With low initial infestations, adequate feeding sites on the watermelon roots are available and reproduction will continue throughout the season. In this situation, peak numbers of nematodes will occur near the end of the season (Fig. 6.4).

Survival of root-knot nematodes between cropping seasons is influenced greatly by soil type, temperature, and moisture.

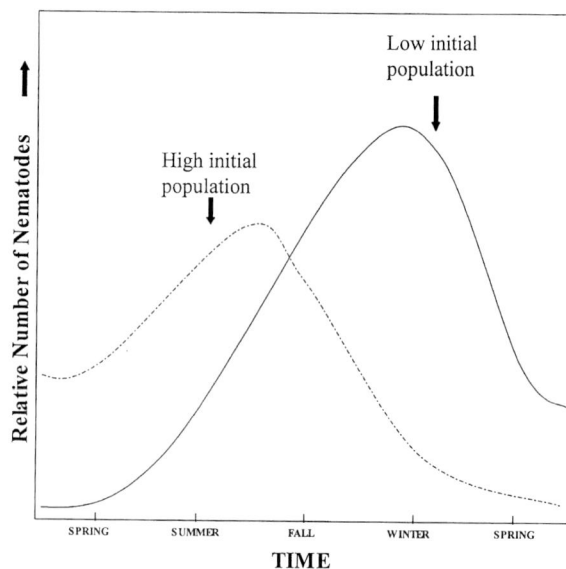

Figure 6.4. General population dynamics of root-knot nematodes, as affected by initial population level and time. Severe decline of high initial population numbers in fall and winter is due to heavy root damage which results in loss of food source for the nematodes.

Populations of *M. javanica* from tropical areas are especially sensitive to cold, but extended exposure of eggs of *M. incognita*, *M. arenaria* or *M. javanica* to freezing also will result in sharp population declines or death. Sunlight and drying combined can kill nematode eggs with a 30-minute exposure. In contrast, eggs and juveniles of these nematodes may survive below the surface of fallow soil for many weeks. Damage on watermelon and other susceptible crops is greatest in sandy and sandy loam soils, but *Meloidogyne* species occur and may cause significant crop damage in a wide range of soil types. Generally, reproduction of these nematodes is greater in loamy sands than in soils with high clay content or in organic soils. A number of host nutrients, including potassium, have been reported to decrease nematode reproduction. However, conditions that favor host-growth usually favor greater reproduction of the nematodes. In general, the relative survival rate of these nematodes between cropping seasons is inversely related to the initial population for a given year (Fig. 6.4). In other words, very high initial nematode populations that result in severe crop damage and therefore loss of nematode food source results in a low percentage survival for the subsequent growing season.

DISEASE COMPLEXES. Disease complexes are diseases caused by two or more pathogens. Root-knot nematodes interact with many types of bacteria and fungi, resulting in numerous root rots and often wilt- disease complexes. Although these interactions have been studied little on watermelon, the root decay associated with these nematodes occurs commonly on watermelon. This decay often occurs as a result of the plant-nematode interactions, resulting in injury and openings for the fungi to enter the roots. Nematodes keep the root tissues physiologically young and direct plants to translocate nutrients and sugars, etc., to the rapidly enlarging galled roots. At least one species of root-knot nematode, *M. arenaria*, interacts with the fusarium-wilt fungus (*Fusarium oxysporum* f. sp. *niveum*) on watermelon, resulting in a more severe disease problem than is caused by this fungus alone. Some nematodes such as the dagger nematode (*Xiphinema americanum*) are able to transmit plant viruses. Although this nematode is sometimes found on watermelon, it has not been associated with virus diseases.

ECONOMIC IMPORTANCE. Root-knot nematodes are the most important nematode parasites of watermelon. Nevertheless, yield losses due to these pathogens may be overlooked or underestimated because reduced plant vigor is subtle, and below-ground symptoms are not considered. Under temperate and tropical production systems, losses can be as high as 50% due to one or a combination of the three root-knot nematode species—*M. javanica*, *M. incognita*, or *M. arenaria*. Watermelon has a low tolerance for *M. arenaria* and *M. javanica*. Damage to plants occurs when the numbers of infective juveniles at the beginning of the season are 10–25 per pint of soil. In contrast, root- knot nematodes usually are of little consequence to watermelon in the upper midwestern or northeastern sections of the United States. For example, where watermelons are grown in Indiana, the predominant root-knot nematode is *M. hapla*, which does not reproduce on watermelon. However, *M. hapla* on suitable hosts is favored by the cooler temperatures in the midwestern states, whereas the prevailing temperature is too low for most other root-knot species. Compared to most vegetable crops, very limited research has been done to determine precise damage to watermelon by root-knot nematodes. It has been taken for granted that root- knot nematodes cause severe yield losses on watermelon. Thus, we have only limited information as to the economic losses caused by nematodes on watermelon in contrast to other vegetable crops such as tomato or beans.

Many other species of plant-parasitic nematodes are known to reproduce on cucurbits, including watermelon. Some of the lesion nematodes such as *Pratylenchus thornei*, attack this crop. These nematodes feed inside the roots and are called migratory endoparasites. Generally, they invade and feed upon the root cortex and cause brown, fibrous lesions on the roots. These nematodes damage fibrous roots, root hairs, and limit the ability of the plant to take up nutrients and water. This injury also results in plants becoming stunted and often chlorotic. Other nematodes that reproduce on watermelon include the burrowing nematode (*Radopholus similis*), spiral nematodes (*Helicotylenchus microlobus*), reniform nematode (*Rotylenchulus reniformis*), *Hirschmanniella imauri*, dagger nematodes (*Xiphinema* species), and other root-knot species such as *M. exigua*. Watermelon has been reported both as a host and a nonhost for the reniform nematode (*R. reniformis*). This situation suggests the existence of host races of this nematode.

Watermelon also is a nonhost for a limited number of nematode species. This includes the sting nematode (*Belonolaimus longicaudatus*) and a false root-knot nematode called *Naccobus*. Thus, watermelon can be used in rotation as part of a management program for these nematodes.

NEMATODE MANAGEMENT

As early as the late 1900s, a wide range of methods were available for nematode management. These included the use of nonhost plants in rotation, use of trap crops (nonhost plants which are invaded by nematodes, resulting in the parasites' death), use of compost, sterilization of soil by starvation (fallow), nematicides, and soil amendments such as hardwood ashes and potash. In the 1930s, a combination of two or more of the following practices were recommended for root-knot nematode control: 1) burning crop residues two or three times, if possible, each preceded by spading or plowing; 2) dry fallow, and/or frequent plowing; 3) one or more well-irrigated trap crops completely destroyed 2 or 3 weeks after sprouting; 4) flooding or moist fallow during warm weather, without weeds; 5) nonhost/resistant crops in rotation, kept free of weeds, and 6) repetition of d and e.

NEMATODE POPULATION ASSESSMENTS. Today, the extent of nematode management practices for watermelon varies greatly in different production regions. Before implementing one or more nematode management practices for given farms or fields, an assessment of the cropping history and magnitude of root-knot nematodes should be carried out. Nematode assays of appropriately collected soil samples can be very useful in this regard where nematode advisory programs are available. Bioassays involving the examinations of susceptible host roots for root-gall development can be a very rapid (2–6 weeks) and reliable method for tracking infestations of these important nematodes. Two types of these assays are used: First, plant growth and presence of galls on roots of susceptible crop plants (e.g., watermelon, tomato, cotton, tobacco), roots can be examined late in the growing season to determine the presence of root-knot nematodes in the field. The amount of root-knot galling on roots can be estimated visually as a percentage of the root system that is galled. If significant galling, 5% or more of the roots with galls, is present over much of the field appropriate nematode control measures should be followed or a resistant or nonhost crop should be planted. For these visual root-gall assessments, at least 20 randomly selected root-systems of the current or old crop should be examined for each 4- to 5-acre section of a field.

Second, for fields where residual root systems have been destroyed, a root-knot bioassay may be done by the grower. First, collect a large composite soil sample (0.5 gallon of soil) consisting of about 30 1-inch soil cores to a depth of 8 inches taken from an X-pattern over a 4- to 5-acre field. The top inch of soil should not be included in the sample. After a brief and gentle mixing, six 0.5-pint units of soil are placed in cups for a bioassay by planting two or more of the plants listed in Table 6.1 (use one type seedling per cup). The remaining soil may be used for nutrient analysis, if desired. This process involves digging or plowing out the root systems, removing soil from the roots (by rinsing in water if necessary), and estimating the percentage of randomly selected root systems that has galls. If one is only interested in watermelon and does not plan to grow other crops in the same field, only two containers of soil are needed with one being used for root-knot susceptible tomato and the second for watermelon. These plants can be grown in a window of a home or any area where they receive adequate light, heat, and water. After about 4–6 weeks, the root systems of the plants should be examined for the presence of root galls. The amount of root system galled is an indication of the amount of injury that will occur to the crop planted in the field where the soil sample was taken.

Where a nematode advisory service is available, soil samples may be submitted to secure a full assessment of the number and type of nematode species present. Where possible, this assay should be done in the fall when population levels are still high (avoids detection failures). Management options would be selected according to the assay result.

CULTURAL PRACTICES. Cropping systems, based on rotating susceptible crops with nonhost crops, have been central to nematode management for more than 100 years. Crop rotation also has the advantage of providing crop diversity as well as separating or dispersing pests over space and time. This practice, however, is of limited value for root-knot nematodes because of their very wide host ranges in crops and associated weeds. Nevertheless, grass fallows such as fescue, orchard grass, bahia grass, and the use of various green manure crops have proven useful in managing root-knot and other nematodes.

HOST RESISTANCE. The ideal and most economical means of nematode control is the use of host resistance, provided product quality and yield are not compromised. Unfortunately, no available root-knot resistant varieties of watermelon have been developed. A few varieties of watermelon, such as 'Sugar Baby', show low levels of resistance relative to the major watermelon varieties, but are still considered susceptible. Although watermelon is highly susceptible to the common root-knot nematodes (*M. arenaria*, *M. incognita*, *M. javanica*), it does support less reproduction of the root-knot nematodes than more susceptible crops such as tomato and tobacco. Hopefully, the promising genetically engineered resistance to root-knot nematodes in experimental plants can be exploited and incorporated into watermelon and a wide range of other vegetables.

NEMATICIDES. In the 1950s through the 1970s, nematicides were used routinely for nematode management on many crops. In fact, these highly effective, low cost, crop protectants were often used as an insurance measure by many farmers. Because of human health concerns and environmental issues, most of the more effective and less expensive nematicides have been removed from the market. In addition, nematicides such as methyl bromide, organocarbamates, and organophosphates are currently under federal review. Nonfumigant nematicides such as aldicarb, oxamyl, and fenamiphos effectively control root-knot nematodes, but only oxamyl (Vydate) is registered for watermelon. Because serious human-health problems have been encountered on watermelon and cucumber treated with aldicarb, these crops should never be treated with this or other products not registered. Thus, great care must be given in using nematicides on watermelon. In fact, only preplant nematicides should be used on this crop. Fortunately, nematodes cause much of their damage to annual crops during the first few weeks after seeding or transplanting. Thus, protection of the crop during this time is critical.

BIOLOGICAL CONTROL. Many fungi and bacteria have potential for control of root-knot and other nematodes, but no practical means of exploiting these antagonists for management of root-knot nematodes of watermelon or other crops is available today. A promising approach for biological nematode management involves the use of certain legume cover crops such as velvetbean that favor the buildup of growth-promoting, antagonistic bacteria. Some of these bacteria have been shown to induce resistance in plants to disease agents, including nematodes such as root-knot species. However, the practical use of biological controls remains to be developed.

OTHER MANAGEMENT PRACTICES. Proper sanitation, including cleaning of equipment after use in a nematode-infested field, is critical for an effective nematode management program. Early planting limits nematode damage on crops that can tolerate cooler conditions. This practice may have some potential on watermelon, and warrants evaluation.

Recently integrated nematode management systems have received attention and a number of success stories of single and multiple-pest management have been published. In North Carolina, for example, an integrated management system that involves rotation with nonhosts, use of crop resistance/ tolerance, and application of nematicides has been very effective in limiting losses caused by root knot on tobacco. With the addition of prompt crop root destruction at the end of the season, periodic discing, and the appropriate cover crop, most associated weeds, viruses, fungi, bacterial pathogens, and insects also are controlled for this crop. Cyst and root- knot nematodes on soybean are controlled in the United States by integrating nematode-resistant varieties with crop rotation. For watermelon, selection of root-knot nematode free fields should be a top priority. This approach, combined with crop rotation and cultural practices such as destruction of residual crop roots, weed control, and the use of a cover crop should limit yield losses of watermelon to root-knot nematodes.

CONCLUSIONS

In contrast to the complexity of nematode communities on many crops such as tomato, tobacco, or potato, the target nematodes for watermelon are primarily three species of root-knot: *M. arenaria*, *M. incognita*, and *M. javanica*. Because of the few available options for managing heavily infested root-knot fields for watermelon production, monitoring of nematode populations should be central in production of this crop where root-knot nematodes are known to be a major problem. The detection and monitoring of root-knot nematodes for watermelon fields can be done through carefully collected soil samples and nematode assays or appropriate bioassays as described herein. Biochemical/molecular techniques are now available for identifying species of root-knot nematodes. These techniques, while important for many crops, are unnecessary for watermelon production since all of the major root-knot species, except *M. hapla*, attack and severely damage this crop. With current technology and resources available, a reasonably effective integrated root-knot nematode management system is available for watermelon. This includes the following: 1) monitoring for these pathogens (determining the level of nematodes present in the soil); 2) cultural practices including rotation with nonhost crops and nonhost cover crops, destruction of residual root systems and control of weed hosts; 3) field selection based on the above; and 4) proper preplant nematicide treatments if necessary. Hopefully, effective root-knot resistance will be added to these limited options in the future.

General References

Acosta, N. 1983. Evaluation of granular nematicides for the control of root-knot nematodes in watermelon. Fungicide-nematicide tests. Amer. Phytopathol. Soc. 39:100.

Barker, K.R. and S.R. Koenning. 1998. Developing sustainable systems for nematode management. Annu. Rev. Phytopathol. 36:165–205.

Evans, K., D.L. Trudgill, and J.M. Webster (eds.). 1993. Plant parasitic nematodes in temperate agriculture. CAB Intl., Wallingford, U.K.

Barker, K.R., G.A. Pederson, and G.L. Windham (eds.). 1998. Plant and nematode interactions. Amer. Soc. of Agron., Crop Sci. Soc. of Amer., and Soil Sci. Soc. of Amer., Madison, Wis.

Duncan, L.W. 1991. Current options for nematode management. Annu. Rev. Phytopathol. 29:249–290.

Luc, M., R.A. Sikora, and J. Bridge. 1990. Plant parasitic nematodes in subtropical and tropical agriculture. CAB Intl., Wallingford, UK.

Nickle, W.R. (ed.). Manual of agricultural nematology. Marcel Dekker, New York.

Sasser, J.N. and C.C. Carter. (eds.). 1985. Advanced treatise on *Meloidogyne*. vol. 1. Biology and Control. N.C. State Univ. Graphics, Raleigh.

CHAPTER 7

DISEASES

D.L. Hopkins and R.X. Latin

Effective management of watermelon diseases involves identifying crop disorders and implementing appropriate control options. Accurate diagnosis is an important first step in disease management. It is important for growers to distinguish between diseases and other types of crop injury and to be familiar with symptoms of chronic diseases that remain a threat each year. This chapter presents symptom descriptions that will aid in diagnosing watermelon disease problems.

Disease prevention is the key to effective control. However, some outbreaks may be unavoidable. In those situations, remedial control measures will be most effective if the problem is recognized early in its development. Growers may be able to detect outbreaks before they become unmanageable by scouting their fields regularly. Early warning of disease outbreaks also may be obtained from weather-based disease forecasting systems. These systems use local weather conditions to determine the disease risk and can improve fungicide application scheduling. While fungicides are essential for some diseases, growers are encouraged to implement as many disease control options as appropriate to reduce the risk of serious crop losses. This chapter emphasizes an integrated approach to disease management because nonchemical options tend to reduce disease pressure and can enhance fungicide performance. Therefore, genetic control options (resistant varieties) and cultural control options (healthy seed and transplants and adequate crop rotations), are addressed in addition to chemical control measures.

INFECTIOUS DISEASES
Alternaria leaf blight

Alternaria (*Alternaria cucumerina*) leaf blight is a foliar disease of many cucurbits including watermelon. The disease can rapidly defoliate plants, causing reductions in bulk yield. Fruit on defoliated vines ripen prematurely and are of lower quality those produced on healthy vines. Yield losses are significant in situations where early season outbreaks occur and prevailing weather conditions favor disease increase and spread.

SYMPTOMS. Alternaria infections occur only on leaves. Petioles, stems, and fruit are not directly affected by the pathogen. Lesions begin as tiny, tan

Figure 7.1. Advanced alternaria lesions with concentric circles. (Source: D.L. Hopkins.)

or brown spots that may appear water-soaked on the underside of leaves. Older lesions are generally round, brown, and may be surrounded by a halo of yellow tissue. Within the brown areas of alternaria lesions are characteristic concentric circles that resemble the growth rings of a tree (Fig. 7.1).

DISEASE CYCLE. The alternaria leaf blight pathogen survives in soils associated with infested crop debris. Prolonged daily wet periods with temperatures that range from 60–75° F will activate fungal growth and spore production. Spores may be rain splashed and windblown to spread the disease. New infections result in lesions that produce many new generations of spores. A disease cycle may be completed in 5–10 days, depending on environmental conditions.

DISEASE MANAGEMENT. Alternaria leaf blight is best managed by integration of nonchemical and chemical control options. Local disease history will play a significant role in determining the need for fungicide sprays targeted specifically for alternaria leaf blight management.

HOST RESISTANCE. Many varieties have good resistance to alternaria leaf blight. Check with university plant pathologists and seed company representatives to avoid susceptible types for fields with a history of the disease.

CULTURAL CONTROL. Crop rotation and tillage will significantly reduce disease risk in subsequent crops. Rotations with noncucurbit crops for at least 2 years are recommended.

CHEMICAL CONTROL. Fungicides

Figure 7.2. Angular anthracnose leaf lesions. (Source: R.X. Latin.)

applied at appropriate rates and intervals will prevent serious losses to alternaria leaf blight. Several contact fungicides are registered and effective. New systemic fungicides may offer improved disease management capabilities. Weather-based disease warning systems can be used to apply fungicides at most appropriate times. Check with university plant pathologists and/or extension specialists for the availability of such systems in various regions.

Anthracnose

Anthracnose (*Colletotrichum orbiculare*) is caused by a fungal pathogen that can affect other cucurbits as well as watermelons. The leaf and stem blighting phase results in rapid defoliation of vines and reduced bulk yields. Fruit infection results in unmarketable melons and/or rejected truckloads of fruit.

SYMPTOMS. Anthracnose infection can occur on stems, leaves, and fruit. Leaf symptoms include irregularly shaped, dark brown lesions. Lesion growth often is limited by leaf veins, giving the lesion an angular or jagged appearance (Fig. 7.2). As lesions expand and their diameter approaches 1/2 inch, the dead brown tissue often cracks and may leave a split or a hole in the lesion. Lesions on watermelon stems are somewhat oval and tan colored, usually with a brown margin. Fruit lesions are round, sunken and tan and most often occur on the sides of infected fruit (Fig. 7.3). Anthracnose symptoms on melon seedlings include sunken tan-orange lesions on seedling stems (Fig. 7.4). Vigilant growers usually first discover a seedling anthracnose problem when distinct clusters of symptomatic plants are evident.

DISEASE CYCLE. Between growing seasons, the anthracnose pathogen can survive with infested crop residue in soils. The pathogen is activated by warm wet conditions. It will grow on crop debris and produce spores that are splash dispersed into the air. Airborne spores may spread and create new infections if deposited in a watermelon field. As long as warm, wet weather persists, the lesions will continue to produce more spores that may be spread to neighboring plants, rows,

Figure 7.3. Anthracnose fruit lesions. (Source: R.X. Latin.)

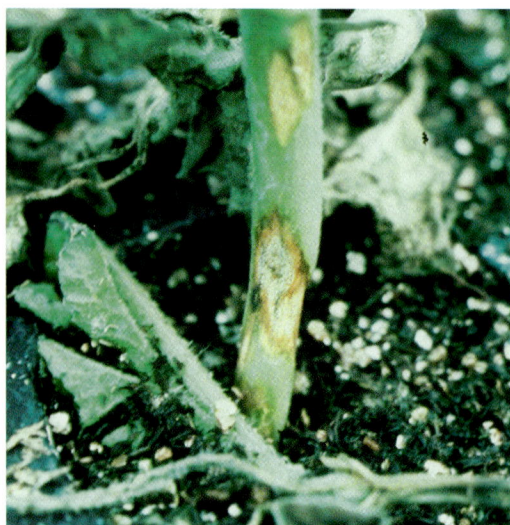

Figure 7.4. Anthracnose seedling lesions. (Source: R.X. Latin.)

and fields. Under favorable environmental conditions, infection by a single spore can result in a lesion that will produce tens of thousands of spores after only a few days. The short time for the completion of the disease cycle explains why anthracnose can increase so quickly in an unprotected crop. The fungus also may be carried on contaminated watermelon seed. In such cases, the disease cycle in transplant production facilities is similar to the field cycle of infection and spore production and dispersal. If symptoms are not detected at an early stage of disease development, an entire seedling crop may be infected in a matter of weeks because of constant warm, wet conditions.

DISEASE MANAGEMENT. Disease management with fungicides is almost always necessary for commercial watermelon crops. Integration of host resistance (where possible) and cultural control options should improve the performance of effective fungicides.

HOST RESISTANCE. Partial resistance has been reported in a few commercial varieties, but will not provide acceptable control without chemical protection.

CULTURAL CONTROL. Rotation and tillage options will help reduce the disease threat in subsequent years, but will not provide acceptable control in fields with a history of the disease without chemical protection.

CHEMICAL CONTROL. Repeated applications of protectant fungicides are necessary for reducing disease-related loss, especially in fields with a history of disease. New systemic fungicides may contribute to improved control. Weather-based systems are being developed and tested for use in scheduling fungicides for watermelon disease control. Check with university extension/research pathologists for their recommendations for use of systemic fungicides and the availability of weather-based disease advisories.

Bacterial rind necrosis

Bacterial rind necrosis (*Erwinia* sp.) is a disease that can render watermelon fruit unmarketable because of internal blemishes. Incidence and severity of the disease is variable from year to year and from field to field and is unpredictable.

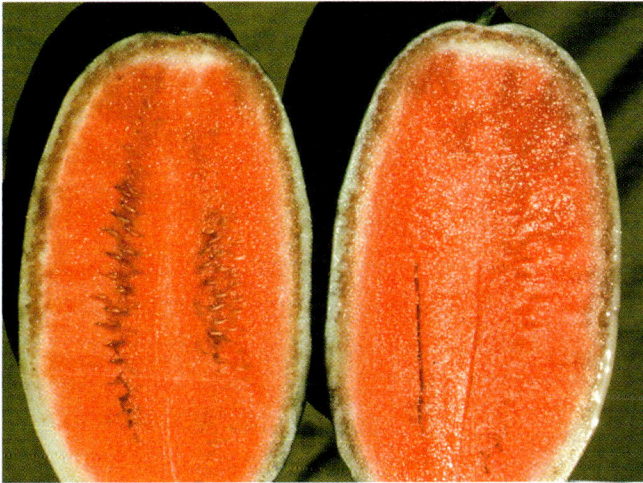

Figure 7.5. Light-brown, dry discoloration symptom of rind necrosis. (Source: D.L. Hopkins.)

SYMPTOMS. Typical rind necrosis is characterized by a light brown, dry, and hard discoloration interspersed with lighter areas (Fig. 7.5). The disease develops in the rind and rarely extends into the flesh. Occasionally the affected area is limited to the vascular bundles, but generally the discoloration spreads, sometimes affecting the entire rind.

DISEASE CYCLE. Bacterial rind necrosis was often more severe in fields where plants were heavily infected with watermelon mosaic virus. This led to speculation that a common vector may facilitate the spread of both diseases. Watermelon bacterial rind necrosis appears to be genetically controlled, but its frequency is affected by an interaction with environment. While there is some uncertainty about the relative importance of bacteria, genetic, and physiological factors in bacterial rind necrosis, several characteristics of the disease are known. *Erwinia* sp. most often has been associated with the diseased rind areas, other bacterial organisms isolated from either diseased or healthy fruit cause typical symptoms at inoculation sites, the incidence of the disease varies among varieties and growing seasons, and varieties may not always respond to the disease in the same way.

HOST RESISTANCE. For the most part, varieties in use today appear not to be as susceptible as those used in the 1970s, suggesting that watermelon breeders have been successful in selecting against the disease. There is no other known control method.

Bacterial fruit blotch

Bacterial fruit blotch (*Acidovorax avenae* subsp. *citrulli*) was introduced to major United States watermelon production areas in 1989 with contaminated seed of a certain watermelon variety. It is suspected that contaminated seed also was responsible for the fruit blotch epidemics of 1992 and 1994. Early season outbreaks can result in total losses. Fields adjacent to severely affected crops can suffer 5%–50% loss, depending on environmental condi-

tions and the crop growth stage at which fruit blotch becomes established.

SYMPTOMS. The characteristic symptom of bacterial fruit blotch is the dark olive green stain or blotch that occurs on the upper surface of infected fruit (Fig. 7.6). Initially the blotch is about the size of a quarter, and then rapidly expands so that much of the fruit surface is covered with the lesion in 7–10 days. As the blotch increases in size, the area around the initial infection site turns brown. The epidermis of the rind ruptures (cracks) in advanced stages of lesion development and frequently oozes a sticky, clear-amber colored substance (Fig. 7.7). Fruit lesions rarely extend into the flesh of the melon; secondary rotting organisms are responsible for the ultimate decay and collapse of fruit. The fruit blotch bacteria also infect leaves, although foliage surrounding infected fruit may appear healthy to the untrained eye. Leaf lesions are small, dark brown, somewhat angular, and generally inconspicuous (Fig. 7.8). When viewed from the bottom of the leaf, the margins of the lesions appear water-soaked, especially in wet or humid weather. Water-soaked lesions also occur on cotyledons and true leaves of infected watermelon seedlings (Fig. 7.9).

DISEASE CYCLE. Disastrous outbreaks of bacterial fruit blotch occur when a significant proportion of young seedlings are infected. This situation arises when contaminated watermelon seed is planted in transplant production facilities and infected transplants are introduced into the field.

Figure 7.7. Cracked rind and clear-amber colored ooze in advanced fruit blotch lesion. (Source: R.X. Latin.)

Figure 7.8. Fruit blotch lesions along leaf midrib. (Source: R.X. Latin.)

Although the pathogen may survive with weed hosts, among infested crop debris in soils, or with remnant seed buried in a field, survival of the bacteria with contaminated seed destined for transplant facilities is clearly most significant. Warm, wet weather favors the spread of fruit blotch. Bacteria produced on lesion surfaces may be splash dispersed and briefly wind borne to quickly spread the disease over short distances. The extent of foliar infection during fruit development influences the proportion of fruit infection. Fewer fruit infections will occur where outbreaks are late season because mature watermelons are protected from infection by a natural waxy coating over the fruit surface.

DISEASE MANAGEMENT. Guidelines for avoiding bacterial fruit blotch were established by a team of university plant pathologists in 1996. The guidelines address disease management from the standpoint of seed production, transplant production, and fruit production. They stress seed/plant health testing, sanitation, and chemical protection where appropriate.

HOST RESISTANCE. Current hybrid watermelons appear to be equally susceptible to fruit blotch infection although those with light colored fruit may express blotch symptoms more severely. Triploid (seedless) watermelons can sustain high levels of leaf infection with comparatively low levels of fruit infection.

CULTURAL CONTROL. Recommended practices include tillage of infested fields after harvest is complete, and crop rotation with grain crops where herbicides will control volunteer watermelons. Fruit blotch infested fields should be planted to

Figure 7.9. Fruit blotch water-soaked lesion on cotyledons of watermelon seedlings. (Source: R.X. Latin.)

Figure 7.10. Circular spots with light-brown centers caused by cercospora leafspot fungus. (Source: D.L. Hopkins.)

noncucurbit crops for at least 2 years following an outbreak.

CHEMICAL CONTROL. Copper sprays applied to protect developing fruit and reduce the rate of disease increase on foliage can limit the extent of infection on fruit. Applications at 5- to 10-day intervals beginning when fruit start to develop are most effective.

Cercospora leaf spot

Cercospora leaf spot (*Cercospora citrullina*) is a disease of the foliage of watermelon grown in tropical and sub-tropical regions and also is common on other cucurbits, such as melon and cucumber. The disease usually causes minor damage with severe economic losses being rare.

SYMPTOMS. Symptoms consist of circular to irregular circular spots with tan or light brown centers on the leaves (Fig. 7.10). Lesions also may appear on the petioles and stems if the environment is favorable.

DISEASE CYCLE. Cercospora overseasons on cucurbit crop debris. Spores are airborne and may be carried considerable distances on wind-driven rain.

CULTURAL CONTROL. Reduce inoculum sources through destruction of crop debris. This can be accomplished with crop rotations of 2–3 years between cucurbit crops.

CHEMICAL CONTROL. Usually, cercospora leaf spot can be controlled by a regular fungicide spray program.

Downy mildew

Downy mildew (*Pseudoperonospora cubensis*) caused by a fungus is one of the most important foliar diseases of watermelon, as well as cucumber, squash, melon, pumpkin, and other cucurbits. Without control measures, it can completely defoliate watermelons. The disease occurs in temperate and tropical areas with low or high rainfall. Sufficient leaf wetness periods for disease development are usually provided by dew.

SYMPTOMS. Symptoms of downy mildew are usually confined to leaves. They appear as small, slightly chlorotic to bright yellow areas on the upper

Figure 7.11. Downy mildew results in chlorotic lesions on the upper leaf surface that become necrotic in the center. (Source: D.L. Hopkins.)

leaf surface with irregular margins (Fig. 7.11). Lesions appear first on the older crown leaves and progress to the younger leaves. The yellow leaf spots later become necrotic and brown. As lesions expand they often coalesce into progressively larger areas of necrosis, resulting in an exaggerated upward leaf curling (Fig. 7.12). In a few days, the entire leaf is necrotic.

DISEASE CYCLE. The fungus causing downy mildew survives from season-to-season only on living cucurbit hosts. Therefore, the source of the disease each year is windblown spores from infected cucurbits in areas where cucurbit plants survive the cold season. Downy mildew outbreaks occur in individual fields after airborne spores from other fields are deposited on the foliage. Spread of the disease within a field usually occurs by wind, but also may be dispersed by rain-splash. When environmental conditions are favorable for the disease, downy mildew can defoliate an entire watermelon field in 2–3 weeks.

DISEASE MANAGEMENT. Optimum control of downy mildew requires an integrated approach including cultural practices and chemical controls.

HOST RESISTANCE. Low levels of resistance are available in a few commercial varieties, but will not provide acceptable control without chemical protection.

CULTURAL CONTROL. Management practices that reduce the presence of free moisture on the leaves lower the incidence of downy mildew. These

Figure 7.12. Severe necrosis with upward leaf curling symptom of downy mildew. (Source: D.L. Hopkins.)

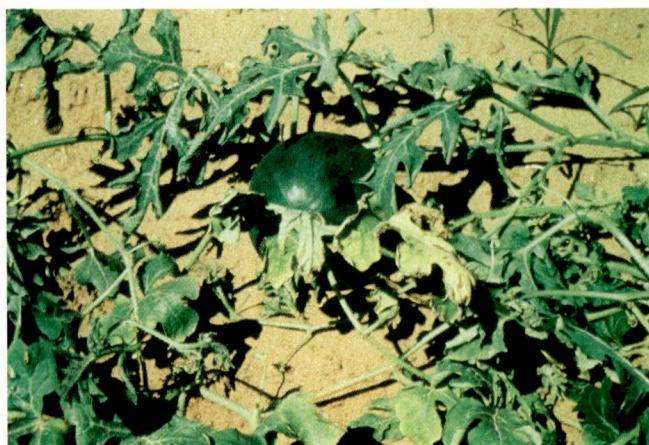

Figure 7.13. Chlorotic, yellow, wilted crown leaves symptom of fusarium wilt. (Source: R.X. Latin.)

include using plant spacings which reduce canopy density and avoiding overhead irrigation, which can lengthen the duration of leaf wetness. The distance from watermelon to potential sources of the downy mildew fungus should be maximized.

CHEMICAL CONTROL. Fungicide sprays are generally required for the control of downy mildew of watermelon. Protectant and systemic fungicides that are effective in controlling downy mildew are available. However, protectant fungicides are less effective when inoculum levels are high and meteorological conditions are favorable for disease development. Weather-based systems are being developed and tested for use in scheduling fungicides for watermelon disease control. Check with university extension/research pathologists for their recommendations for use of fungicides and the availability of weather-based disease advisories.

Fusarium wilt

A soil fungus causes fusarium wilt (*Fusarium oxysporum* f. sp. *niveum*) of watermelon. Losses to fusarium wilt have been reduced substantially in recent years with the introduction of resistant varieties. However, the disease occurs to some extent each year in locations with a history of wilt, especially in traditional sandy soil production areas. Yield reductions in severely affected fields can exceed 50%.

SYMPTOMS. Fusarium wilt is most readily identified after young plants begin to produce runners, but before the initial harvest. Affected plants appear in clusters and are often (but not always) located in low areas of a field where drainage is less than optimal. Infection by the fusarium pathogen may result in a relatively slow wilt of the plant, or may result in rapid wilt in young or stressed plants. Leaves close to the crown of the plant usually wilt first. Chlorosis, or yellowing, of the crown leaves also may occur (Fig. 7.13). Close inspection of the lower stems of infected plants reveals narrow brown streaks or lesions along the vines. Affected stems may appear symptomless or appear cracked and exude a red, brown, or black gummy substance. Because fusarium wilt affects the plant's vascular system, the vascular bundles of infected plants assume a brown discoloration (Fig. 7.14).

DISEASE CYCLE. The fusarium pathogen survives as persistent, long-lived spores for indefinite periods of time between crops. The spores germinate in the presence of active watermelon roots, penetrate root tissues and colonize vascular elements. The vascular disease restricts water transport from roots to foliage resulting in wilt and death of the plant. The pathogen progresses through a single disease cycle since there is no plant to plant spread of the disease in a growing season.

DISEASE MANAGEMENT. Severe losses associated with fusarium wilt can be avoided by nonchemical means.

HOST RESISTANCE. Good, usable, stand-alone resistance to fusarium wilt is available in many commercial varieties. Because host resistance depends on the nature of the prevailing fusarium races or biotypes, check with university pathologists and seed company representatives for varieties that are suitable for production in certain areas.

CULTURAL CONTROL. Long-term (more than 5 years) rotations with non-cucurbit crops are recommended to reduce the disease threat in the field. However, because overwintering spores may survive indefinitely, the disease threat will never be eliminated in fields with a history of the disease.

CHEMICAL CONTROL. In some circumstances, depending on the intended watermelon variety and the disease history of the field, chemical fumigation will help limit the extent of fusarium infection. Effective fungicides are not available for fusarium wilt control.

Gummy stem blight

Gummy stem blight (GSB) (*Didymella bryoniae*) is caused by a fungus that attacks watermelons and other cucurbits. On fruit, this disease is known as black rot. Most yield loss due to GSB occurs as a result of rapid defoliation of vines, but fruit infection and subsequent decay is possible.

SYMPTOMS. Symptoms of GSB on leaves often appear as irregularly

Figure 7.14. Brown discoloration of vascular bundles symptom of fusarium wilt in stem cross-section. (Source: R.X. Latin.)

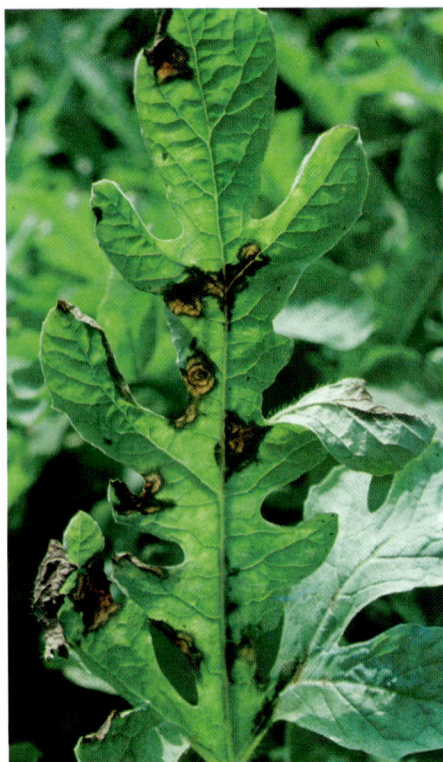

shaped brown areas (Fig. 7.15). Infected petioles and stems first appear water-soaked. As the infection progresses, an elongated, tan-colored lesion develops. Mature GSB lesions appear corky and cracked and often exude an orange-red-brown gummy substance (Fig. 7.16). The key diagnostic feature of GSB is the presence of small black fungal structures called pycnidia embedded in the diseased tissue. Pycnidia are smaller than a period printed on this page and often occur in groups or clusters within the lesion. A 10× hand lens should be used to view the pycnidia clearly. Gummy stem blight also can occur on seedlings raised in transplant production facilities. The diagnostic seedling symptom is the water-soaked stem, well above the soil line, and just below the cotyledons.

Small, water-soaked spots develop on watermelon fruit, enlarge, and exude gummy material (Fig. 7.17). As the symptoms develop, fruiting bodies of the fungus may appear as black specks on the lesions. In the tropics, fruit infection can occur through blossom scars and begin to decay inner fruit tissue, with no visible symptoms on the surface of the watermelon. The decay eventually will progress to the stem end and reach the surface of the fruit.

DISEASE CYCLE. The GSB fungus remains dormant in infected crop residue between growing seasons. Warm wet weather will activate growth

Figure 7.16. Gummy stem blight results in corky, cracked crown lesions exuding red-brown gummy substance. (Source: R.X. Latin.)

Figure 7.17. Fruit lesions of gummy stem blight. (Source: D.L. Hopkins.)

and spore production. Spores may be rain-splashed and briefly windborne to neighboring plants, rows, and fields. New infections result in lesions that will continue to produce an abundance of spores until the crop is destroyed. Under favorable environmental conditions, the disease spreads rapidly throughout the field.

DISEASE MANAGEMENT. Effective GSB management can be achieved with an approach that integrates all possible control options with a sound fungicide program.

HOST RESISTANCE. There are claims that some watermelon varieties are less susceptible than others to GSB infection. However, such 'resistance' alone is not effective in preventing severe epidemics and crop defoliation.

CULTURAL CONTROL. Cultural control options such as tillage of severely affected fields, rotating fields with nonsusceptible crops for at least 2 years, and avoiding fields with a history of the disease may contribute to more effective and efficient chemical control.

CHEMICAL CONTROL. Fungicides are essential for GSB control in watermelon production regions that experience prolonged periods of hot humid weather. Application of protectant fungicides at 7- to 14-day intervals beginning when vines of adjacent plants touch within rows is standard procedure. Fungicide applications should be initiated sooner if infection was discovered in transplant production facilities. New systemic fungicides may contribute to satisfactory control with fewer applications. Weather-based systems are being developed and tested for use in scheduling fungicides for watermelon disease control. Check with university extension/research pathologists for their recommendations for use of systemic fungicides and the availability of weather-based disease advisories.

Monosporascus root rot and vine decline

Monosporascus root rot and vine decline (*Monosporascus cannonballus*) of watermelon is a recently described disease. Melons also are highly susceptible; cucumber, squash, and gourd may also be affected. Monosporascus is adapted to hot, arid climates and, to date, appears limited to areas with this climate.

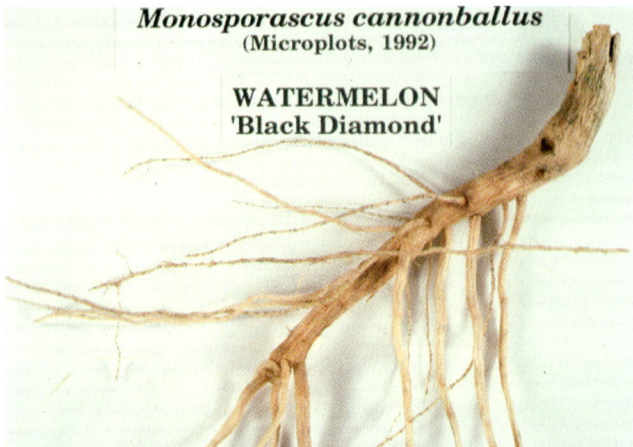

Figure 7.18. Root lesions and loss of feeder roots symptoms of monosporascus root rot. (Source: R.A. Martyn, Purdue University, West Lafayette, Ind.)

SYMPTOMS. Although often overlooked, the first symptom is stunting of young plants. Within 2–3 weeks of harvest, the older crown leaves begin to turn yellow and then necrotic. Chlorosis and death of leaves proceeds rapidly toward the tips of the vines. From onset of foliar symptoms to death of most of the canopy may require only 5–10 days. Root lesions, root rot, loss of smaller feeder roots (Fig. 7.18), and, in some cases, death of the taproot may be observed below ground. Lesions begin at the junctions of secondary or tertiary roots or at the tips of young roots as discrete, dry areas of necrosis.

DISEASE CYCLE. Young roots in the upper part of the soil are affected first in the early part of the season. Colonization of the plant is favored by high soil temperatures later in the season, resulting in the vine decline symptoms. Monosporascus survives long-term in the soil and spread probably occurs through the movement of infested soil or infected plant material. Spores of the fungus may be moved by water flows from furrow irrigation or heavy rainfall. There is no known secondary spread of monosporascus during the season.

CULTURAL CONTROL. Do not plant in fields known to be infested with *M. cannonballus* and maintain a long-term rotation with noncucurbit crops. Practices that enhance plant growth are good cultural control methods, such as drip irrigation, plastic mulch, and good field drainage.

CHEMICAL CONTROL. In infested fields, preplant fumigation can reduce stunting and increase fruit yields.

Phytophthora root, crown, and fruit rot

Phytophthora root, crown, and fruit rot (*Phytophthora capsici*) affects a wide range of vegetable crops, including cucurbits. Losses to this pathogen are sporadic, but can result in total loss of individual fields in warm temperate, subtropical, or tropical climates.

SYMPTOMS. The first visible symptom is a sudden, permanent wilt of infected plants. Plants often die in a few days after first symptoms, or following excessive rain or irrigation. Roots and the stem near the soil surface turn light- to dark-brown and become water-soaked and soft. Infected stems collapse and roots are destroyed. Diseased plants are pulled from the soil with little resistance, since lateral roots are often sloughed off.

Fruit symptoms begin as a water-soaked, often depressed, spot. Frequently, the area of the fruit in contact with the moist ground is affected first, but symptoms also can develop on the upper surface, following rain or overhead irrigation which provides splashing water to disperse the pathogen. In older lesions, a mass of white mycelium that contains sporangia may develop (Fig. 7.19). Infected fruit can decay rapidly and collapse. Fruit decay may continue after harvest.

DISEASE CYCLE. The fungus survives for at least 2 years in the soil. Spores are spread by wind and water, in infected transplants, and through contaminated soil and equipment. Surface moisture is required for motile zoospores to reach and invade the host. Therefore, disease is most severe in warm, wet weather and in low, waterlogged areas of fields. Disease is promoted by heavy rainfall, excessive irrigation, and poorly drained soils.

CULTURAL CONTROL. For disease control, rotation with nonhost crops is recommended, avoiding rotations with pepper, tomato, and eggplant. Management of soil moisture by selecting well-drained fields, avoiding low-lying fields, and not overirrigating is the most effective control strategy. Other good management practices to limit disease include the elimination of volunteer crop plants and weeds, roguing infected watermelon plants, and decontaminating equipment.

CHEMICAL CONTROL. When combined with good cultural practices, fumigation and preventive fungicides may help suppress disease.

Pythium damping-off and root rot

Damping-off and root rot (*Pythium* sp.) of watermelon and several other cucurbits can be caused by any one of several species.

SYMPTOMS. In seedlings, a watery rot develops at or near the soil line, resulting in sudden wilting

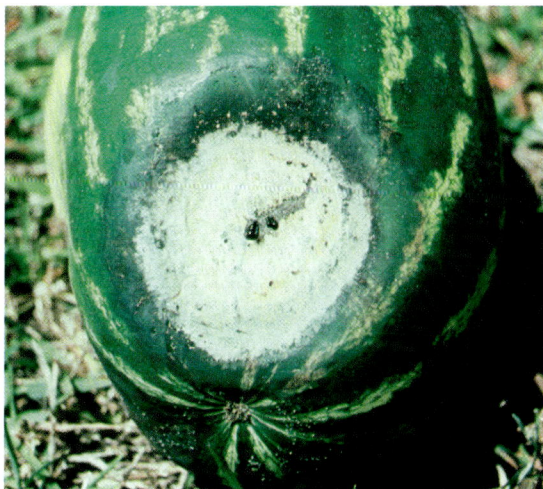

Figure 7.19. Depressed fruit lesion with a mass of white mycelium caused by *Phytophthora*. (Source: D.L. Hopkins.)

Figure 7.20. Clusters of infected plants is an initial symptom of powdery mildew. (Source: D.L. Hopkins.)

and death. When pulled, these seedlings break at the soil line, leaving the roots in the ground. In mature plants, the crown leaves may become chlorotic and then necrotic, proceeding outward from the crown to the runner tips. Sudden wilt also may be a symptom, with healthy-appearing plants wilting in the heat of the day. On these mature plants, brown lesions develop on roots and feeder roots may be destroyed.

DISEASE CYCLE. Infection of seedlings occurs soon after germination when soils are wet and favorable environmental conditions exist, such as foggy, rainy weather. Conditions favorable for disease varies somewhat with the pathogen species, but cool, wet conditions contribute to seedling damping off in the early spring. Mature plants often are infected following irrigation or wet weather preceded by plant stress. Hot weather and low humidity increase the severity of symptoms.

CULTURAL CONTROL. Control of root rot can be achieved by avoiding excessive irrigation and improving drainage by planting on raised beds.

Powdery mildew

Powdery mildew (*Sphaerotheca fuliginea*) is a major disease of cucurbits throughout the United States. The disease has been reported regularly on watermelons in southern states, but seems to occur less frequently in northern production regions. The powdery mildew pathogen does not infect watermelon fruit. However, severe early season outbreaks will result in rapid defoliation of vines, reduced fruit per acre, and poor quality fruit.

SYMPTOMS. The initial obvious field symptoms of a powdery mildew outbreak are a few small clusters of affected plants scattered throughout the field (Fig. 7.20). Close inspection of individual affected plants reveals the presence of numerous chlorotic spots and the characteristic white mold of powdery mildew infection (Fig. 7.21). The mold occurs on both sides of the leaves.

DISEASE CYCLE. The powdery mildew pathogen will survive year round on cucurbit weeds in warm climates (e.g., Gulf Coast states). In northern production regions, it is likely that the pathogen overwinters as weather resilient spores

Figure 7.21. Characteristic white mold symptom of powdery mildew on leaves. (Source: D.L. Hopkins.)

among debris in affected fields. The disease cycle involves spore production as suitable weather persists, infection of leaves and stems, more spore production, and widespread dispersal of spores on wind currents. Unlike other foliar pathogens, the powdery mildew fungus does not require precipitation and long dew periods for infection and spread.

DISEASE MANAGEMENT. Fungicides may not be necessary to avoid losses caused by powdery mildew infection unless outbreaks occur early during fruit development. All control options should be considered in developing a powdery mildew management strategy.

HOST RESISTANCE. It is likely that some commercial varieties possess stand-alone resistance to powdery mildew. Check with university extension specialists and seed company representatives for lists of resistant varieties in various production regions.

CULTURAL CONTROL. Rotation and tillage options will have only a minor effect on powdery mildew control in areas where the pathogen is active year round. Sound cultural practices will reduce the threat of early season epidemics in northern regions where the pathogen is dormant during winter months.

CHEMICAL CONTROL. Effective systemic fungicides are available. Initial sprays should be applied prior to the appearance of outbreaks in fields or immediately upon the discovery of clusters of affected plants. If initial outbreaks occur late in the season (after the harvest begins), the cost of fungicide applications may exceed the potential yield benefit associated with late season disease control.

Southern blight

Southern blight (*Sclerotium rolfsii*) is caused by a soilborne fungus with a broad host range. The disease occurs on watermelon in tropical, subtropical, and warm temperate areas.

SYMPTOMS. The first symptoms are a yellowing and wilting of individual runners. Symptoms include the presence of white, nestlike, fungal mycelium

Figure 7.22. Southern blight results in watery decay on fruit. (Source: D.L. Hopkins.)

with tan to brown specks (sclerotia) on stems and fruit that are covered with or in contact with the soil. A watery decay occurs on the stems or fruit (Fig. 7.22).

DISEASE CYCLE. The causal fungus builds up on susceptible crops and survives in the soil in plant debris and as sclerotia. Soil deposition over watermelon runners and warm, moist conditions favor disease development.

DISEASE MANAGEMENT. Chemical control is generally not effective and resistance is not available.

CULTURAL CONTROL. The most effective control is to not plant watermelon after a crop in which southern blight was present. Rotate watermelons with a nonhost crop. Deep plowing may help to control southern blight by burying infected plant material and sclerotia. Liming acid soils to pH 7.0 also contributes to disease control.

Virus diseases

Virus diseases of watermelon may be caused by a number of pathogens: cucumber mosaic virus (CMV), papaya ringspot virus (PRSV-W), tobacco ringspot virus (TRSV), watermelon mosaic virus-2 (WMV-2), squash mosaic virus (SqMV), and zucchini yellow mosaic virus (ZYMV). These viruses also affect other cucurbits. On watermelon, CMV and SqMV occur rarely, although the effects of SqMV can be especially severe because the virus can be seed-borne. ZYMV is identified occasionally and also can result in severe losses.

The extent of crop loss due to virus disease is highly correlated with the crop growth stage at which the virus becomes established in the field. Watermelon plants infected early in their development (near or before the time of flowering) are severely affected and produce few (if any) fruits. However, plants infected four or more weeks after harvest begins may not show any yield loss. Late-season melons are especially prone to losses associated with virus diseases.

Figure 7.23. Mottled, abnormally shaped leaves caused by WMV-2. (Source: S.E. Webb.)

SYMPTOMS. Regardless of the virus pathogen, early season infections usually result in stunted plants and reduced yields. Virus symptoms first appear on new growth, shortly after infection occurs. The most common symptoms of virus-infected melon plants are abnormally shaped and have yellow/green mottled leaves (Fig. 7.23). Watermelon fruit from infected vines often are irregularly shaped, off-colored, and express certain surface abnormalities such as mottling, warts, or a very rough rind (Fig. 7.24).

DISEASE CYCLE. The viruses that affect watermelon generally have a broad host range and can survive with a variety of weed hosts in fencerows, wooded areas and non-cultivated fields. Transmission of viruses to watermelon plants is accomplished by insect vectors (including aphids and cucumber beetles), nematodes, and by mechanical transfer of plant sap from infected hosts. It is not unusual for mechanical transmission to occur during crop cultivations. The rate of spread may be dependent on the environmental conditions that influence vector activity.

DISEASE MANAGEMENT. Virus diseases are the most difficult to manage. The most successful strategy is to try to avoid circumstances that favor infection, spread and serious losses.

HOST RESISTANCE. All watermelon varieties are not equally susceptible to the virus diseases. Check with university plant pathologists and seed company representatives for varieties that are suitable in specific regions.

CULTURAL CONTROL. Because the most serious losses occur when virus infection occurs early in crop development, late-planted watermelons have the greatest risk of exposure to vectors and viruses. Planting early will help avoid

Figure 7.24. Mottling from WMV-2 on watermelon fruit. (Source: S.E. Webb.)

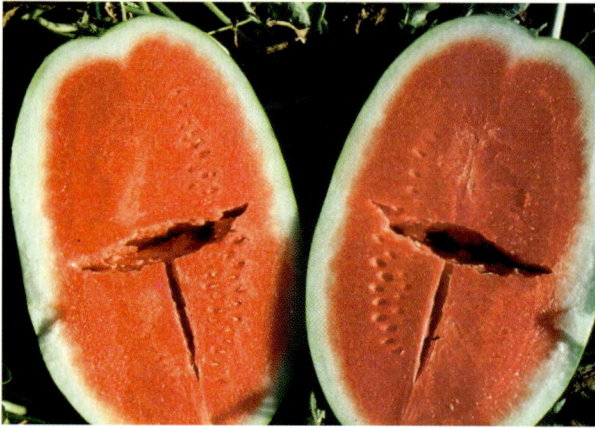

Figure 7.25. Separation of flesh within watermelon is expressed as hollowheart fruit. (Source: D.N. Maynard.)

losses because the crop will be more advanced when the normal exposure to vectors occurs. Rigorous weed control programs in and around fields will reduce the number of hosts that may harbor viruses, thereby limiting the risk of virus infection. Reflective mulches may help discourage aphid vectors from feeding in a field, but their effectiveness often is inconsistent.

CHEMICAL CONTROL. Use of insecticides against aphid and cucumber beetle vectors may be effective only where vector pressure is light. Nematicides and fumigants may contribute to a reduction in the incidence of nematode transmitted virus (TRSV).

PHYSIOLOGICAL DISORDERS

HOLLOWHEART. This disorder is manifested by the separation of flesh within the fruit (Fig. 7.25). It occurs in every production area, but frequency and severity vary considerably among areas and seasons. Occasionally, however, loads are rejected because of hollowheart. It is very difficult to externally identify hollowheart fruit. Sometimes, they can be distinguished by a rough rind and irregular shape, but this is not always the case.

Most watermelon experts agree that there is a higher incidence of hollowheart in crown-set fruit than in lateral-set fruit, that triploid (seedless) varieties have more hollowheart than diploid (seeded) varieties, and that there are differences among varieties in hollowheart susceptibility. Beyond that, there is much speculation as to the role of water and fertilizer management, temperature, pollination, and other factors.

Figure 7.26. Blossom-end rot results in dark-brown, sunken leathery lesion on blossom-end of fruit. (Source: D.N. Maynard.)

Figure 7.27. Constricted growth at stem-end of fruit caused by poor pollination is called bottleneck. (Source: D.N. Maynard.)

BLOSSOM-END ROT. Symptoms begin as a softening and shriveling of the blossom-end of partially grown fruit and progress to a dark-brown, sunken, leathery lesion (Fig. 7.26). Varieties producing elongated fruit are more susceptible to blossom-end rot than those producing round fruit.

The incidence of the disorder is increased under low calcium regimes. Recommendations for control of blossom-end rot include liming of soil according to soil test results and maintenance of an adequate, uniform soil moisture through irrigation management.

BOTTLENECK. Constricted growth at the stem end of the fruit characterizes this disorder (Fig. 7.27). It is attributed to inadequate pollination either because of a low bee population or to poor conditions for bee activity such as cold, wet, or windy weather. The cause of the misshapen fruit can be verified by a cut fruit which will show an absence of seed at the stem end of the watermelon.

SUNBURN. This disorder appears on the upper fruit surface as a gray area where the rind pigment has been destroyed by high temperature (Fig. 7.28). Sunburn damage may be avoided somewhat by selection of varieties with light colored rinds which are less subject to sunburn than dark-rinded varieties. The best means of circumventing sunburn damage, however, is to provide conditions for good vine growth which shades the watermelon fruit.

DISORDERS OF UNKNOWN ORIGIN

CROSS STITCH. This disorder appears as a series of 0.5–1 inch

Figure 7.28. Sunburn results in destroyed pigment in the rind. (Source: D.N. Maynard.)

Figure 7.29. Cross stitch is expressed as necrotic lesions or cracks that are perpendicular to longitudinal axis of fruit. (Source: D.N. Maynard.)

Figure 7.30. Circular, raised, olive-green areas on surface of rind are called greasy spot. (Source: D.N. Maynard.)

Figure 7.31. Target cluster is the result of target-like configurations on the rind. (Source: D.N. Maynard.)

long necrotic wounds that are perpendicular to the longitudinal axis of the fruit (Fig. 7.29). It was observed in Indiana in the late 1980s and early 1990s and in Florida in 1990 where the name was coined.

GREASY SPOT. Relatively inconspicuous raised, circular, olive-green areas on the rind surface characterize this disorder first described in Florida (Fig. 7.30). Greasy spot occurs rarely and is thought not to be of economic concern.

TARGET CLUSTER. Distinctive target-like configurations occur on the rind surface, usually in clusters of three or more. It has been suggested, because of their unique appearance (Fig. 7.31), that the causal organism may be a ringspot virus, but this has not been confirmed.

General References

Latin, R. 1993. Diseases and pests of muskmelon and watermelon. Purdue Univ. Coop. Ext. BP-44. West Lafayette, Ind.

Maynard, D.N. and D.L. Hopkins. 1999. Watermelon fruit disorders. HortTechnology 9:155–161.

Zitter, T.A., D.L. Hopkins, and C.E. Thomas (eds.). 1996. Compendium of cucurbit diseases. APS Press, St. Paul, Minn.

CHAPTER 8

INSECT AND MITE PESTS

S.E. Webb, D.G. Riley, and G.E. Brust

Insects and mites can cause severe problems in the production of watermelon, either through direct damage to the crop or through transmission of disease agents, such as the aphidborne mosaic viruses. New insect pests have recently become established: silverleaf whitefly in the United States (particularly serious in the southwest), Mexico, and Central America and *Thrips palmi* in Florida and Hawaii. In this chapter, we discuss both major and minor pests of watermelon in the United States. The importance of a particular insect varies geographically (Table 8.1), and management options may also differ. Not every insect is listed. For example, field crickets and a complex of darkling beetles are common on fall crops in the southwest. There are many excellent state and regional publications that will provide more specific guidelines for a particular area and pest.

Table 8.1. Status of watermelon pests in the United States by region.

Pest	S. Florida	N. Florida	Southeast	Region[z] Northeast	Midwest	Mid-south	Southwest
Melon aphid[y]	Major	Major	Major	Major	Major	Major	Occasional
Whitefly	Major	Occasional	Minor	Rare	Rare	Minor	Major
Squash bug	Minor	Minor	Minor	Minor	Occasional	Major	Rare
Rindworm complex[x]	Major	Occasional	Major	Minor	Rare	Occasional	Major
Cucumber beetles	Rare	Rare	Major	Major	Major	Major	Rare/Minor
Twospotted spider mite	Rare	Rare	Minor	Major	Major	Occasional	Major
Leafminers	Occasional	Minor	Minor	Minor	Rare	Minor	Major
Thrips	Major[w]	Occasional[v]	Occasional[u]	Minor	Rare	Minor	Minor
Flea beetles	Rare	Minor	Minor	Minor	Rare	Minor	Major
Grasshoppers	Minor	Minor	Minor	Minor	Minor	Minor	Minor
Seedcorn maggot	Rare	Minor	Occasional	Major	Major	Minor	Major
Wireworms	Rare	Minor	Minor	Minor	Occasional	Minor	Rare
White grubs	Rare	Minor	Minor	Minor	Minor	Minor	Rare
Whitefringed beetle	Not found	Minor	Minor	Not found	Not found	Not found	Not found
Mole crickets	Rare	Minor	Rare	Not found	Not found	Rare	Not found

[z]Regions correspond roughly to the National Watermelon Promotion Board Districts, I through VII, from right to left. Mid-South is based primarily from information from Oklahoma, South Texas is included in Southwest.
[y]Pest status is due to role as virus vector in addition to direct feeding damage.
[x]Complex includes beet armyworm, cabbage looper, granulate cutworm, corn earworm and others, depending on location and season.
[w]*Thrips palmi*.
[v]Tobacco thrips (*Frankliniella fusca*).
[u]Western flower thrips (*Frankliniella occidentalis*).

Figure 8.1. Adult green peach aphid. (Source: *Compendium of Cucurbit Diseases*, APS Press, St. Paul, Minn.)

BENEFICIAL INSECTS

Bees are essential for watermelon production. It has been determined that eight or more visits per blossom are necessary for optimum fruit set and normal fruit development. The morning hours are most critical for pollination, but bees will continue to forage into the afternoon, so application of insecticides harmful to bees should be done in the late afternoon or evening during the flowering season. Biological and cultural controls should be used as much as possible to preserve, not only bees, but other beneficial insects. Some of the predators and parasites important in the management of insect and mite pests are mentioned in the following sections.

INSECTS THAT FEED ON PLANT SAP
Melon aphid

Melon aphid (*Aphis gossypii*), also known as cotton aphid, is common throughout the country. In addition to being a major pest of cucurbits and cotton, it also attacks a wide variety of other plants such as eggplant, pepper, potato, citrus, okra, many ornamentals, and many weed species. Green peach aphid (*Myzus persicae*) (Fig. 8.1) and cowpea aphid (*Aphis craccivora*) (Fig. 8.2) occasionally may be found on watermelon but will not be discussed here.

DESCRIPTION AND DAMAGE. Melon aphids are soft-bodied insects, almost egg-shaped when viewed from above (Fig. 8.3). The largest ones are about 1/16 inch long. Their color can vary from pale yellow to orange to dark green to almost black. A pair of small tubelike structures called cornicles extend backward and upward from the posterior of the aphid, above a small taillike structure (cauda). The first

Figure 8.2. Cowpea aphid. (Source: *Compendium of Cucurbit Diseases*, APS Press, St. Paul, Minn.)

Figure 8.3. Parasitized (tan, swollen) and normal melon aphids. (Source: G. Brust).

individuals to colonize a plant will usually have wings, but then wingless aphids become the dominant form until crowding occurs or the plant deteriorates. Then winged aphids will be produced again to disperse to other plants.

Melon aphids reproduce very rapidly, because, in most of the United States, no males are produced and female aphids give birth instead of laying eggs. Thus, their offspring begin feeding immediately and, in 7–10 days, also begin to give birth to more aphids. Average temperatures of 78–80 °F are highly favorable for aphid development. Aphids will grow and reproduce more slowly at cooler temperatures. They feed by inserting their long, piercing- sucking mouthparts into the plant's vascular system and sucking out the plant sap. In doing so, they excrete large amounts of sugary, sticky honeydew. Honeydew is a source of food for a black fungus known as sooty mold and for ants. The ants will actually protect the aphids from attack by other insects and may move them to other leaves. On watermelon, the first sign of aphid damage is a downward curling and crumpling of the leaves which also appear thickened and may glisten with sticky honeydew. If plants are attacked when very young they may be killed. This aphid is also involved in the spread of several viruses which affect watermelon.

MONITORING. The presence of curled, thickened, crumpled leaves is a good indication of the presence of melon aphids. The undersides of leaves should be examined. If an average of more than 5–10 aphids per leaf are found on 20–50 leaves taken throughout the field, it may be necessary to institute control measures. Data from Texas indicates that maintaining aphid levels below 10 per leaf (between the 3–9 leaf nodes) prevents losses due to aphid injury in the absence of virus.

MANAGEMENT. If the infestation is localized, spot-treatment with a recommended insecticide or removal of the infested plant or plants may solve the problem. In some areas, aphids have become resistant to particular insecticides, so it is important to consult local extension offices for recommendations. Some newer chemicals which are fairly specific for sucking insects are proving to be effective and safe and should soon be available for use on cucurbits. The use of some insecticides that are not effective in killing aphids may actually result in increased populations because they eliminate the insects that normally feed on aphids. These beneficial natural enemies include lady beetles, lacewings, and larvae of syrphid flies. Tiny wasps lay their eggs in aphids. The wasp larva matures inside the living aphid and finally exits, leaving a gold or tan shell (aphid mummy) behind (Fig. 8.3). In some areas of the country, fungi commonly infect aphids, drastically reducing populations. When monitoring for aphid infestations, it is important to note the presence of predators and parasites which may be all that is needed for control.

MANAGING VIRUS SPREAD BY APHIDS. Neither insecticides nor natural enemies will prevent virus spread by aphids. Melon aphid, green peach aphid and cowpea aphid can be involved but many other winged aphids that do not actually reproduce on watermelon, but are only passing through, may be more important in spreading watermelon mosaic virus 2, zucchini yellow mosaic virus, and the watermelon strain of papaya ringspot virus. Aphids must land and taste plants by probing briefly with their mouthparts to determine if the plant is a suitable source of food. By doing this, they can either pick up virus from a plant that is already infected, or, if they have just come from an infected plant, they can introduce or transmit virus into the healthy plant. These viruses are transmitted in a nonpersistent manner which means that the aphid quickly loses the virus it is carrying. Insecticides cannot kill the aphid fast enough to prevent virus transmission, which can take as little as 10 to 15 seconds. Reflective mulches which repel aphids and highly purified mineral oil sprays which interfere with attachment of virus to the aphid's mouthparts may reduce virus spread.

Whitefly

DESCRIPTION AND DAMAGE. Silverleaf whitefly (*Bemisia argentifolii*) has become a major pest in watermelon in the southwestern United States, affecting the crop directly by its feeding and by acting as a vector of viruses such as squash leaf curl virus. It attacks many other crops and weeds, in addition to watermelon. The silverleaf whitefly adult is small, less than 1/16 inch long, and has solid white wings held in a tentiform position over a yellow body while at rest (Fig. 8.4). Greenhouse whitefly (*Trialeurodes*

Figure 8.4. Adult silverleaf whitefly. (Source: D. Riley.)

Figure 8.5. Greenhouse whitefly adults. (Source: *Compendium of Cucurbit Diseases*, APS Press, St. Paul, Minn.)

vaporariorum) is similar except that it holds its wings flat or horizontally at rest (Fig. 8.5). Immature stages begin with a pointed oblong yellow egg which darkens at the tip just before hatching (Fig. 8.6) A mobile first instar or crawler stage settles on the leaf and develops through sessile second, third, and fourth instars, which look like semitransparent, flat, oval scales. Later instars, more yellow and more easily seen without the aid of a hand lens, typically have very distinct eye spots and are referred to as red-eyed nymphs. The life cycle from egg to adult can be as short as 2 weeks under very warm temperatures. Degree days for total life cycle development on cantaloupe are reported to be 250 with minimum threshold for development of 55 °F. Eggs and early immature stages of whitefly are generally found on the undersides of younger leaves. Whitefly adults also concentrate on younger leaves where they lay the most eggs. Larger nymphs are typically more numerous on older leaves. Whiteflies feed in the plant vascular system (phloem) through a stylet similar to that of aphids and, like aphids process a relatively large volume of plant sap by excreting excess liquid in the form of honeydew.

In the southwestern United States, a rapid increase and decline in adult whitefly migration has been correlated with the development and decline of the cotton crop. Peak migrations of whitefly occur when a large acreage of a host crop, such as cabbage, melon, or cotton in the spring or summer, begins to decline. Whiteflies have been reported to transmit the geminivirus, squash leaf curl virus, in watermelon. Sweetpotato whitefly (*B. tabaci*), which has been displaced in most parts of the country by the silverleaf whitefly, transmits a closterovirus called lettuce infectious yellows virus. Fortunately, silverleaf whitefly appears to be an inefficient vector of this virus.

MONITORING. Adults are gener-

Figure 8.6. Silverleaf whitefly nymphs. (Source: D. Riley.)

ally monitored using yellow sticky traps or by carefully turning over leaves to examine the underside where whiteflies typically feed and lay eggs. This is best done during the coolest part of the day when whiteflies are least active. The younger leaves (third to fifth leaf nodes) of many crops are more preferred by adult whiteflies than older leaves, but any fully expanded leaf from the youngest third of the runner can be chosen for examination, except for the very youngest. The largest nymphs are usually found on older leaves. Established thresholds for whiteflies in muskmelon are three adults per leaf at the third leaf node or 0.4 large nymphs per square inch of leaf area. If viruses transmitted by the whitefly (squash leaf curl virus or lettuce infectious yellows) are present, then this threshold should be lower.

MANAGEMENT. The use of insecticide is the primary tactic for whitefly control in commercial agriculture; however, it can be expensive and complicated by insecticide resistance and disruption of natural enemies. Natural sources of mortality for the whitefly include predation by green lacewing or lady beetle larvae, parasitization by wasps such as *Encarsia* or *Eretmocerus* species, and infection by insect pathogens such as *Beauveria*, *Paecilomyces*, or *Verticillium* species. Cultural control options include destroying crop residues to reduce whitefly and virus carryover, using physical barriers such as row covers, or repellants such as reflective mulches, adjusting planting dates, and selecting field locations in respect to potential sources of whiteflies. Although action thresholds for the control of whiteflies in muskmelon using contact insecticides have been reported at three adults per leaf at the third leaf node from the growing point, no thresholds have been developed specifically for watermelon. Several insecticides, including 1% to 2% oil solutions, that are applied to foliage control whiteflies to varying degrees. Systemic insecticides can be very effective. Local recommendations should be followed.

Squash bug

DESCRIPTION AND DAMAGE. Squash bug (*Anasa tristis*) is reported as a primary pest of cucurbits, including watermelon, in Oklahoma and other areas in the United States. The adults and nymphs feed on plant sap, severely stressing the plant when bugs occur in high numbers. Studies in Oklahoma suggest that pumpkin and squash are much better hosts for squash bug than watermelon. Also, development time of squash bug is longer on watermelon than pumpkin and squash. Adult squash bugs emerge in the spring and can attack seedlings. Later, oblong eggs are laid in uniform clusters on the undersides of leaves, appearing creamy white (initially) to metallic bronze (Fig. 8.7). The squash bug develops through five nymphal instars, requiring 30–45

Figure 8.7. Squash bug eggs and nymphs. (Source: *Compendium of Cucurbit Diseases*, APS Press, St. Paul, Minn.)

days to develop to the adult stage from an egg. Adults are dark brown to ash black, about 1 inch long, with light patches on the anterior margins of dark abdominal segments that are mostly covered when the wings are folded (Fig. 8.8).

MONITORING. Squash bug adults are located within the plant canopy, on stems and often congregate near the base of the plant. Small nymphs are generally around the cluster of eggs from which they hatched. Egg clusters are usually on the undersides of leaves.

MANAGEMENT. Cultural controls include removal or destruction of crop debris infested with squash bug and avoiding host plants late in the year that may contribute to an overwintering population. In the spring, seedlings should be scouted regularly to detect movement of adults into the field from overwintering sites. Chemical control is typically used for squash bug and effective treatment can be attained by targeting small nymphs. Since these often occur on the undersides of leaves, good spray coverage with sufficient spray volume can improve control with an effective insecticide. A healthy, vigorous watermelon crop can withstand low infestations of squash bug without reductions in yield.

FOLIAGE AND FRUIT-FEEDING INSECTS AND MITES
Rindworm complex

DESCRIPTION AND DAMAGE. Any caterpillar (larval stage of moth) that feeds on the surface of watermelon fruit is considered a rindworm, although many of these insects feed primarily on stems and foliage. Scarring of the fruit is economically more important, however. The white to tan blotches left after the caterpillar feeds on the upper layers of the rind make the fruit less marketable.

At any given time and location, vari-

Figure 8.8. Squash bug adult and nymph on squash. (Source: J.L. Capinera, University of Florida, Gainesville.)

Figure 8.9. Cabbage looper moth resting on watermelon leaf. (Source: W.C. Adlerz (deceased), University of Florida, Leesburg.)

ous species may be present. Currently, in Florida and southern California and Arizona, beet armyworm (*Spodoptera exigna*) and cabbage looper (*Trichoplusia ni*) (described in more detail in the following paragraphs) are the most abundant, but other species may be important at other times. Control measures may vary for each species so it is important to identify them properly. In general, it is much easier to control these insects when they are small.

Cabbage looper feeds on a variety of crops, including cabbage and related plants, potato, spinach, tomato, cucumber, watermelon, cotton, and soybean. They overwinter in Florida and adjacent states and migrate north each year. The adults are night-flying moths with brown, mottled forewings marked in the center with a small, silver figure eight (Fig. 8.9). They lay their eggs (small, ridged, round, greenish-white) singly on both upper and lower leaf surfaces. The eggs hatch into larvae that are green with white stripes running the length of their bodies (Fig. 8.10). The caterpillar has three pairs of slender legs near its head and then three pairs of thick prolegs near the end of its body. It moves in a characteristic looping motion, alternately stretching forward and arching its back as it brings the back prolegs close to its front legs. After feeding for 2–4 weeks, the caterpillar, about 1 1/4 inches long when fully grown, spins a cocoon and pupates. The adults emerge 10–14 days later. There can be several generations per year depending on climate.

Beet armyworm also feeds on many crops and weeds and is a particularly serious pest of cotton. It ranges through most of the southern United States, including California. The highly mobile adult moth has dark forewings with mottled lighter

Figure 8.10. Cabbage looper and feeding damage to watermelon. (Source: W.C. Adlerz (deceased), University of Florida, Leesburg.)

Figure 8.11. Beet armyworm feeding on watermelon rind. (Source: W.C. Adlerz (deceased), University of Florida, Leesburg.)

markings and hind wings thinly covered with whitish scales. Each female can lay over 600 eggs, generally in masses of about 100 on the undersides of leaves in the lower plant canopy. Very young caterpillars feed in groups and then disperse as they grow older (third instar). The dull green caterpillars (Fig. 8.11) have wavy, light-colored stripes lengthwise down the back and broader stripes on each side. After feeding from 1–3 weeks, they construct a cocoon and pupate, emerging as adults about 1 week later. Beet armyworm survives the winter in south Florida and can complete many generations a year there. From south Florida, adults migrate into north Florida and other parts of the southeast.

MONITORING. Fields should be monitored for the presence of caterpillars and feeding damage. Although plants can tolerate a certain amount of feeding on leaves, damage to the fruit may reduce marketability and control measures should be taken.

MANAGEMENT. Many beneficial insects and insect pathogens help keep populations below economically damaging levels, especially if it has not been necessary to use foliar applications of insecticides to control other pests. In Florida, cabbage loopers have been found naturally infected with an insect virus (nuclear polyhedrosis virus), and granulate cutworm has been found infected with a protozoan (*Microsporidium* sp.). Nuclear polyhedrosis virus and fungal pathogens also infect beet armyworm. Beet armyworm is also attacked by many parasitoids, both wasps and tachinid flies. A number of small wasps and a tachinid fly parasitize caterpillars or eggs of cabbage looper. Predaceous bugs may consume eggs and small caterpillars as will wasps, green lacewings and spiders.

Many different forms of *Bacillus thuringiensis* are available that are highly specific for caterpillar pests and will not harm beneficial insects. However, only small caterpillars are highly susceptible. Specific insecticide recommendations for older larvae, which are hard to control, may vary from state to state.

Cucumber beetles

DESCRIPTION. There are two species of cucumber beetles that attack

Figure 8.12. Striped cucumber beetles massing on seedling. (Source: G. Brust.)

watermelon: striped (*Acalymma vittatum*) (Fig. 8.12) and spotted (*Diabrotica undecimpunctata howardi*). Both species are about 1/4 inch long and are yellow-green. The spotted cucumber beetle has 12 black spots while the striped has three black stripes on its back.

DAMAGE. Adult beetles feed on emerging watermelon plants or transplants as soon as they appear in the field. Feeding damage can occur very quickly with cotyledons usually being fed on before foliage. Both species can transmit *Erwinia tracheiphila*, the causal agent of bacterial wilt in some cucurbits, but not in watermelon. Beetles can also feed on watermelon stems below the plastic, when plastic mulch is used. Plants will begin to wilt and then collapse due to the stem feeding. The larva of the cucumber beetle (Fig. 8.13) feeds on roots and stems and can cause severe damage to very small plants, but less damage to larger plants with more fully developed root systems. Later in the season, beetles can feed on watermelon rind causing mostly cosmetic damage to the fruit, which may reduce marketability.

Striped cucumber beetle adults overwinter along fence rows or wooded areas and become active in the spring. Spotted cucumber beetles become active in late spring in the midwest but much earlier in their southern range. At temperatures above 55 °F, striped cucumber beetle adults start to move about. When temperatures reach 60 °F or above, they take flight. Adult beetles will feed on wild hosts, i.e., sunflower, dandelion, Rosaceae family, until cucurbits are available. Once plants emerge or are transplanted, cucumber beetle adults can appear in the field in large numbers in a matter of hours. Beetles are most active in the morning and late afternoon. Beetles begin to disperse throughout the field and females begin to lay eggs at this time. After dispersal in the midwest, the adult population begins to decline, but never disappears. Eggs hatch in 6 to 9 days while the larval stage lasts 2 to 3 1/2 weeks. Pupation takes 6 to 10 days. Adults emerge in late June or early-mid July and remain

Figure 8.13. Striped cucumber beetle larva. (Source: G. Brust.)

active through autumn. There is one generation in the northernmost part of their range and two in the southern range.

MONITORING. Because beetles can attack watermelon plants at anytime they are in the field, plants should be monitored as soon as they are present (direct seeded or transplanted). Because watermelon is not susceptible to bacterial wilt, plants can stand some feeding damage before controls are necessary. Controls are necessary if there are five beetles per plant or moderate stem or rind feeding.

MANAGEMENT. There are no biological controls that work very well for either cucumber beetle, therefore, synthetic insecticides applied when beetles reach the threshold is the best procedure. A possible cultural control is the use of squash around the perimeter of the field as a trap crop. The cucumber beetles should prefer to feed on the squash and, once concentrated on these plants, can be sprayed.

Twospotted spider mites

DESCRIPTION. Twospotted spider mites (*Tetranychus urticae*) are very small (1/80–1/60 inch) arthropods that are closely related to insects. The body is a light green-yellow with two dark spots on either side. Mite eggs are very small, spherical, straw-colored and shiny. Immatures look similar to adults. Twospotted spider mites are almost ubiquitous as they feed on hundreds of different plants. Adults move into fields from the edge in early to midsummer where they feed and can rapidly reproduce. In the fall, mites move out of fields to fence rows or wooded areas where they overwinter.

DAMAGE. Mites feed on the undersurface of leaves. Mites feed by shredding small areas of leaf and sucking the juices. Light mite feeding looks like tiny scratch marks on the upper surface of the leaf. As mite feeding intensifies, the scratch marks begin to coalesce. The upper surface of these leaves have an interveinal yellowing (chlorosis). The underside of leaves are tan and have a crusty texture. Mite infestations usually start at the edge of a field and slowly move into it. On individual plants, mites tend to establish themselves on the crown leaves and these are the first to show symptoms of mite feeding. Watermelon fruit from heavily infested plants have a coarse surface. Mites reproduce rapidly in hot (>80 °F), dry (<50% RH) conditions. Water-stressed plants are more prone to infestations and damage. Mite feeding dam-

Figure 8.14. Severe damage to watermelon plants caused by twospotted spider mite. (Source: G. Brust.)

age can kill plants (Fig. 8.14) or reduce their vigor to the point where fruit does not mature properly due to lack of water or have enough sugars to be marketable. When mite populations build, they produce a protective webbing around their feeding area which makes contact with insecticides even more difficult.

MONITORING. The crowns of plants should be watched closely for any signs of mite feeding. The undersides of crown leaves from plants located along the edge of fields should be examined for mite activity weekly in mid-June (south) or early to mid-July (north). Ten plants from ten locations along the field edge should be checked. Since there are other causes for chlorosis and interveinal yellowing of crown leaves, such as magnesium deficiency, ozone damage or water stress, the presence of mites must be confirmed. There are many natural enemies of mites such as predatory thrips, minute pirate bugs and predatory mites. These predators are present in fields that have not had many insecticide applications. Since conservation of these predators is essential for good mite control, insecticides should not be applied on a weekly basis but only as needed for control of other pests. If mites are found along edges of fields the rest of the field also should be checked. Early feeding should be watched to see if mites expand within individual plants or into the field. Often, natural enemies or the weather, i.e., rain, can control these early small populations. If, however, mites begin to expand on marked plants along the field edges or into the field, then a foliar application directed at, but not solely to, the crown of the plant is warranted.

Leafminers

DESCRIPTION AND DAMAGE. Leafminers (*Liriomyza sativae* and *L. trifolii*) have been reported as a major pest of watermelon in Hawaii and occasionally in south Florida. The responsible leafminers are larvae of agromyzid flies that establish themselves within the foliage after adult flies (Fig. 8.15) lay eggs directly in the leaf tissue. Larvae feed between the leaf surfaces, creating meandering mines that enlarge as the larvae increase in size (Fig. 8.16). After about 2 weeks in warm weather the larva completes development and leaves the mine, dropping to the ground to pu-

Figure 8.15. Serpentine leafminer adult resting on leaf. (Source: Alton Sparks, Texas A&M University, Weslaco.)

Figure 8.16. Mining on a melon leaf by leafminer larva. (Source: *Compendium of Cucurbit Diseases*, APS Press, St. Paul, Minn.)

pate. On plastic-mulched beds, pupae accumulate underneath melons on top of the plastic film. Infestations can be more severe late in the growing season, particularly if adults migrate out of nearby crop residue into late planted fields. Defoliation of the crop late in the season can lead to sunburned fruit.

MONITORING. Plants are usually monitored for leafminers by examining leaves with mines for live and parasitized larvae. Treatment thresholds for leafminers on watermelon have been reported in Hawaii at 20 live leafminer larvae per leaf when vines are less than 20 inches long, and afterward, 15 larvae per two consecutive sample dates or 35 live larvae per leaf on a single sample date.

MANAGEMENT. Leafminers are controlled in large part (75% control reported in Hawaii) by several parasite species, including *Chrysonotomyia punctiventris*, *Halticoptera circulus*, and *Ganaspidium hunteri*, especially if insecticides have not been needed to control other pests. The danger of crop defoliation late in the season can require pesticide applications to prevent sunburn damage to the fruit. It is important to note that certain contact insecticides are only effective against the adult stage and the systemic materials may be required to control the larvae within the leaf tissue. Local control recommendations should be followed.

Thrips

DESCRIPTION AND DAMAGE. Thrips are very small (1/25–1/10 inches long), slender insects that, depending on the species, feed on leaves, pollen, and flower parts. Tobacco thrips (*Frankliniella fusca*) adults appear dark in color while melon thrips (*Thrips palmi*) are lighter. It is usually not possible to identify thrips to species level without the aid of a microscope.

Melon thrips is by far the most serious thrips pest of watermelon. So far, in the United States, it has been reported only in Hawaii and southern Florida where it attacks a number of vegetable crops. In watermelon, its feeding causes bronzing of foliage and destruction of vine tips leading to limited canopy development. Tobacco thrips has been mainly reported as a pest of seedling watermelon plants. Feeding damage to developing leaves leads to scarring that is reminiscent of abrasion by blowing sand. It is not known if the early damage affects later yields.

MONITORING. In areas where melon thrips is present, leaves and vine tips should be examined for the presence of thrips. In Hawaii, this has been done by shaking the vine tip (still attached to the plant) vigorously against the inside walls of an 8-ounce paper cup and then examining the inside of the cup for the presence of thrips. For areas where tobacco thrips is a problem, the seedling can be tapped and gently shaken over a stiff piece of paper. A hand lens is helpful for examining leaves for the presence of thrips. In Hawaii, insecticides were applied if eight active melon thrips were found per leaf or if 20% of the vine tips were infested.

MANAGEMENT. Preservation of natural enemies such as pirate bugs (*Orius* sp.) that feed on thrips is desirable because many insecticides are not very effective for control of melon thrips. Heavy, widespread infestations of tobacco thrips may require chemical control.

Flea beetles

DESCRIPTION. Flea beetle (Chrysomelid species) adults are small (1/10–1/4 inch) jumping beetles of various colors and patterns. The larvae are usually root feeders which are elongate and white. Flea beetle adults can attack a field very rapidly. Most damage occurs within the first 2–3 weeks crops are in the field. Beetles feed and then lay eggs in the soil, where larvae feed on underground plant parts. There are two to three generations per year.

DAMAGE. Most of the damage is due to the adults chewing numerous small round holes in foliage. This feeding can be so intense on seedlings and small plants that it causes stunting, reduced yields, and death of plants.

MONITORING. Plants should be watched for shot-hole feeding damage soon after transplanting or emergence. Beetles are usually most active on clear, warm, calm days. Small plants can take 30%–40% defoliation with little effect on yield and therefore, treatment is justified only if beyond this defoliation level.

MANAGEMENT. In general, it is rarely necessary to control flea beetles. In the event that chemical control measures are necessary, pyrethroids are effective.

Grasshoppers

DESCRIPTION. Grasshopper (*Melanoplus* sp.) adults are large brown-green hopping/flying insects that most people are very familiar with. Immatures, which resemble adults, but cannot fly, develop from eggs that were laid in grain or grassy areas the year before. In spring, immatures feed on any close

Figure 8.17. Damage to stem by seedcorn maggot. (Source: G. Brust)

available plants, usually grasses. In summer, adults begin to mate and lay eggs. Several warm dry seasons in a row are favorable for grasshopper outbreaks.

DAMAGE. Adults can feed on foliage, stems or any upper part of the plant. A few grasshoppers are not a problem; it is when there are thousands that damage can be severe.

MONITORING. Grasshopper populations should be monitored if watermelon fields are located near large areas of pastures or grazing areas for livestock. Large grasshopper populations in these areas during periods of drought can result in mass migration into nearby fields.

MANAGEMENT. Fortunately, there are many natural enemies such as ground beetles, anthomyiid flies, bee flies, flesh flies, various parasites, birds, and mammals that usually keep grasshoppers under control. Foliar insecticides will give some control during large migrations.

SOIL INSECT PESTS

Seedcorn maggot

DESCRIPTION AND DAMAGE. Seedcorn maggot (*Delia platura*) adults are the size of small houseflies and are grayish-brown. The immatures are pale, yellowish-white, legless maggots that are 1/4 inch long when full sized. There are three instars. Adults lay eggs at the base of transplants in fields with soils high in organic matter such as plowed-under cover crops or manure. Eggs hatch quickly and first instar maggots bore into seed or the stem of plants (Fig. 8.17). Often this initial damage is not noticeable. Once inside the stem (Fig. 8.18), the feeding injury causes the plant to wilt and eventually die. Stems that have been fed upon appear shredded. During a cool wet spring, as much as 50% of the plants can be destroyed by maggot feeding.

Figure 8.18. Seedcorn maggots in stem of transplant. (Source: G. Brust.)

In early spring, in the midwestern and the northeastern United States, flies become active and begin to search for organic matter in which to lay their eggs. Fields that have a cover crop that has just been plowed under are very attractive to flies. Flies prefer cool, moist conditions for their activity. Eggs hatch quickly and maggots feed on any organic matter for 2–3 weeks. They will concentrate their feeding on plants or seeds, if present. There are three generations a year, with the first being most important for causing injury. Once warmer temperatures arrive, flies will retreat to wooded areas. Seed corn maggot overwinters in the wooded areas in the pupal stage.

MONITORING. At the present time there are no good ways to monitor fly populations before they become pests. Any organic matter should be plowed into the soil at least 2–3 weeks before transplanting. Transplanting or direct seeding should be delayed until maximum soil temperatures are above 72 °F at a 4-inch depth. Lower soil temperatures will increase the likelihood of damage. If planting takes place before soils are warm, the use of plastic mulch (especially clear or infrared-transmitting) will heat the ground much faster and reduce seedcorn maggot injury. In some areas of the country, carbofuran can be used under the plastic, which will reduce, but not eliminate, damage. The midwest and northeastern parts of the United States have more consistent seedcorn maggot problems than the rest of the country.

Wireworms

DESCRIPTION AND DAMAGE. Wireworms (*Agriotus* sp., *Melanotus* sp., and other Elateridae) are hard-bodied wirelike larvae of the click-beetle. Larvae are brownish yellow and 1/2–1 1/2 inches long. Adults are large, brown beetles that make a clicking sound when they try to right themselves after being on their backs.

Depending on species, wireworm larvae can stay in the soil for 1–5 years. Eggs are laid singly in soil 1–6 inches deep in spring or summer. Hatching takes place in 2–4 weeks. Because of the long egg-laying period, overlapping generations with larvae of different sizes are present. Adults prefer to oviposit into grassy areas, which include rye, wheat or oat plantings, mixed pastures, old fields, and even potato.

Figure 8.19. Wireworm and damage to transplant. (Source: G. Brust.)

Larvae drill into seeds, stems, or roots of watermelon plants (Fig. 8.19) causing plants to wilt soon after transplanting.

MONITORING. To determine if wireworms are present before planting, four to five bait stations should be placed in the field 4–5 weeks before planting. A station is a hole, about 6 inches deep, with a cupful of untreated wheat and corn. The hole is covered and in 2–3 weeks is dug up and checked for the presence of wireworm larvae. One wireworm per station justifies a treatment.

MANAGEMENT. If wireworms are present, then use of a soil insecticide is warranted. However, none of the labeled insecticides do a very good job of controlling wireworms. Wireworms do not thrive in hot soils; therefore, use of plastic mulch and a later planting date will ensure a warm soil and reduce the threat of wireworm damage. If planting takes place before soils are warm, the use of plastic mulch, especially clear or infrared-transmitting, will heat the ground much faster and reduce wireworm injury. In some areas of the country, carbofuran can be used under the plastic which will reduce, but not eliminate, damage. The midwestern and northeastern parts of the United States have more consistent wireworm problems.

White grubs and whitefringed beetle

DESCRIPTION AND DAMAGE. White grubs (*Phyllophaga* sp.) (larvae of May and June beetles) and whitefringed beetle (*Graphognathus* sp.) larvae can occur at damaging levels if watermelons are planted into fields where grassy sod or small grains were grown in previous season. Soil insects usually take some time to establish in a field. For example, white grubs such as *P. anxia* spend up to 3 years in the soil from egg to adult, usually developing on the fibrous roots of grasses. A watermelon planting following a row crop, such as soybean, is much less likely to have problems with soil insects. Mature white grubs are 1/2–1 inch long, depending on species, and can be recognized by their typical C-shaped, grub-like appearance.

Whitefringed beetle has been reported as a nuisance pest of watermelons in the southeastern United States, but its occurrence in commercial watermelon fields has

Figure 8.20. Whitefringed beetle adult. (Source: Russell Ottens, University of Georgia, Tifton.)

not been reported recently. The larval stage or grub, which can cause serious damage by boring into and destroying the taproot of seedlings, is cream-colored with a small, recessed, reddish-brown head. It can be up to 1/2 inch long. Adult weevils (Fig. 8.20) are dark gray, about 1/2 inch long, and appears to have a white fringe along the outside edge of the body. Adults live 2–5 months, laying eggs in masses of 11–60 eggs on plant debris. The insect overwinters as a grub (or sometimes in the egg stage) and pupates in the spring. The weevil cannot fly but spreads by crawling or by movement in commerce. Whitefringed beetles generally have one generation per year and preseason control is only recommended if a preplant sample or previous history of the field suggests that a problem exists.

MANAGEMENT. For most of the root feeding insects, preplant sampling and preventative controls are the best solutions. Curative insecticide treatments of white grub and whitefringed beetle grubs are not effective after the crop is established. Cultural controls, such as avoiding sod fields for new watermelon plantings, are generally practiced, except in central and north Florida where it is common to plant in long rotations with Bahia grass pasture to avoid the soilborne fungus, *Fusarium oxysporum*. In general, it is difficult to control many of the soil insects effectively with insecticides currently registered for use in cucurbit crops. Soil fumigation can be very effective and in general, where plastic mulch with bed fumigation is used, insect root feeders do not occur in watermelon.

Mole crickets

DESCRIPTION. Of the 10 species of mole crickets, only a few are pests. The tawny mole cricket (*Scapteriscus vicinus*) is the most damaging to vegetable crops. The southern mole cricket (*Scapteriscus acletus*) has also been reported to attack vegetable seedlings in Florida. The tawny mole cricket is also a major pest of turf and pasture. It was introduced into the United States from southern South America around 1900, and now occurs in Florida, Georgia, South Carolina, North Carolina, Alabama, Mississippi, Louisiana, and Texas. The presence of mole crickets can be detected by the meandering tunnels they create. About 1/2 inch in diameter, tunnels are just below the surface and

Figure 8.21. Mole cricket tunnels in watermelon field. (Source: W.C. Adlerz (deceased), University of Florida, Leesburg.)

Figure 8.22. Earwig feeding on mole cricket. [Source: W.C. Adlerz (deceased), University of Florida, Leesburg.]

resemble miniature ground mole tunnels (Fig. 8.21).

In the southeastern United States, there is one generation per year. Eggs are laid in chambers, 4–12 inches underground, from April through June. Eggs hatch after about 3 weeks. The adults of the previous generation die off during May and June and most of the new generation reaches the adult stage in the fall and early winter. These adults overwinter and breed in the spring. For 2–3 months in the spring, tawny mole crickets are most commonly seen during their brief mating flights which begin shortly after sunset.

DAMAGE. Mole crickets mainly feed on plant roots. At night, in warm, wet weather, they will also feed on stems and leaves at surface level. Their tunneling in, around, and under the developing root system, in addition to feeding, is particularly damaging to young seedlings. Bahiagrass is a preferred food and watermelon fields that were in bahiagrass pasture the previous year may harbor large populations.

MANAGEMENT. In areas where mole crickets are known to cause problems, a preplant application of a soil insecticide that is incorporated into the soil is the most useful control measure. Because of the damage done to pastures and turf, much effort has gone into finding additional natural enemies of this pest in South America and releasing them in the United States. Native predators such as earwigs (Fig. 8.22) also attack mole crickets.

General References

Davidson, R. and W. Lyon. 1987. Insect pests of farm, garden, and orchard, 8th ed. Wiley, New York.

Foster, R. and B. Flood (eds.). 1995. Vegetable insect management, with emphasis on the Midwest. Meister, Willoughby, Ohio.

Hoffman, M. 1993. Manual on natural enemies of vegetable insect pests. Cornell Resources, Ithaca, N.Y.

McKinlay, R. 1992. Vegetable crop pests. CRC Press, Boca Raton, Fla.

Metcalf, R.L. and W.H. Luckman. 1994. Introduction to insect pest management, 3rd ed. Wiley, New York.

CHAPTER 9

WEED MANAGEMENT

W.M. Stall and J.W. Shrefler

Watermelon is extremely sensitive to competition by many different weeds and yield and quality may be severely restricted because of weed competition. Weeds compete for water and nutrients as well as light and space which restricts crop growth and yield. Weeds may affect crop yield by interfering with procedures used to control other pests. Because watermelon plants must be widely spaced for optimum yield, a large area between plants is available for weed emergence and growth with no competition from the crop early in the season. Later, vine cover and the extensive root system of watermelon plants does allow watermelon plants to be much more competitive with weeds.

WEEDS

There are numerous weedy species that are found commonly in fields used for watermelon production including monocots, dicots, and sedges. For each of these types, there may be annual and perennial species. Often, one or several weed species will constitute the major weed problem in a crop. As few as 24 goosegrass (*Eleusine indica*) plants per 30 ft of row reduces watermelon yield compared to weed free rows. Watermelon should be maintained free of large crabgrass (*Digitaria sanguinalis*) for at least 6 weeks to avoid yield reduction. Large crabgrass emerging after that time does not restrict yield or quality of the fruit. Watermelon yield is reduced by 7% for every additional week during the 6-week period that large crabgrass is present. Season long competition reduces yield by more than 70%.

Early weed control in watermelon is extremely important. Even small weeds germinating and growing for a week in the row of young watermelon plants may reduce yield. Late in the season, when vines are growing vigorously, emerging weeds may not have a direct effect on crop yield. Control methods obviously should be geared for early season weed control. However, certain weeds late in the season may interfere with the application of pesticides and may hinder harvesting.

Season-long competition of only six smooth pigweed (*Amaranthus*

Figure 9.1. Ten percent of the potential watermelon yield has been lost by smooth pigweed competition at this growth stage. (Source: W. M. Stall)

hybridus) plants between watermelon plants resulted in total crop failure. If the pigweed emerges at the same time as the watermelon and grows for 5 days before being removed, final yield is reduced by 10% (Fig. 9.1). If, however, watermelon fields are kept free of emerging smooth pigweed for 4 weeks, no yield is lost due to any emerging plants after that time.

One of the major problem weeds in watermelon crops is yellow nutsedge (*Cyperus esculentus*) (Fig. 9.2). If allowed to grow season long, yield is reduced 98% by 21 yellow nutsedge plants in the bed around a watermelon plant (82 ft^2). Watermelon yield is reduced 20% by five nutsedge plants per square yard or about one nutsedge per 2 ft^2. If the watermelon crop is maintained free of yellow nutsedge for 5 weeks, no yield reduction occurs from nutsedge that emerge after that time.

METHODS OF WEED CONTROL

Weed control in watermelon typically includes combinations of two or more of the following means of control: mechanical, cultural, or chemical.

MECHANICAL CONTROL. Field preparation by plowing or disking, cultivation, mowing and hoeing or hand pulling of weeds are examples of mechanical control. Seedbed preparation by plowing or disking exposes many weed seeds to variations in light, temperature, and moisture. For some weeds this process breaks seed dormancy, making possible early-season control with herbicides or additional cultivation. Where fields are known to contain a large number of hard-to-control weeds, a fallow treatment before planting watermelon can reduce the weed seed bank and the subsequent number of weeds emerging in the crop.

Figure 9.2. Yellow nutsedge, if allowed to grow season long, will reduce watermelon yield 98%. Yield will not be adversely affected if the nutsedge is removed at this stage of watermelon growth. (Source: W. M. Stall)

Fallowing, whether all mechanical or a combination of mechanical and chemical, can reduce pests that may survive on weeds growing in the field. Mechanical fallowing is allowing weeds to germinate and emerge and then disking them under before they have a chance to propagate. When this is done several successive times, the seed bank of many weeds in the soil is significantly reduced. Successive diskings is the key since some weeds such as nightshade (*Solanum* sp.) complex will not all germinate uniformly because allelopathic compounds given off by the emerging weeds keep a proportion of the remaining nightshade seeds dormant. These dormant seeds will not germinate until the growing weeds are killed. Other weed seeds must be either scarified or be near the soil surface to germinate. Several mechanical diskings can cause these seeds to germinate. With some propagules, such as the nutsedges (*Cyperus* sp.), mechanical fallowing must be supplemented with chemicals. Disking every 2 weeks for 2 years was required to eliminate nutsedges in one study. In another study, nutsedges hoed every week for 14 weeks reduced nutsedge populations by 76%.

Weed populations were greatly reduced when nutsedges and perennial grasses received a systemic, nonselective herbicide and were disked after the herbicide translocated throughout the plant (usually 2 weeks), and the process was repeated. If this process is repeated more than twice a higher proportion of nutsedges can be removed.

Because most watermelons are grown on widely spaced beds, cultivation between the rows is a preferred method of weed control before the vines run. Lay-by cultivation and fertilization is usually accomplished by the fourth or fifth week after seed emergence or transplanting. Care should be take at this time not to cultivate too deep. Watermelon roots normally are out as far as the ends of the vines. Incorrect cultivation can prune roots and reduce yield.

Hoeing weeds in the beds is an acceptable method of weed control if enough labor is available; at least two hoeings are needed before the vines run off of the bed. The weed species present generally dictates the timing of the hoeings. Pigweeds (*Amaranthus* sp.), nightshades and some other broadleaf weeds require hoeing the weeds out earlier after emergence than with grasses and nutsedges.

CULTURAL CONTROL. There are several methods that can be used to reduce weed competition in watermelons. These include polyethylene mulches, crop rotation, and cover crops. The use of polyethylene mulch warms the soil for earlier yields, reduces fertilizer leaching, helps in water conservation and aids in weed control. Black or other opaque mulches suppress many grass and broadleaf weeds. Nutsedge, however, will germinate and pierce through the mulch. Clear mulches allow the soil to warm faster than opaque or black mulches. Weeds, however, grow under the clear and opaque mulches.

Crop rotation if used correctly can enhance weed control. Watermelon formerly was grown on an 8-year rotation with pasture in the south because of soilborne diseases such as fusarium. The advent of fusarium resistance in newer varieties along with more frequent use of fumigation reduced the importance of long term rotations. Rotations of watermelon onto crop land that has established weed problems can cause yield reductions. Knowledge of the weeds present in a field and growing a crop that has labeled herbicides that will control those weeds or using a crop whose growth habit will smother or shade out the weeds are long term planning processes that can reduce weed competition. Growing watermelon after crops where long residue herbicides have been applied should be avoided. This is a factor growers need to consider in planning for watermelon and rotation crops. In the South, for example, peanut (*Arachis hypogaea*) is often grown in rotation with watermelon. Growers using this practice need to select a weed control program for peanut that will not include residual herbicides that may injure watermelon grown the following year. The same is true for any rotational crop with watermelon.

Some cover crops such as annual ryegrass or small grains can be used for windbreaks between rows early in the watermelon growing season and be killed later when the vines begin to run. Cover crops can also be used to reduce weed buildup in fields. Cover crops can shade out certain weeds, compete with weeds, and cause them not to flower or seed, or in some cases be allelopathic to weeds and kill them.

HERBICIDES. At the present time there are a limited number of herbicides labeled for use in watermelons. They are classified by timing of applications, area of application, and use patterns.

Preplant herbicides. Preplant refers to applications made before the crop is planted. In most cases these materials are incorporated into the soil and are called preplant incorporated treatments (PPI). The greatest advantage to incorporated treatments is that the herbicide is moved into the zone where most weed seeds germinate. For incorporated herbicides the crop must be very tolerant, in that the herbicide is in contact with the germinating crop seed. The incorporation procedure adds an extra cultural operation that increases costs.

Preemergence herbicides. Preemergence treatments (PRE) are usually made after watermelon seed is planted but before emergence of the crop and the weeds. Preemergence herbicides are applied to the soil surface and usually require irrigation or rainfall to move the herbicide into the soil before it is degraded by photodecomposition or lost by volatilization.

The label should be followed carefully, in that preemergence to the crop does not mean pretransplant. Stunting and damage to watermelon transplanted into the treated soil will occur if this precaution is not followed. Herbicides applied preemergence to weeds will have specified on the label if it can be applied pretransplant or posttransplant to the crop.

Postemergence herbicides. Postemergence treatments are applied following emergence, however, it should be specified whether as to postemergence to the crop or to the weed. There are several herbicides that may be applied over the top of watermelon plants to control emerged weeds. Postemergence grass herbicides will control actively growing grass weeds but usually have no residual effect. Other herbicides may be applied over the top of watermelon plants and usually will control small emerged weeds and may or may not have residual control.

Most PPI and PRE applications in watermelon are made as band applications. Band application refers to treating a narrow area directly over the row. This reduces the amount of herbicide required and therefore the cost per acre. Weeds may be controlled between the herbicide bands by cultivation and/or cultivation and a directed application at lay-by.

Several herbicides are labeled on watermelon as directed or directed-shielded applications. The directed applications are usually made to the row middles after the last cultivations and are preemergence (to weeds) herbicides to control weeds emerging late in the season. The directed- shielded treatments labeled are with nonselective postemergence or foliar herbicides that will control emerged weeds in the row middles. Directed-shielded applications are made where mulch is used and weeds close to the mulched bed cannot be controlled by cultivation.

HERBICIDE LABELING FOR WATERMELON. To expedite establishing pesticide tolerances on minor crops, without having to carry out residue trials on each commodity, the Interregional Research Project No. 4 (IR-4) requested the Environmental Protection Agency (EPA) to rule on crop groups. EPA has ruled on this and has established crop grouping under 40CFR. This ruling has been amended and expanded several times. The EPA crop grouping definitions provide for tolerances for a pest control agent from one crop to include other closely related crops. Watermelon falls into the cucurbit vegetable group and the melon subgroup. To establish a tolerance for a herbicide on watermelon, the residue analysis would probably be done on cantaloupe. The tolerance established then would cover all cantaloupes, honeydews, casaba, crenshaw and others in the melon group as well as watermelon. The label developed after the tolerance establishment then may say melons. The term melons on a label signifies use on both watermelon and the group.

The IR-4 project was established to obtain clearances for minor use pest control products on food and ornamental commodities where economic considerations preclude private sector involvement. IR-4 relies on commodity producers, state and federal research scientists and extension personnel to submit pest control needs important to the agricultural community. Many of the active labels of herbicides used on watermelon have been established through the IR-4 program. Needs and requests for research on herbicides on watermelon should be sent through the IR-4 liaison representative in each state or directly to IR-4 Headquarters, Center for Minor Crop Pest Management, Technology Center of New Jersey, New Brunswick, NJ 08902-3390.

General References

Stall, W.M. 1999. Weed management, p. 45–46 In: D.N. Maynard (ed.). Watermelon production for Florida. Fla. Coop. Ext. Serv. SP 113.

Stall, W.M. 1992. Weed management, p. 73–77 In: D.N. Maynard and G.J. Hochmuth (eds.). Vegetable production guide for Florida. Fla. Coop. Ext. Serv. SP 170.

CHAPTER 10

HARVESTING AND POSTHARVEST HANDLING

J.W. Rushing, J.M. Fonseca, and A.P. Keinath

Watermelon harvesting and handling systems are relatively simple in comparison to the procedures used for many other fruits and vegetables. Nevertheless, attention to management in all steps in the system are needed to restrict postharvest losses, maintain quality and increase profitability. Watermelon quality is attained by timely and careful harvest and transport to the central packing area, uniform grading, rapid packing, cooling and transport to the destination market.

HARVEST

MATURITY DETERMINATION. Several changes take place in watermelon fruit as they reach maturity. The ground spot changes from white to pale yellow. In some varieties, tendrils nearest the fruit turn brown and dry. The surface of the fruit also may become a bit irregular and dull rather than glossy. Some folks believe that when the fruit is thumped or rapped with the knuckles, immature fruit will give off a metallic ringing sound whereas mature fruit will sound dull or hollow.

Watermelons do not continue to ripen or become significantly sweeter after they are removed from the vine, so they must be horticulturally mature when harvested to assure that good quality fruit are delivered to the market. Determining the most appropriate time to harvest is an imprecise procedure at best. The most reliable way of assessing watermelon maturity is to visually examine fruit for the changes described above, then cut a few fruit in scattered areas in the field to evaluate internal color development and flavor. Some buyers, particularly those that purchase fruit for use in salad bars, require watermelons to have some minimum sugar content. In this case a refractometer is needed to measure the °Brix, which is a reliable indicator of the percentage of soluble sugars in the fruit.

HARVEST PROCEDURES. Mechanical harvesters for watermelons have not been developed. Typically, all of the handling is done by hand. Because of the size and bulk of watermelons, harvest containers such as bags or buckets cannot be used effectively.

Figure 10.1. Watermelons being selected for harvest and placed in a row in the field to be collected later. Note that a fruit has been cut to inspect maturity. (Source: J.W. Rushing.)

In commercial harvesting operations, one experienced person typically is given the task of selecting fruit that are mature and ready for harvest. Fruit with symptoms of disease should not be selected for marketing. Other workers with knives will accompany the spotter through the field and cut the stems from the selected melons. Watermelon stems do not form a well-defined abscission layer and slip as do cantaloupes. Thus, they should be cut with a sharp knife rather than being pulled, twisted, or broken off which can cause the removal of a small piece, or plug, of tissue from the fruit itself. A plugged fruit is more likely to decay around the damaged area. Bacterial soft rot is a particularly troublesome disease that can become established in such a harvest injury.

Once the fruit are cut, they may be moved to a drive row to be picked up later and placed on a truck or trailer (Fig. 10.1). Alternatively, a group of workers pass through the field and literally toss the melons from one worker to the next, eventually tossing them to a person on the transport vehicle (Fig. 10.2). A harvest aid consisting of simple mobile conveyor belt is sometimes used to move the melons. Any fruit that is dropped during this process should not be loaded, even if it did not break when it was dropped. Further, workers should not walk or ride on top of a load of watermelons. Watermelons can be bruised and the bruising injury may not be apparent for some time after the injury occurs, so a fruit that appears to be in good condition in the field may be rejected later in the market.

Watermelons should not be stacked on the stem end or blossom end during transport. Many commercial handlers believe that the internal flesh is more likely to be damaged by shock and vibration if the fruit are stacked in this fashion.

Figure 10.2. Watermelons being tossed from one field worker to the next to be loaded on a field trailer. Fruit that are dropped should not be loaded. (Source: D.N. Maynard.)

Figure 10.3. Loading an over-the-road vehicle from a field trailer. Fruit are sorted as they are loaded. (Source: D.N. Maynard.)

Watermelons are susceptible to sunburn before and after they are removed from the vine. Once the stem is cut, fruit should be removed from the field as quickly as possible. Sunburn can occur very rapidly preharvest—within a couple of days—if there are a few days of wet, cloudy weather followed by a sudden increase in light intensity just before harvest. The damage is more evident in varieties with dark rinds. Some growers report that field applications of a sun protectant, which is a suspension of a clay material, can help reduce the incidence of sunburn. During harvesting and handling, the clay powder is easily wiped off of the fruit and does not create a marketing problem unless a surfactant is used when the protectant is applied, which makes the powder stick to the fruit surface. Buyers may object to the presence of the residue.

POSTHARVEST HANDLING
Preparation for shipment

BULK SHIPMENT. It is common practice to transfer watermelons from the field truck or trailer to over-the-road vehicles at some convenient spot near the fields (Fig. 10.3). In some cases, watermelons are placed directly from the field into bulk trailers and transported to market in the same vehicle. This is essentially a form of field packing. Any time a product is field packed, special attention should be given to harvest management to exclude decayed or defective fruit from the shipment.

WASHING. Watermelon fruit are usually not washed. If washing is required to remove excess soil or to enhance the appearance for a particular market niche, wash water quality must be managed carefully. An approved disinfectant should be included in the wash water to reduce the potential for spread of disease. Chlorine gas, sodium hypochlorite (household bleach), calcium hypochlorite, chlorine dioxide, and ozone all are presently approved for sanitizing wash water. Each chemical has its own special management requirements. Sodium hypochlorite is most commonly used because it requires very little investment by the handler, is easy to prepare in solution, and is effective against decay organisms when used at a rate of about 100 ppm free chlorine in water with pH near neutral. As wash water becomes contami-

Figure 10.4. Watermelons being inspected, packed into fiberboard cartons, and weighed. (Source: D.N. Maynard.)

nated with soil and organic matter, the efficacy of the chlorine is diminished, so tanks should be washed and filled with clean water each day. Handlers who need to wash watermelons should be sure that the disinfectant they use is approved and that they understand the management procedures needed for optimal sanitizing.

PACKING. Watermelons often are taken in bulk from the field to a packing shed for grading and packing. Experienced workers usually size the fruit visually, look for defects, and place them on a packing table where other workers sort them into more precise size groups and pack them. Table surfaces should be covered with a nonabrasive material, such as carpet, to help avoid scratching the fruit. Some packing operations have conveyor belts with an automated scale for sizing by weight.

Corrugated boxes containing from three to six watermelons, depending on fruit size and shape, have become popular with many receivers (Fig. 10.4). Since watermelon fruit are so heavy, specially designed inserts should be used inside the carton to help support the weight. Corrugated bins with a capacity of about 1,000 lb also are used (Fig. 10.5). These may be manufactured with colorful graphics and used for display purposes inside retail markets. Whenever corrugated materials are used in wet or humid conditions, they can absorb moisture, which reduces the strength of the material. Waxed, moisture-resistant cartons are available at higher cost, so managers must consider the cost and benefits when choosing a shipping container.

GRADES AND STANDARDS. The U.S. Department of Agriculture (USDA) descriptors for standards of watermelons state that fruit should

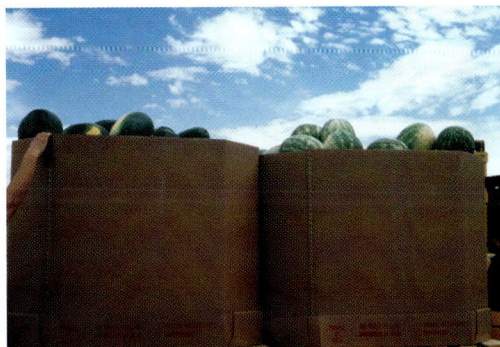

Figure 10.5. Corrugated bins that are placed on pallets and filled with about 1,000 lb of watermelons. Note that the bins are overfilled and cannot be stacked on top of one another. (Source: J.W. Rushing.)

be mature but not overripe, fairly well formed with similar varietal characteristics, and free from anthracnose, any type of decay, sunscald, whiteheart, or mechanical injury. Internal quality requirements are optional. Buyers may specify some minimum °Brix, absence of hollowheart, or a tolerance for the numbers of seeds found in seedless types. In general, the difference between U.S. Fancy, U.S. No. 1, and U.S. No. 2 grades is simply the tolerance for the percentage of fruit that do not meet the minimum criteria stated in the descriptors for each quality characteristic. Individuals needing guidance on quality criteria should obtain a copy of the USDA Standards for Grades of Watermelons.

SPECIAL INSPECTION REQUIREMENTS. Watermelons destined for export must be carefully inspected. Freight costs may constitute the greatest single expense when shipping to an offshore market and it is critical that all fruit of inferior quality be excluded from the shipment. The presence of disease, insects, soil or vegetative matter can result in failure to meet phytosanitary requirements at the destination and lead to rejection of the entire shipment. A less severe, but still costly, penalty would be a requirement for reinspection and thus repacking of every individual fruit before they can be released for distribution in the receiving country. These problems can be avoided by adequate inspection during packing. At the packinghouse, a simple conveyor belt can be utilized to transport the watermelons in a single row past workers who can examine each fruit individually before they are placed in shipping containers. If the inspection is done on a stationary table, the surface should be covered with carpet or some other material that will prevent scratching of the fruit surface. Inspection areas should be kept clean and surfaces should be disinfested periodically with chlorine solutions or other approved disinfectants to reduce the risk of spreading pathogens.

SPECIAL PACKAGING TECHNIQUES. Studies with plastic carton liners and individual shrink wrap packaging have not revealed significant benefits for the storage or shipping quality of watermelons. The apparent non-climacteric nature of the fruit, i.e., no significant increase in respiration during ripening, suggests that little benefit could be derived from modified atmosphere packaging techniques in general. Further, the growth of microbial colonies on the fruit surface was enhanced by the high humidity conditions that were created within lined cartons and beneath shrink wrapping. Certainly there are opportunities for special packaging applications on fresh cut product (discussed later) but the use of expensive plastics for intact watermelons must be weighed carefully against any benefits that could be expected in marketing.

PRECOOLING. Watermelons are almost never precooled, but there is evidence that storage quality would be enhanced if field heat could be re-

Figure 10.6. Room cooling of palletized boxes of watermelons. Note the placement of pallets to allow for adequate air circulation between the rows. (Source: J.W. Rushing.)

moved quickly after harvest. Forced air cooling would be the preferred method. Cooling schedules for watermelons are not available, but extrapolating from cantaloupe data, it would require from 6 –12 h to effectively remove field heat from watermelons in cartons. In common room cooling, good air circulation between palletized boxes is essential (Fig. 10.6). Fruit that are placed in fiberboard bins would be much more difficult to precool because of the difficulty in circulating air through the bin.

Transportation

As mentioned earlier, many watermelons are transported unrefrigerated in bulk. If distance to the market is not excessive and the condition of roads is good, fruit usually arrive with acceptable quality. Problems with compression and impact injuries have been observed in eastern markets with fruit that were transported from Mexico or Central America by truck. Sometimes watermelons are hauled uncovered in open trucks which is the least desirable method of transportation as the fruit on top of the load are subject to sunburn. Refrigerated trailers are preferred. Boxed fruit should be stacked to permit adequate air flow through the load. Note that refrigeration units on trailers are designed to maintain the temperature of properly precooled product and do not normally have sufficient capacity for removing field heat. Before loading, trailers should be examined for damage that would result in poor cooling, such as damaged or defective door seals, bulkhead, air delivery chute, or side walls and ceilings. Trailers should be clean and free of trash or debris. Watermelons should not be mixed in a load with high ethylene-producing commodities, such as ripening tomatoes or cantaloupes.

Storage

Watermelon varieties and types, i.e., seeded vs. seedless, vary in their storage potential, but in general none are suited for very long term storage. Watermelons should be consumed within 2 or 3 weeks following harvest. In the absence of decay, quality deterioration is gradual, with softening and fading of flesh color being the most obvious changes. The ideal storage conditions are in the range of 50–60 °F with about 90% relative humidity. All watermelons are susceptible to chilling injury (described later) at low temperatures and at higher temperatures, decay will develop faster. In actual practice, there is seldom any attempt to control humidity in a storeroom.

PHYSIOLOGICAL DISORDERS

ETHYLENE SENSITIVITY. Exposure to as little as 5 ppm ethylene induces cell wall modifications that result in softening and rind thinning. Flesh color fades and has the appearance of being overripe. Higher concentrations of ethylene result in more rapid injury to the fruit. Ethylene absorbents, catalytic generators, ozone, or other techniques may be used to inactivate ethylene in enclosed areas. Avoiding ethylene exposure is the simplest approach to avoiding ethylene injury.

Perhaps the most troublesome source of ethylene in postharvest handling systems is forklifts powered by internal combustion engines, especially if used in an area that is not well ventilated. Electrically powered forklifts are recommended for handling watermelons in storerooms. Storing the fruit in an area near other commodities that produce ethylene or in proximity to the ventilation of ripening rooms also should be avoided. This can be a problem in supermarket distribution centers that have all of the produce in one large storeroom and may have banana ripening rooms nearby.

CHILLING INJURY. Watermelons develop chilling injury when stored below about 50 °F for more than a few days. Symptoms appear as surface pitting and brown-staining of the rind, fading of flesh color, loss of flavor, and increased susceptibility to decay upon warming. Conditioning fruit at 86 °F for about 4 days to allow for some water loss (curing) before cooling has been shown to induce some tolerance to chilling, but it does not alleviate the problem completely. Fruit may sustain chilling injury in cold storage without exhibiting symptoms until they are warmed, when the symptoms develop rapidly and the fruit becomes more susceptible to decay.

HOLLOWHEART. Hollowheart (see Fig. 7.25) is a disorder of preharvest origin, but when it is prevalent the postharvest consequences are significant simply because it is a marketing problem. Using appropriate production practices that help avoid the occurrence of hollowheart is the most effective way of ensuring that it does not appear in the marketing chain.

POSTHARVEST DISEASES

Watermelon fruit blotch (*Acidovorax avenae* subsp. *citrulli*) (see Fig. 7.6) was a problem in the marketing chain for one or two seasons in the United States. The disease is not easily transmitted from one fruit to another during postharvest handling, so proper attention to grading to remove diseased fruit during harvest and packing is essential. Appropriate temperature management during shipping and storage can virtually eliminate fruit blotch from postharvest handling systems.

With good disease control in the field, anthracnose (*Colletotrichum orbiculare*) (see Fig. 7.3) and black rot (*Didymella bryoniae*) (see Fig. 7.17) rarely develop on watermelon fruit. Anthracnose has been a concern for fruit exported to Europe and a postharvest inspection protocol, described earlier, is implemented when necessary. Postharvest rots caused by *Fusarium* sp. and *Phytophthora capsici* (see Fig. 7.19) are a more serious concern because currently available methods for disease control in the field are often inadequate. Both fungi can infect fruit directly; fusarium also invades wounded tissue. The first spots usually occur on the underside of the fruit, but may also occur on the upper surface. These fungi reproduce quickly, so the potential exists for postharvest spread during unrefrigerated transport.

In the absence of approved chemical measures to control postharvest decay on watermelon, the primary defense against the occurrence of decay is the exclusion of diseased fruit from the marketing chain through careful selection at harvest and appropriate grading during packing.

FRESH-CUT WATERMELON

Regional distribution of fresh-cut watermelon, including slices and cubes, has been limited by the high perishability of the product. Typically the quality shelf life is about 2 days under retail display conditions. Consequently, most processing has been done in back rooms of supermarket produce departments. Some guidelines for handling fresh-cut product are based on recently published research.

Only ripe watermelons with 8 °Brix or higher should be selected for cutting. Seedless fruit yield more cubes with pulp of marketable quality than seeded varieties.

Sanitation is key for all processing steps. Before cutting, the exterior of the watermelons should be washed with detergent, rinsed with a solution of 100 ppm chlorine, and dried. Fruit should be processed in a refrigerated room at about 37 °F that is constructed of materials that are easy to clean and sanitize. The room and all utensils should be sanitized and workers should wear hairnets, masks, gloves, aprons, etc., in accordance with guidelines for all fresh-cut vegetable processing operations. The most appropriate method of sanitizing the cut surfaces of the pulp still has not been identified. Chlorinated water is reported to be unsatisfactory for this purpose. Studies are in progress with ozonated water, ultraviolet light, and other methods.

Cubes must be placed in a rigid container to avoid crushing the flesh and causing excessive juice leakage during handling and storage. In simulated transit tests with various packages, quality deterioration due to shock and vibration has been an overriding factor. To minimize handling, the container should be suited for retail display. Modified-atmosphere packaging may prove to be useful for extending the quality shelf life of watermelon cubes, but the most effective concentrations of oxygen and carbon dioxide have not been clearly identified.

The recommended temperature for storage and display of fresh-cut watermelon is 37 °F. Lower temperatures promote the development of chilling injury and at higher temperatures the population of microorganisms increase. At the retail level, refrigerated display cases are more effective than a bed of crushed ice in maintaining the appropriate product temperature.

To develop a handling system that is suitable for regional distribution of fresh-cut watermelon, more research is needed in several areas. Sanitation methods are required that reduce microbial load on the processed product without adversely affecting quality. Packaging must be identified that will protect the product from shock and vibration stress during transport.

General References

Close, E.G., J. Varick, and L.A. Risse. 1971. Comparative methods of handling watermelons—Bulk and cartons. Fla. Dept. Agr. Consumer Serv. Ser. MA 1-71.

Elkashif, M.E., D.J. Huber, and J.K. Brecht. 1989. Respiration and ethylene production in harvested watermelon fruit: Evidence for non-climacteric respiratory behavior. J. Amer. Soc. Hort. Sci. 114:81–85.

Hardenburg, R.E., A.E. Watada, and C.-Y. Wang. 1986. The commercial storage of fruits, vegetables, and florist and nursery stocks. USDA-ARS Hndbk. 66.

Picha, D.H. 1986. Postharvest fruit conditioning reduces chilling injury in watermelons. HortScience 21:1407–1409.

Rushing, J.W., A.P. Keinath, and W.P. Cook. 1999. Postharvest development and transmission of watermelon fruit blotch. HortTechnology 9:33–35.

Sargent, S.A. 1998. Fresh-cut watermelon. Citrus Veg. Mag. 62:26–28, 44. Vance Publications, Tampa, Fla.

Snowdon, A.L. 1992. Color atlas of postharvest diseases and disorders of fruits and vegetables. vol. 2. Vegetables. CRC Press, Boca Raton, Fla.

CHAPTER 11

MARKETING

E.A. Estes

United States consumers spend about $100 billion to purchase fruits, vegetables, and melons each year. Government analysts estimate that farmers receive less than 20% of total expenditures, leaving about $80 billion spent annually on marketing. The United States food distribution network is among the most efficient in the world, allowing Americans, on average, to spend less than 12% of annual disposable income for food. Although the precise retail value of United States watermelon purchases is unknown, extrapolation of farm value data suggests that Americans spend from $1.2–$1.5 billion each year to buy watermelons. Watermelon is a popular food with Americans who consume about 17 lb each year. During the past two decades, consumption growth in fruits, vegetables, and melons was remarkable and unmatched by any other food group. Recent increases in production, shipments to market, consumption, and farm price suggest an optimistic future for the domestic watermelon industry. But, as the industry prepares for business in a new century, the marketing system remains complex and confusing. Rapid daily, weekly, monthly, and seasonal price fluctuations create income uncertainty and market risk. Seemingly unrelated production considerations such as genetic modification, computer technology, precision farming techniques, food safety considerations, environmental stewardship, and sustainable farming practices impact sales, marketing practices, and profits. Veteran watermelon producers know that past market success is not a good indicator of future success. In contrast to regulated or program crops, watermelon producers must make market decisions based on limited price information, are not eligible for nonrecourse loans or subsidy payments, and spend more money to grow, harvest, and sell their crop. Watermelon brokers, distributors, and wholesalers must minimize flow-to-market time, offer buyers a maximum selection at competitive prices, and discover new sales opportunities while operating on thin profit margins. For all participants in the watermelon industry, market success depends heavily on information acquisition, knowledge about market opportunities, and the flexibility to adapt to rapidly changing market situations.

SUCCESSFUL MARKETING

Experience and intuition are valuable assets in marketing watermelons. Yet, experience and intuition fail at times because new competition emerges, consumer tastes, preferences, and buying habits change, and critical market information is unavailable. The traditional view of marketing was sell what you have while today's markets require that an individual have what sells. Growers often focus on the technical aspects of watermelon production and raise high quality watermelons. In the marketplace, however, consumers want to buy watermelon plus other features such as better health, improved nutrition, and convenience. Market participants must learn about what consumers are buying in addition to the commodity to make a sale. Knowledge about consumer preferences is just as important as knowledge about cultural practices and how to grade watermelons. Each market participant, from grower to retailer or institutional user, needs to appreciate and understand market interdependencies. Sometimes, acquisition of knowledge about marketing is thought to be an exercise only for the inexperienced seller or as a necessary evil done primarily out of fear. Inattention to market planning arises from the belief that market success depends on luck, circumstances, or the vagaries of weather. Too often, market success is viewed as the agricultural equivalent of hitting the lottery, that is, financial reward is the result of circumstance rather than planning. Occasionally, luck influences price received and impacts financial success. More often, however, individuals who plan for marketing have regular success while people who do not develop a marketing strategy or depend on hitting the lottery win occasionally but fail more often. Unfortunately, there is not one formula for marketing success that can be prescribed because management skills, market opportunities, and resource availability vary considerably among individuals. Marketing is more art than exact science since it involves creative thought and application of multiple principles rather than a formula to be used in all situations.

Over time, successful marketers simply spend more time acquiring market information, assess the situation correctly more often, understand system interactions, and supply the bundle of attributes desired most often by buyers. In marketing, one common key to success seems to be an ability to put acquired knowledge to work. In effect, successful sellers are able to work smarter and not just harder than their competitors. Smart work is the acquisition and use of relevant market knowledge. Marketing cannot sell watermelons to people who do not want to buy watermelons. In addition to learning about genetic modifications and postharvest physiology, marketers also must learn what customers want, who are potential customers, and where buyers are located, how to evaluate market prospects, how to use market assessment aids such as market window information, and understand why competitive and economic forces motivate buyer actions. The process of market plan development helps to focus knowledge collection efforts, provides insight on how markets work in certain situations, develops sales skills needed for success, reduces financial risk, and increases the likelihood of sustainable profits. However, creation of a market plan, spending more time thinking about marketing, and working smarter will not always guarantee success. It can reduce the chance for failure. The intent of this chapter is to identify various marketing services provided by watermelon market participants, to provide insights about factors that influence watermelon marketing, to explore market analysis aids such as market window tools that provide sales insights, and to discuss marketing options available that influence outcomes. Topic discussions attempt to demonstrate that it is the market system that links farmer with retailers with the common objective of satisfying consumer wants. If one link in the chain is weak or fails, then the entire market network fails. Discussions and examples are applicable to any participant in the market network but particular focus is directed toward producers and first-handlers since they must develop the basic market plan and their decisions impact the sales options available to brokers, distributors, dealers, wholesalers, retailers, and institutional users.

MARKETING OPTIONS

In general, watermelon production and sales occur in a diverse set of locations throughout the nation. Because watermelon production is scattered but most consumers live in urban areas, watermelons must be moved from inconvenient production locations to convenient purchase locations. Marketing is the system of independent processes that coordinates production, handling, transportation, pricing, and selling activities. The marketing options available to watermelon sellers are depicted in Fig. 11.1. During the process of movement, watermelon load ownership can change.

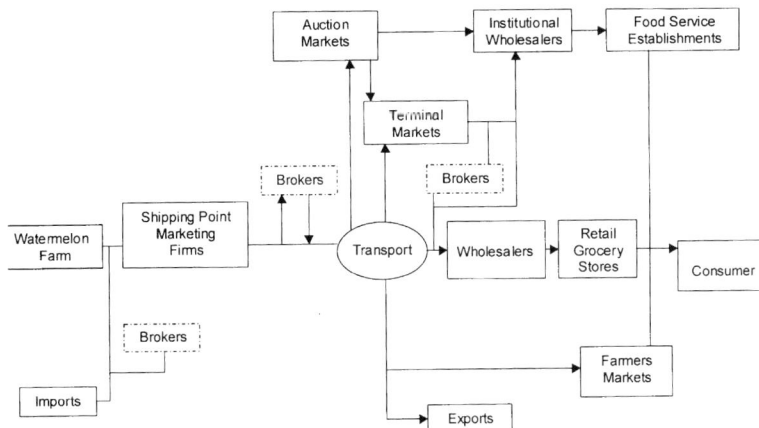

Figure 11.1. Watermelon marketing systems, 1999.

It is the responsibility of the individual who owns the watermelon to locate a new buyer, receive payment, arrange resale logistics, and then expedite transport to the location desired by the new buyer.

The process of sale and resale begins with the grower. Growers can retain ownership but assign various marketing tasks such as hauling or selling to other individuals, but until ownership is transferred, remain responsible for marketing the melons. Watermelon owners can employ additional individuals such as brokers, commission merchants, truckers, and shipper-packers to provide necessary marketing services or the owner can perform all necessary marketing tasks themselves. In most cases, brokers, commission merchants, and truckers work for the seller or buyer but do not actually own the melons. In watermelon marketing, a system can exist where few ownership transfers (the grower sells directly to a retailer or the consumer) occur or there can be many ownership transfers (grower to shipper to wholesaler to retailer). The simplistic marketing system of local producers selling watermelons to a local retailer or directly to consumers is straightforward and there is little need for a market intermediary. However, imbalances between area consumer demand and area watermelon availability create profit opportunities in distant locations so market intermediaries can facilitate the market balancing process. The coordination of product movement is complex and poses a difficult challenge for individuals unfamiliar with the process. Inexperienced individuals must learn standard operating procedures or the mechanics involved in moving perishable items to buyers, acquire information about prices and buyers, learn precise meanings for sales and marketing terms so communication is facilitated, and know how buyers source loads. Early in the market evaluation process, growers must identify feasible sales options.

Typical sales options can be categorized into three main areas: 1) sales to local packers, shippers, retailers, specialty stores, or directly to consumers such as farmers' markets; 2) sales to regional assembly point markets such as an auction market or a cooperative, local grocery store, or institutional users such as restaurants, cafeterias, or schools; and 3) bulk sales to national market buyers such as large chain stores, wholesalers, dealers, commission merchants, terminal market distributors, and commodity jobbers. Wholesalers are the group of buyers who purchase watermelons exclusively for the purpose of reselling them. There are, however, many categories and types of wholesalers. Wholesalers can be located in or near the production area or in or near a large consumption area. Most often, wholesalers are located in urban areas. Terminal market wholesalers are receivers located in produce receiving centers. Terminal market companies specialize in receiving and distributing a wide variety of produce. Terminal markets are the urban opposite of shipping point assembly markets. Terminal market operators receive truckload shipments of produce from production areas and then redistribute smaller loads to various buyers in the urban market area. Arriving loads are often presold to dealers on a terminal or wholesale market. In other instances, however, loads arrive from shipping point markets but buyers have not been identified. In this circumstance, sellers employ companies such as commission merchants to identify buyers, negotiate price, and arrange delivery. Commission merchants receive a percentage of the sales price in return for their services. Most loads of watermelons are sold to chain store retailers who represent a special type of wholesaler. Chain store warehouses receive and redistribute watermelons intended for retail sale at affiliated stores. Most often, chain store warehouses receive shipments directly from large growers or shippers who can meet their larger volume sales requirements. If direct shipment quantities are inadequate, then many chain store buyers purchase additional watermelons from terminal market wholesalers. While sale terms are arranged before shipment to a terminal market, perishability considerations sometimes dictate that loads are shipped to terminal markets but sales terms and buyers are not identified as yet. Distributors are a specific type of wholesaler that have special or exclusive rights to resell particular brands of watermelons. For example, certain distributors may have the exclusive right to sell 'Sun World' watermelons in an area or region. Purveyors are a type of wholesale buyer that specialize in delivery of produce to food service companies such as restaurants, cafeterias, or prisons. Finally, a jobber is a wholesaler that specializes in delivering preordered loads of watermelons to a specific set of clients such as independent grocery stores, hospitals, and dealers.

While the quality, maturity, and shipping requirements can differ by option, wholesaler category, and type, volume requirements tend to increase when moving from local markets to national market distribution. As volume increases, price becomes a more important consideration in the buy decision. Thus, each market option differs from another because of volume, price, quality, maturity, and frequency of delivery considerations. In all cases, buyers seek exceptional value (highest quality for the price), consistency in quality (both within and across loads), timely delivery of loads, and the longest possible shelf life to minimize waste and loss.

Which marketing option is best? The answer depends on the resources available, individual preferences, and the likelihood of profit. The advisability and feasibility of each option depicted in Fig. 11.1 should be examined through collection of relevant market assessment information. What is relevant market assessment information? Marketing information is relevant and of value only if it is 1) timely and applicable to a particular situation; 2) can be used to make a decision; 3) the added cost of acquiring the information is less than or equal to the anticipated benefit of using the information; and 4) it provides answers to questions you did not know the answers to before you started. Growers and brokers may have general knowledge that United States watermelon consumption is increasing but unless it is accompanied by more specific information such as retailers need additional supplies of larger watermelons in mid-summer, then consumption information is interesting but not useful. Similarly, knowledge that consumers eat more watermelon at picnics is less important than information that buyers increase purchases before July 4th. At any point in the marketing system, sellers need relevant marketing information such as 1) how much volume is sold each week during the expected harvest period; 2) when are local, regional, and national supplies expected to be most abundant and least available and most abundant; 3) who is my competition; 4) what are my acquisition or production costs; and 5) who buys large loads of watermelons and what drives the marketing system. Some basic market information can be obtained at a low cost through off-season visits to local retailers, attendance at educational programs, and tours to central receiving and distribution points. Personal visits to potential buyers can provide answers to basic volume questions, store or chain procurement practices, expected price, packaging, and delivery frequency information. Names of potential buyers, handlers, and brokers can be identified through purchase of the trade publications such as the Red Book (Vance Publishing, Inc.) or the Blue Book (Produce Reporter Company). In some states, State Department of Agriculture marketing specialists can also assist individuals locate potential growers, truckers, distributors, brokers, wholesalers, and retailers. Conversations with farmers and county extension agents could support or refute possible market opportunities. In certain market circumstances, it may be more important when you have watermelons for sale than how many are available for sale. For small volume suppliers, local and regional market niches may exist. For niche markets, timing of crop availability is often important. Market window analysis can assess the potential payoff from earlier or later than normal harvest periods. Finally, sales within the marketing network operate on reliability and trust. Reliability and trust are dependent on regular and open communication between a buyer and a seller. If the buyer and seller create a business and personal relationship, then it is easier to satisfy customer requirements. Collection of market information is both tedious and time-consuming but is a task that can be done well by dedicated individuals.

PREPARING A MARKET STRATEGY

After an assessment of market options, a marketing strategy should be developed. Marketing frustration often arises from the belief that there must be a better or more exact way to market watermelons than the current practice. There are different expectations about what the marketing system should provide. Growers want a marketing system that provides them with a fair price, rewards cost-effective production, and an assurance that someone will buy their crop. Brokers and wholesale buyers want the marketing system to provide the highest volume of product available from the fewest sources that satisfy their sales needs at the best value. Retailers, of course, want watermelons that are requested by consumers and allows them to realize the greatest possible net profit. Market participants sometimes perceive the conflicting wants of market participants as an adversarial contest that results in economic winners and losers. In its simplest terms, however, market participants really have the same objective of meeting consumer expectations so they will want to buy. Everyone in the market system from the producer to the retailer needs to be responsive to the consumer. The market system is simply the method used to communicate consumer wants throughout the system. Through marketing, producers obtain information about consumer wants from the wholesalers and first-handlers, who, in turn, obtain information about consumer wants from retailers and institutional users. Knowledge about consumer preferences is the important determinant to market success. In a system that only occasionally rewards hard work and production efficiency, marketing success also requires creativity, knowledge about consumer preferences, and ways to outthink your competitors. Hard work is not always synonymous with success and this outcome perplexes many individuals. A buyer or consumer wants to compensate a farmer on the basis of work effort, but usually they do not know the amount or extent of effort expended. Instead, buyers and consumers observe only indirect measures of effort such as appearance, size, and price.

Marketing should not be thought of as more than just the process of selling and moving high quality watermelons to eager consumers who want to buy them. A building is not a market unless buying and selling occurs. Instead, marketing should be thought of as the coordinating economic force that communicates consumer preferences as well as guides, directs, motivates, and controls business decisions. It is important to recognize the market will not consistently provide a profit for whatever is grown and whenever it is harvested. While growers may think about marketing efforts during the off-season, usually there is little thought about marketing before planting. Instead, thoughts about marketing seem to intensify several weeks before harvest as several phone calls are made and sales options are considered. While this marketing approach is common, it is usually inadequate to ensure the crop is sold at the highest available price. Harvest-time marketing works for some growers but its success depends primarily on an individual's price negotiation skills, knowledge about current market conditions, and accurate predictions about the impact of weather on supply levels. Alternatively, if marketing is viewed as an extension of production activities, then it is necessary to have a marketing plan established before planting, to develop multiple sales options, identify specific target markets and marketing methods, and consider how flow-to-market activities can be timely and rapid.

In short, marketing includes not only selling or delivery but also the performance of all activities that direct the flow of goods and services from the farm to the place where a consumer buys the melon. Marketing involves buying and selling but also grading, load assembly, transportation, risk-taking, financing, and the collection of market information. Market prospects are affected by nearly every production and handling decision. Since many aspects of marketing involve the activities of many individuals, market information should be collected. With market intelligence, better decisions can be made and the result can be that watermelons are in the right place, at the right time, and in the right form for the buyer. Thus, the market planning process begins with the grower and should begin months before planting time. Future market and sales prospects are influenced by the variety planted, the cultural method employed, the quality grown, the time of harvest, the experience of the sales individual, the density of watermelon production in the area (facilitates load assembly), total and per unit costs, and the proximity of buyers and brokers to the farm operation. Careful consideration of all production aspects provides a starting basis for development of a marketing strategy. A marketing plan is the result obtained from development of a market strategy. The first stage in formulation of a marketing strategy is examination of long-run industry trends, often identified as a market situation and outlook assessment. The market assessment should be done during a period when time allows an individual to collect information and visit buyer facilities. Basic assessment information includes collection of information about consumption trends, who and where competitors are located, identification of marketing advantages, estimation of costs, and when sales opportunities look favorable.

MARKET RESEARCH. Analysis of recent watermelon trend data suggests that sales, revenue, and income will continue to expand modestly during the next decade. From 1986–91 watermelon consumption stagnated somewhat as many consumers seemed hesitant to purchase traditional larger-sized melons (such as the 'Charleston Gray' types). Consumer purchase decisions likely were influenced by factors such as smaller average family size, increased consumption of cantaloupe, and increased availability of exotic and specialty fruits. Since 1991, however, United States consumers have reacted positively to watermelon promotion efforts, the availability of smaller icebox melons, and the introduction of seedless fruit. During the 1990s, watermelon output, crop value, and consumption have increased regularly. The watermelon industry likely benefited from generic industry-wide promotional programs such as the "5-a-Day" campaign, innovative marketing efforts coordinated by the National Watermelon Promotion Board, and media attention on health and nutrition issues such as consumption of cancer-inhibiting foods. Since 1980, the fresh fruit and vegetable sector has experienced about 50% growth in consumption but over the same period watermelon consumption expanded even more rapidly. Supermarket and institutional sales of value added watermelon contributed greatly to increased consumption. Value added innovations included sales of watermelon chunks on salad bars, containerized fresh-cut melon snacks, and shrink-wrapped sliced wedges. Demand expansion permitted increased watermelon production without severe adverse price effects for growers or distributors. Since 1995, the rate at which Americans eat fresh fruits and vegetables has slowed somewhat but watermelon consumption continues to expand at an average annual rate of 3%. Beyond value enhanced sales, Americans continue to purchase watermelon for traditional consumption at summer holiday outings, family picnics, and special occasion meals.

As the new century begins, however, watermelon marketing and promotion efforts need to intensify because of changes in the market environment. In particular, watermelon marketing will be more competitive, consolidation in the number of retailers, wholesalers, and brokers will continue, and market access will be more difficult and elusive for many growers and shippers. While a variety of sales options can exist for watermelons, the principal buyer and seller of watermelons is the supermarket distribution channel. Supermarket purchases are often controlled by a small group of centralized supermarket produce buyers. It is the responsibility of the supermarket buyer to minimize costs, control produce and watermelon procurement practices, oversee merchandising and promotion efforts, and meet company profit expectations. Supermarket buyers obtain market assessment information through conversations with growers and shippers, through company employees who provide field assessment and quality information, from shipping point brokers, and from wholesalers and dealers located in terminal markets or other central receiving locations. Most often, chain store buyers purchase loads through the use of specialty brokers. Brokers can act as agents for the buyer or the seller or occasionally both. A broker is an individual who negotiates specific elements of a contract between a seller and a buyer. The broker does not work strictly for the seller or the buyer (usually) but sells market information and knowledge (who has watermelons and who wants watermelons). If this individual acts only as a broker, then the broker does not own the watermelons. However, often a broker performs other duties such as arranging truck transport, remitting invoices and bills of lading to buyers, etc. Occasionally, brokers purchase watermelons and resell them. If the broker owns the melons, then the broker performs additional tasks beyond brokering and operates more like a wholesaler. The seller is charged a separate fee for each service performed. Brokers earn fees by selling product (a flat rate per unit sold or a percentage commission of the price), arranging transportation, and billing and receiving payment from the buyer. Thus, sellers should be alert as to when and if ownership transfers. If the seller elects to hire a broker, then it is essential that the seller and broker trust each other. The basis for a successful partnership is truthful communication. Establishment of a good relationship often takes time and is a difficult task. Sellers should ask and answer the following questions before employing a broker.

- What volume of product is needed each day, week, and season?
- Who is responsible for expenses such as telephone calls?
- Are sales to be made in the broker's name and will the broker pay you immediately?
- Does the broker have a good credit worthiness rating?
- Are broker references available?

Contact brokers by letter first; explaining what tasks you want performed. When and if the broker responds, be prepared to ask questions about the brokerage business and be willing to answer specific questions about your operation.

Frequently brokers want specific information about the commodity such as the variety, the exact volume available over time, and the quality or grade. Sellers should communicate honestly with the broker. A seller response of more than 20 bulk bins is a poor answer to the question How many watermelons are available for sale, especially if you have 60 bulk bins. The broker may request specific information about postharvest handling practices and the availability of short-term cold storage. In general, watermelon sales opportunities and transport patterns follow south to north rather than across country (there are of course important exceptions). The shipment pattern follows the seasonal harvest pattern as locations further south have watermelons available sooner than more northern locations. Transportation expenses can be reduced and price prospects enhanced through use of the south-to-north pattern. This pattern breaks down during August and September since watermelons are available in most regions. Sellers should examine shipment and unload data to identify niche opportunities for sales.

MARKET COMPETITION. After market trends are assessed, the competitive environment of the watermelon industry should be evaluated. As consumption expanded, additional sales spurred increased plantings. From 1992–97, national watermelon output and consumption expanded about 8%, imports more than doubled, and United States average annual farm price increased 28%. Watermelon production is most concentrated in four states that supply about 70% of all domestically grown watermelons. In 1998, Florida, California, Georgia, and Texas producers harvested nearly 29 million-hundred-weight of watermelons. However, USDA statistics reveal that commercial watermelon production occurs in only one-third of the states. Expanded utilization and favorable prices has created a more competitive market environment for the industry. Increased competition is evident through examination of several market factors.

First, market competition for watermelons from other fruit and vegetable products has intensified. The number of items stocked by the average supermarket produce department increased from 133 items in 1981 to 360 items in 1999. The mix and array of new produce offerings continues to increase as new and exotic produce is available from both domestic and foreign suppliers. In addition, consumers continue to spend less time ingredient shopping and will focus on ready-to-eat meal solutions offered by retailers. The popularity of lightly processed snacks such as peeled carrots, celery sticks, and grape tomatoes also present competitive challenges to melon suppliers. Second, the success of new format retailers such as Wal-Mart and Kmart Supercenters (Super K's) has expanded the number of sales outlets available for produce suppliers including watermelon growers but at the same time has increased buyer price bargaining leverage and consolidated market power. Large volume buyers want and expect watermelons to be available from courteous and professional suppliers who deliver ordered quantities of safe-to-eat melons in a timely manner. In agriculture, there are a large number of experienced and new growers, shippers, and handlers who seem willing to satisfy buyer expectations and demands. Third, the introduction and use of scanner-based data coupled with retailer loyalty cards has provided retailers with store-specific data about what was sold, when it was sold, at what price, and who bought it. Advances in computer technology, store loyalty cards, and inventory management advances have allowed chain store retailers to base purchase decisions on sales performance and net profit contributions rather than previously used intuition-based sourcing methods. Competition within the produce industry remains intense because produce sales are an important component in the overall financial success of a supermarket. For the average supermarket, the produce department accounts for 11% of total store sales and occupies less than 13% of the store floor space but provides 17% of store profits. Produce Business, a produce industry periodical, reported that two-thirds of all 1998 supermarket customer transactions included a produce purchase. Consumer surveys also reveal that shoppers choose to shop at a particular store because of the quality and selection available in the produce department. Thus, an increasing competitive sales environment requires that the commercial watermelon industry must devote more time and attention to development of sound watermelon marketing practices if they are to maintain or expand per capita consumption.

MARKETING ADVANTAGE. Market trend information and competitive assessment findings can be used to discover possible market advantages. Sales transactions occur because of fundamental economic motivations and are most frequently based on one or more market advantages. A market advantage can be based on either a competitive or a comparative advantage. Competitiveness is the ability of a watermelon grower to secure business from a buyer despite the best efforts of another grower to secure that business. For the most part, competitive success is a measure of the capability of supplying product to a market at a cost below the prevailing market price. Success is measured in economic and monetary terms. Alternatively, a comparative advantage is an ability to out-hustle a competitor in the production of watermelons such as higher yield per acre. The purpose of comparative analysis is to reinforce strengths, eliminate weaknesses, and improve output efficiency. Comparative assessments do not involve money but focus on physical efficiency. The identification of comparative strengths leads to on-farm improvements that allow for successful competition in the marketplace.

Marketing advantages originate from discovery of comparative advantages and lead to competitive marketing advantages. A grower or region can have a competitive marketing advantage if the total cost per unit for producing and harvesting watermelons is always less than another grower's cost or the average cost in a competitive supply region. Lower costs allow growers and intermediate market handlers to realize a transaction profit but also result in lower consumer prices. Large volume buyers expect to purchase larger quantity loads from low cost regions. Lower cost production regions such as the russet potato production in southeastern Idaho and the vine-ripe tomato production area in southern California are examples of regions that have established reputations among buyers as low per unit cost areas. In effect, large volume buyers seek volume suppliers from this area and thus have established a competitive marketing advantage. Of course, transportation costs can affect the delivered cost of a load so they can offset possible production cost advantages. For example, Texas watermelon growers likely have lower production costs but higher transport costs for melons sold to Michigan retailers than Indiana watermelon growers. Competitive advantages arise from comparative advantages. A comparative advantage is a relative measure of an activity that is done better than other activities. Each seller possesses a relative comparative advantage. The seller's task is to identify and improve on comparative advantages so competitive market advantages will exist. For example, if a farmer grows both field corn and watermelons, on a comparative basis, then the farmer does a better job of production (as indicated by yield) for one crop relative to the other. The farmer possesses a comparative production advantage in growing the higher yield crop relative to the lower yield crop. Comparative advantage identification leads to a competitive advantage. In the earlier example, Texas watermelon growers have a competitive production cost advantage but a competitive transport disadvantage for sales to Michigan markets. Production costs and transport costs impact the total competitive advantage. (See Appendix 4 for production costs in several states.)

Second, a competitive market advantage can exist if the price received is relatively higher than the average market price. In certain instances, high prices are associated with name brands. For example, sweet onion growers located in Georgia (Vidalia), Washington (Walla Walla), Hawaii (Maui Sweet), and Texas (Sweets) often receive price premiums for branded sweet onions compared with sweet onions grown by North Carolina, New York, or Florida growers. Beyond branding, a comparative marketing advantage can exist because of the timing of harvest. Perishability considerations preclude long-term storage of watermelons, so seasonal movements in supply availability correspond directly with seasonal price movements. Prices are highest when supply availability is least. In watermelons, a marketing advantage exists most often because of seasonal supply variations rather than the market dominance of a low cost supplier. About 50% of all watermelons grown in the United States are sold during June, July, and August. Retailer experience indicates that peak watermelon sales and consumption occur during the hottest summertime weather. Prices change frequently over this period and knowledge about any systematic movement in prices can help sellers eliminate some price uncertainty. For example, if late afternoon sales command slightly lower prices than early morning sales, then focus sales efforts on morning sales. Beyond daily and weekly price fluctuations, there are seasonal patterns for price movements. Early and late season prices are more often greater than mid or peak season prices. A comparative market advantage exists for sellers who obtain supplies during off-peak periods. Examination of periods when more favorable market prices exist is often characterized as market window price analysis.

MARKET WINDOW ANALYSIS. The fourth step in development of a market plan is to discover possible market timing advantages. Market window analysis is the identification of one or more periods of time during a sales period when an opportunity for higher relative prices most likely occurs. Market window periods change from year-to-year because of weather influences and vary by geographic location, target market, and season of the year. At least two types of market windows occur: 1) the cyclical late fall, winter, and early spring seasonal window that is associated with below-freezing temperatures in most parts of the United States and 2) short-run transition windows where quantities available decline in one harvest area and before-peak harvest begins in another region. Daily and weekly harvest fluctuations create temporary periods of surplus and shortage. Changes in product availability levels result in short-run price increases and decreases. Of course, unusual weather influences also disrupt supply availability patterns but after planting there are few things that a grower can do to influence significantly the harvest date. Since unanticipated market shortages and surpluses do not create predictable price advantages, market window analysis is not intended to examine situations where weather-induced shifts in supply occur. However, if unusual weather patterns seem to exist every year, then use of multiple year prices will capture some of the weather influenced impacts on prices. Weather-related market window opportunities certainly exist and benefit growers but we are most concerned with predictable impacts on prices. Charting weekly price data can provide a visible measure of price fluctuations. Market window analysis operates on the simple premise that all other things being equal, sellers will obtain the highest average price when supplies are relatively low. Of course, the logical extension of this analysis is that most watermelons should be grown in the winter months since supplies are least and prices are highest. However, winter consumption of watermelon is less, import competition exists, and production costs are higher, so extension of window analysis to an extreme position is not intended. In addition, if a significant number of growers produced earlier crops, then the low price period would shift to an earlier date. Nevertheless, market window analysis does represent a simple but effective approach to identification of higher price periods. Growers, of course, can adjust harvest periods somewhat through manipulation of controllable production factors. Harvest times are influenced most directly by weather (uncontrollable) and by changes in the planting date, the variety utilized, and the set of cultural practices used. Often, combining methods such as the use of an early maturing variety with plastic mulch and drip irrigation results in earlier harvest. If an early market window opportunity exists, then growers likely will manipulate planting times and cultural practices to ensure that harvest begins earlier. For growers, an earlier planting date increases the risk of frost or freezes but the tradeoff is easier sales and higher prices. Growers should consider, however, the possibility that manipulation of a planting date and/or cultural practices will result in higher costs, lower yield, and/or poorer quality. Mild temperature locations such as the southern portions of Texas, California, and Florida afford growers an opportunity to reap favorable market prices with minimal additional risk exposure. To determine if a market window exists, watermelon growers need to collect multiple years of weekly or monthly wholesale price data during the expected harvest period, estimate production cost information, calculate marketing and shipment costs, and estimate expected yield. Information for the market window analysis should be collected before seed purchase. Oftentimes, price and quantity data are available from state Departments of Agriculture and World Wide Web sites. While market window information provides useful marketing information, it should be noted that market window techniques remain a guesstimate about what will happen next season. Market window analysis is another piece of information that should be used to analyze the market potential of watermelons. An example of a market window developed to explain the idea behind watermelon window analysis is shown in Fig. 11.2. Wholesale prices were collected for the Raleigh, N.C., wholesale market.

The first phase in construction of a market window is collection of reported wholesale price data. In the above example, average wholesale price data for the Raleigh market were obtained from North Carolina Department of Agriculture and Consumer Services (NCDA & CS) records. Average reported weekly wholesale prices were collected for watermelons sold over a 4-year period between the third week of June (week 24) and the last week in August (week 34). Multiple year prices were used to calculate the average weekly wholesale price so that unusual or

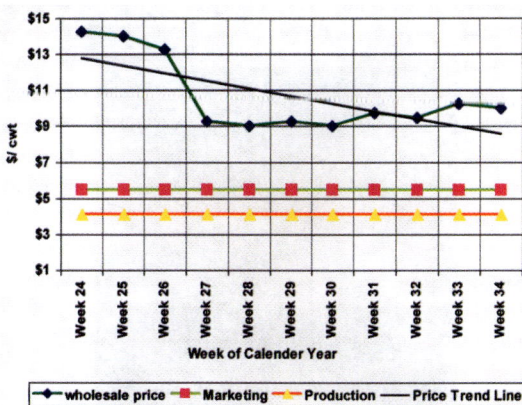

Figure 11.2. Average wholesale price, production cost, and marketing cost for watermelons sold in Raleigh, N.C., between 14 June and 30 Aug. 1995–98.

one-season effects did not distort the analysis. Growers who wish to construct a market window that is applicable to their own situation should 1) use weekly wholesale prices covering 3–5 years; 2) select a specific target market location (city or state) where expanded watermelon sales seem possible; and 3) weekly reported market price data is available for the target market. When considering a target market location, perishability considerations suggest that market opportunities may exist for areas north where harvest has not begun or areas south where peak harvest has already occurred. Next, the watermelon cost per unit of production must be estimated. Based on North Carolina Cooperative Extension Service enterprise budgets, the estimated production cost is $4.10 per hundredweight (cwt). In addition, transport costs from eastern North Carolina to Raleigh, field sorting, and marketing expenses were estimated to be about $1.40/cwt. The breakeven, delivered cost for watermelons grown in eastern North Carolina for sale to wholesalers located in Raleigh was $5.50/cwt. Chart data indicated that average price paid to growers exceeded the total cost of production, delivery, and marketing during all weeks considered. However, the greatest difference between total cost and average wholesale price most often occurred before 4 July (weeks 24, 25, and 26) and after mid-August (weeks 33 and 34) based on the prices reported over the past 4 years. In this situation, a market window exists for eastern North Carolina watermelon growers to sell watermelons on the Raleigh wholesale market before 4 July and after mid-August. Of course, market window analysis provides insights concerning only one probable outcome and realized actual can differ from expected outcomes because of shifts in harvest times due to weather influences and/or unexpected increases in local or aggregate supplies. Nevertheless, the example market window data indicates that eastern North Carolina watermelon growers can expect to receive higher-than-average prices if harvest begins earlier than the usual mid-July harvest date or extends later than usual through late August. With this information, growers should explore production actions than will result in earlier and later harvests. Available options would include staggered planting dates, multiple varieties, and the use of plastic mulch and drip irrigation. Growers should also recognize that the efforts to change the initial harvest date likely will increase production expenses but also increase net returns and profits in most years.

DEVELOPING A MARKETING PLAN

VALUE-ADDED TREND. In development of a market plan, opportunities to add service and market value provide market access. Market intelligence research and market window evaluations suggest that access to large volume buyers is very competitive and difficult. The simplistic focus of many marketing plans is simply to sell watermelons to nearby, large volume chain store warehouses or wholesalers. Of course, this plan may work for a few but not many growers, shippers, and first-handlers. There are limits as to how many watermelons local retailers (even large chains) can sell in a short time. Just as farm operations have become fewer and larger, the number of wholesale and retail firms has declined while the sales per firm have increased. In part, computer technology and the value-added process encouraged wholesalers, distributors, and retailers to explore new sales methods and formats. Today, the result is an invasion of new terms and abbreviations into a watermelon grower's vocabulary. Everyday low prices (EDLP), efficient consumer response (ECR), electronic data interchange (EDI), price look up (PLU), category management (CM), and continuous replenishment programs (CRP) are industry promoted programs designed to improve sales and automate the food distribution system from supplier to checkout. While designed to minimize waste, improve handling logistics, and reduce system costs, the overriding intent of the alphabet programs was to bring better value to customers and increase consumer satisfaction. Implementation of some aspects of alphabet programs have lagged in produce but the industry now accepts the need to reduce system waste and loss while improving coordination between supplier and receiver. Marketing has become less adversarial and more collaborative in its implementation. Grower-shippers need to adjust to changes in the produce procurement process and move away from selling commodities toward selling both commodities and wanted services. Of particular note to the watermelon industry has been the emergence of two competing retail produce pricing policies. First, the overwhelming success of Wal-Mart's EDLP program suggested that sales growth could be achieved through low product prices for every item sold in their stores including fresh fruits and vegetables. Alternatively, the EDLP strategy was not universally adopted. Selective retailers believed sales growth could be achieved by competing on the basis of value added services, meaning that many buyer purchase decisions are not driven exclusively by price. For example, there is little disagreement that the per unit price of fresh cut watermelon sold in pint containers is significantly higher priced per unit than whole watermelons sold individually. In effect, the value-added dimension can permit sellers to satisfy consumer needs, increase selling price per unit, and still maintain a competitive price image. Competition, market segmentation, and sales growth can be enhanced to the extent that value added services focus on supplying other desired quality attributes such as convenience, maturity, and extended storage life that are considered by buyers. For watermelon growers, it is important to recognize differences exist among wholesaler and/or retailer formats so that an appropriate set of features and attributes (low price, quality, value-added services, etc.) can be provided to customers.

PUTTING A PLAN TOGETHER. After market research is conducted, market feasibility issues are evaluated, market options examined, and a market strategy developed, then there is sufficient information to complete a market plan. One of the most difficult tasks is simply getting started. It is best to set aside a specific amount of time each day to work on marketing and to start marketing research and market planning efforts during slack times. The amount of detail contained in a market plan depends on the marketing experience of the seller, seasonal or time of year considerations, the number of viable sales options available, and who is responsible for marketing logistics.

As indicated earlier, a market plan considers a wide number of interrelated production, harvesting, and selling factors ranging from variety selection (seeded vs. seedless) to cultural practices, postharvest treatment, load assembly, containerization (if at all), and sales. Perishability, cultural practices, temperature and precipitation patterns, harvest timeliness, on-farm and off-farm volume availability, import competition, the bulkiness of the product, and buyer definitions of quality are elements considered in the plan. The market plan should also consider production or resource limitations such as hired labor availability, equipment and machinery complements, cash flow needs, risk, and when money is needed for planting, harvesting, and family living expenses. An overriding consideration is the watermelon marketing plan is its perishability. Quality begins to deteriorate from the moment of harvest and continues throughout the marketing process. Perishability considerations affect sales and price negotiations since both buyers and sellers recognize that watermelons cannot be held for long periods while sellers attempt to discover a better price offer.

Analysis of cost records provides insight about the marketing options that should be considered. Growers should estimate expenses for seed and include cash outlays for fertilizer, pest control, cultural practices, land use, harvesting, marketing, general overhead, interest on money borrowed, and hired labor. Other market sellers should consider acquisition costs, handling, labor, waste and loss, precooling, delivery, telephone, and equipment expenses. Cost and return information should be developed for each operational phase. Detailed hired labor, management time, and equipment requirements should be developed. These estimates should include the operation to be performed, the equipment needed, the total amount of labor needed as well as when (day or week) the task should be done. Compare internal costs with cost estimates available from competitive areas. Low cost suppliers will have a competitive market advantage that may provide access to distant, high volume markets.

How are prospective customers identified? Potential customer names can be discovered at trade shows, association meetings (such as the National Watermelon Association, Produce Marketing Association, or United Fresh Fruit and Vegetable Association), or personal visits to retailers. Telephone books and trade association directories also identify supermarkets and restaurants in an area. Public libraries often have telephone books for cities in other states. Retailers and other buyers track sales volume throughout the year and estimate weekly sales based on comparable sales of the same week a year ago. Last year's weekly sales provide a rough estimate for expected weekly sales volume for this year. Sales collection efforts should focus on the varieties sold, grades, quality, size and volume desired, delivery arrangements, transportation costs, postharvest handling requirements such as precooling needs, containers requested, price adjustment policies, and payment terms. Next, subscribe to electronic, paper, or other price reporting services so that price trends can be identified. Breakeven cost and price information serve as guidelines in establishment of target and minimum prices.

The oldest and most effective way to identify new sales opportunities is to make a personal visit to buyers. Face-to-face sales calls are difficult but an individual can acquire the needed communication skills over time. Personal visits are easier if sellers are thoroughly prepared, stress economic reasons as to why they should buy (such as they will make money), and provide a list of services available with load purchases. Basic rules of business and courtesy always apply when visiting potential buyers. Appointments should be scheduled and you should provide literature, business cards, references, and pictures or videotapes of your operation. Sellers should obtain from buyers specific daily, weekly, and monthly volume requirements as well as an expected price. Price discussions should focus on price determination processes such as identification of a common representative market price rather than discuss specific values. After this meeting, sellers should know the minimum volume requested by the buyer, what quality and grade is requested, and the time, days, and frequency of delivery.

Finally, a system of follow-up and feedback from buyers should be established. Did promises match performance and if not, why not? Did quality meet expectations? Can additional services or commodities be provided? Was the sale profitable? Seller focus should be on continuous improvement in the delivery of watermelons and the associated market services. If buyers indicated that they are not interested, then determine why not. If the reasons for rejection fit a pattern, then efforts should be redirected toward fixing any controllable problem areas. Each month and year the market plan should be reviewed and adjusted to reflect modifications. Over time, the process of marketing planning will become less cumbersome, more useful, and provide answers to questions before they are asked.

INTERNATIONAL MARKETING

For large volume suppliers of watermelons, international sales both increase opportunities for sales and expand competition. For most of agriculture, trade does not just involve movement of product across borders. International joint ventures and partnerships have created global opportunities for sales. Increased consumer demand for uninterrupted supplies of produce and improvements in transport technology have resulted in rapid expansion of international produce trade. Horticultural crops are the third most important agricultural commodity exported, trailing only feed grains and oilseeds in export value. For watermelon growers, enactment of the North American Free Trade Agreement (NAFTA) has resulted in both increased competition from Mexican imports and created additional sales opportunities in Canadian markets. Of course before NAFTA, Mexico and Canada were the primary trading partners for United States in fruit, vegetable, and melon suppliers but trade barriers have been reduced or eliminated. After enactment of NAFTA, the volume of in-season (1 Apr.–31 Oct.) watermelon imports from Mexico increased dramatically. Between 1993 and 1997, the quantity of in-season Mexican watermelons shipped to the United States increased 214% while the quantity of winter season (1 Nov.–31 Mar.) watermelons increased only 73%. About 90% of all United States watermelon imports are obtained from Mexico. Alternatively, NAFTA also created additional sales opportunities through increased shipments of watermelons to Canada. Between 1993 and 1997, United States watermelon exports to Canada increased about 3% per year. About 96% of all U.S. watermelon exports are shipped to Canada. The net effect of NAFTA was to increase in-season watermelon supplies and exert additional downward price pressure.

The volume of international watermelon trade is influenced by weather conditions, exchange rate differences, relative production cost differences, transport costs, and the existence of economic or phytosanitary trade barriers. Offshore sales of watermelons likely require use of an export broker or freight forwarder, the establishment of a letter of credit, phytosanitary certification, and special labels on packages. However, the perishability of watermelons, the availability of truck transport, and the proximity of Canada usually limit exports to nearby Canadian cities. Because watermelons are bulky and expensive to transport, international and domestic sales of watermelons must consider transport costs on the delivered price of melons to buyers. Trade agreement negotiations similar to the process that began in Uruguay during 1986 that led to the General Agreement on Trade and Tariffs (GATT) agreements that were enacted worldwide in 1994 are held periodically. It is unlikely that the watermelon industry will be impacted greatly by future trade agreements but overseas export markets could become more important for the watermelon industry so developments should be monitored closely.

For watermelons, transport costs are most directly linked to the distance from the pickup point to the drop-off destination as well as the overall availability of trucks. Freight rates are designed to cover fixed costs such as the initial purchase of the truck as well as variable costs such as fuel, tires, layover expenses, and driver time. Other important influences on transport rates also include the destination or region for the delivery, the number of intermediate pickups and drop-offs and the value of the commodity hauled. In general, long distance hauls command a higher rate per trip than shorter hauls. However, the rate per mile charged decreases as the transport distance increases. Multiple pickups and drop-offs affect both driver time and total mileage so carriers often add a flat-rate surcharge if an intermediate stop is necessary plus they impose additional per mile charges for increased distance traveled. The type of commodity transported also influences the rate. While all fresh market fruits and vegetables are perishable, carriers often distinguish among perishable commodities by their degree of perishability. Freight rates for watermelons are often less than for more perishable tomatoes or snap beans. The market destination can increase the rate charged, however, if few backhaul opportunities exist or traffic congestion increases a driver's waiting or delivery time (delivery to New York City). Watermelons are normally sold with a F.O.B. origin designation. This designation means that the receiver (buyer) assumes responsibility for the load at the point of origin (shipment). If a load has a F.O.B. destination designation, it means that the shipper (seller) is responsible for the load until it arrives and is accepted by the buyer. In F.O.B. origin sales, the buyer usually arranges for transport since they have financial responsibility for the load. Buyers may own a fleet of transport trucks or they could utilize the services of a truck broker. Truck brokerage fees range from 5%–10% of the total freight bill. Separate truck loading and unloading fees are usually charged. While per-mile transport rates vary greatly because of the specific reasons noted earlier, rates are usually highest during the summer. The increased volume of produce and the limited supply of trailers combine to permit carriers to increase rates during peak demand periods. General information about truck rates and per-load charges for watermelons and other selected produce items are published weekly in The Packer. International marketing information can be obtained from various state Departments of Agriculture, from state regional trade groups (such as the Southern United States Trade Association known most often as SUSTA), the Horticultural and Tropical Products Division of the Foreign Agricultural Service in USDA, the U.S. Customs Service, and the Export Counseling branch of the U.S. Department of Commerce.

DIRECT MARKETING OPTIONS

If production volume is limited, then direct marketing may be the best viable sales option. Direct farmer-to-consumer sales of watermelons represent a small but important source of income for many rural farm operators. Direct sales offer several advantages including immediate cash payment at the time of sale and it provides the producer with an opportunity to obtain a considerably higher price than would be realized from wholesale sales. In exchange for a higher price, direct sellers spend more time and effort in marketing activities such as servicing customers, transporting, and selling watermelons. A limitation of direct sales is that lower volumes are usually sold. Direct sales are a good marketing option for watermelon growers in areas where there are few established commercial watermelon operations but populated urban areas are nearby. For example, during 1998, eastern North Carolina growers were able to sell more than 118,500 individual watermelons direct to consumers at the Raleigh Farmers' Market facility at an average price of $2.50 per melon. In North Carolina, there are four state-sponsored farmers' markets plus 80 smaller community farmers' markets that are located throughout the state. Many states operate one or more state-sponsored farmers' market facilities and all states have community markets that provide an opportunity to sell watermelons directly to consumers. Fewer watermelons are sold via other direct selling methods such as roadside stands and u-pick facilities but producers with farms located on or near high traffic roads often find that watermelons can be sold easily to tourists and locals. Direct marketing requires that producers acquire merchandising, pricing, display, and selling skills. In effect, producers must examine and understand why consumers elect to buy watermelons from one seller rather than another. Sales displays, promotion activities, and price are important considerations in the where-to-purchase decision. Sales displays should feature freshness, ripeness, and the fact that the watermelons are locally grown. The first harvest of new crop watermelons should be featured and displayed prominently as customers enter your sales space. In addition, there is increasing consumer concern about the safety of the food that they eat. If chemicals are applied, then consumers should be reassured that the watermelons are safe to eat, that residues are not a problem, and proper field sanitation practices were followed. Promotion activities can feature contests, free melon giveaways, taste tables, and class trips for school children. Cut watermelon can provide customers with a visual confirmation of the quality and ripeness of the melon and offering taste samples will cause shoppers to pause in their shopping routine. Availability of limited quantities of unique melons such as yellow- fleshed varieties is another type of promotion that creates product diversity, provides color contrast in displays, and attracts shopper attention. How do you determine the selling price? First, you need to know your full production and handling costs. Then you need to determine the prices of nearby competitors such as other market sellers or the local grocery store price. Watermelons should be bulk displayed and priced competitively with other suppliers and local grocery stores. Prices should be displayed prominently and provide discounts for volume buyers. Different size categories of watermelons should be priced appropriately but can be sold on an each or per pound basis. Whole melons are often sold using a "any melon in this size category is the same price" policy.

SUMMARY

Expanded watermelon consumption has attracted increased interest from growers, wholesalers, brokers, food service operators, and retailers who want to increase income and sell products sought by consumers. The change to fewer, larger integrated buying operations has furthered the development of larger, high volume wholesalers, shippers, and production operations. As the watermelon marketing system increases in complexity, consumers will demand improved performance from both the production and marketing sectors. Responding to the needs and wants of consumers is not an easy activity but coordination of many marketing activities is facilitated through development of a market strategy and plan. Marketing planning requires that sellers obtain and manage information about consumer and buyer wants. Development of a market plan will not ensure marketing success but can reduce the chance for failure. One of the first steps in development of a market plan is to ensure production competency, that is, develop a comparative production advantage that leads to a marketing advantage. Marketing competency can be developed by the seller while some elements of marketing (sales, delivery, pricing) can be purchased in the marketplace through utilization of brokers, dealers, and other market intermediaries. However, overall marketing responsibility remains with the owner of the watermelons until the sale is completed and owner transfers to the new buyer. Frequent communication is essential among all market participants and sellers are encouraged to identify ways to work smarter than their competitors. Market rewards will be realized by sellers who can become efficient in the handling system, provide economic incentives for buyers, and recognize the collaborative nature of the current watermelon marketing system.

General References

Best, M.J. and J.R. Brooker. 1991. Market window analysis and price risk: Considerations for Tennessee vegetable growers. Tenn. Agr. Expt. Sta. Res. Bul. 681.

Estes, E.A. 1996. Creating a marketing plan. Agr. and Resource Econ. Rpt. 11, Dept. of Agr. and Resource Econ., N.C. State Univ., Raleigh.

Food Marketing Institute. 1998. Food markets in review, 1998–99: Fresh fruits. Food Mktg. Inst., Fair Lawn, N.J.

U.S. Department of Agriculture. 1996. Food Marketing Review, 1994–95. U.S. Dept. of Agr., Food and Consumer Econ. Div., Agr. Econ. Rpt. 743.

Gibson, E. 1994. Sell what you sow: A growers guide to successful produce marketing. New World Publ., Carmichael, Calif.

McLaughlin, E.W. and D.J. Perosio. 1994. Fresh fruit and vegetable procurement dynamics: The role of the supermarket buyer. Food Ind. Mgt. Prog. Res. Bul. 94-1, Cornell Univ., Ithaca, N.Y.

Powers, N.J. 1994. Marketing practices for vegetables. U.S. Dept. of Agr. Econ. Res. Serv. Agr. Info. Bul. 702.

Vance Publishing Corp. 1999. The red book. Vance Publ. Corp., Lexana, Kans.

Produce Reporter Co. 1999. The blue book. 1999. Produce Reporter Co., Wheatley, Ill.

Weinstein, B. 1999. Category management. Produce Bus. 15(5):30–34. Phoenix Media Network, Boca Raton, Fla.

CHAPTER 12

PROMOTION AND MERCHANDISING

L.J. Zanoni

The introduction and promotion of new products from watermelon to lap top computers involves a rich history of individuals acting as entrepreneurs, groups of individuals working independently or together with organizations or associations. The promotional activities that were initiated by these individuals or groups were short-lived and effective for the communications and technology available at that time. Using a historical perspective, this discussion highlights certain events that contributed to the promotion of watermelon, which refers to all activities from the field to the fork that results in the increased per capita consumption of watermelon.

The merchandising of watermelon is one of many activities used in the promotion of watermelon. Merchandising in this text refers to those activities used by the retail and food service industries in presenting, displaying and featuring watermelon with the end result of causing consumers to purchase more watermelon.

European botanists of the 16th and 17th centuries described the wide ranges of fruit sizes, shapes, rind patterns, seed and flesh colors of watermelon. Some of these watermelons were brought to America by the earliest colonists and were grown in Massachusetts as early as 1629.

Consistent with the definition of promotion and merchandising, the first time these early colonists bragged about the uniqueness, sweetness, and size of their garden prizes may have been the first watermelon promotion in North America. These farmers were also the first watermelon horticulturists. Farmers independently mixed and selected new and unique fruits from a wealth of genetic material. Selections were made for large size, desirable shape, outer rind color, flesh color, and sweetness.

By the 19th century new horticultural types were passed on to other farmers as 'Markham's Selection', 'Froese's Pride', and seeds from Jerome B. Rice. By the early 1900s, the catalog of the Jerome B. Rice Seed Company, Cambridge New York listed 'Coles Select', 'Georgia's Rattle Snake Melon', 'Dixie Original', 'Honey Watermelon', and others. Many farmers saved their own seeds but the development of seed saving specialists were the forerunners of today's seed industry.

Watermelon producers in market gardens gave birth to the promotion of watermelon and contributed to the development of the seed industry as well. Barn raisings, church gatherings, and the more official borough, township, county and state fairs were probably the first opportunities that one's seed selections, and strains were officially promoted.

The next major contribution to the promotion of watermelon came from state and federal experiment stations. Along with collecting world wide sources of new seeds and the mixing and reselecting of this genetic material to identify specific traits and new horticultural types, horticulturists associated with the Land Grant Colleges, Universities, and the U.S. Department of Agriculture (USDA) are credited with introduction of the watermelon promotional activities used today with extensive trialing, field days, wide scale communications to producers and receivers, and the release of new watermelon varieties. Seed For Today. A Descriptive Catalogue of Vegetable Varieties prepared by Asgrow Seed Company listed the varieties offered for sale in the 1960s and 1970s include 'Black Stone', 'Florida Giant', 'Striped Klondike', 'Blue Ribbon', 'Charleston Grey', 'Chilean Black', 'Congo', 'Crimson Sweet', 'Peacock', 'Jubilee' and 'Sugar Baby'.

County and state fairs across the country and the many cities and towns particularly those in the southeast claiming to be the watermelon centers and capitals (Fig. 12.1) across the country were the precursors of more modern watermelon promotion and merchandising that we know today. Prizes were awarded for the biggest and the smallest watermelon fruits, unusual fruit sizes, shapes, rind colors and stripe patterns, and the sweetest watermelon. These events featured parades and local spokespersons from the community and the beginning of watermelon queen contests.

The first commercial watermelon promotion that involved the media with consumer activities was by Asgrow Seed Co. with the introduction of 'Mirage' hybrid seeded watermelon in the early 1980s. 'Mirage' was the second hybrid watermelon introduced. The first high volume commercial hybrid watermelon introduced was 'Royal Sweet' by Petoseed. This introduction was timely because the market was showing a

Figure 12.1. Cordele, Ga., proclaims that it is the watermelon capital of the world with roadside banners. (Source: D.N. Maynard.)

preference for the crimson sweet stripe pattern and 'Mirage' provided the crimson sweet stripping pattern with an elongated shape. Promotional activities included fruit stickers, local and regional TV appearances by garnishing chef Harvey Rosen, retail distribution of consumer leaflets on decorative melon carving, in store sampling, cooperative producer/broker retail ads and numerous editorials and news releases in grower magazines.

Fruit stickers were used to identify the hybrid as being unique in the market place and to point out the advantage that hybridity provided with more consistency in fruit size, shape and internal quality. The fruit stickering, cooperative ads and other programs the producers and handlers independently conducted with select retailers greatly contributed to the promotion of watermelon. Market tests that evaluated the value of fruit stickers conducted by Asgrow during this period revealed that consumers would select a stickered fruit over nonsticker fruits seven times out of ten.

Fruit quality in itself is a promotion that serves to enhance sales. In 1987, a new variety called 'Sangria' from Novartis Seeds (now Syngenta Seeds) was released which changed dramatically the consumer perspective of watermelon appearance and eating quality. 'Sangria' is considered an Allsweet type, that is the outside of the rind is dark green with a light green stripe. The fruit shape is elongated and the average fruit size is 20–22 lb. The internal quality of 'Sangria' is what helped to sell this major variety to the public as it has a unique balance of flavor and texture along with high sugars and a deep red flesh. 'Sangria' continues to be the standard of high quality to which new varieties are compared. In fact, market reports list 'Sangria' type to include all Allsweet type varieties and other red meat to include all other seeded varieties. Often, there is a price premium paid for the 'Sangria' type fruit.

The availability of high quality seedless watermelon in the late 1980s took watermelon promotion and merchandising to a much higher level. With seedless fruits, consumers could clearly differentiate the products as unique and different from seeded fruit. Having access to 'Tri-X-313' seeds and developing unique produce distribution channels, Sun World Corp. became a major factor in the introduction of seedless watermelon to the produce industry. Sun World designed and featured creative ads in produce receiver as well as consumer publications. In store promotions included point of purchase materials, product testing, consumer leaflets, cooperative retail ads as well as other promotional and merchandising ideas. Half and quarter cuts of seedless fruit were often displayed along side cut seeded fruit for easy comparison.

With many major seed companies now offering seed of triploid hybrids,

Figure 12.2. Outdoor displays attract customers entering and leaving stores. (Source: D.N. Maynard.)

Figure 12.3. Bins with decorative color graphic attract buyers. (Source: D.N. Maynard.)

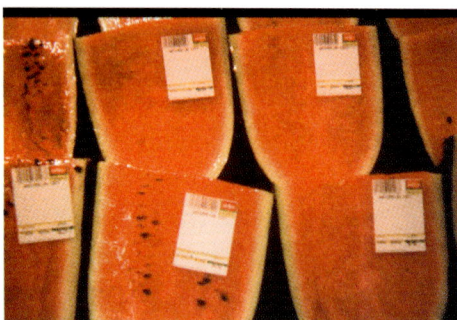

Figure 12.4. Cut fruit enhance watermelon sales. (Source: L.J. Zanoni.)

Figure 12.5. Fresh-cut watermelons are displayed with other fruits. (Source: L.J. Zanoni.)

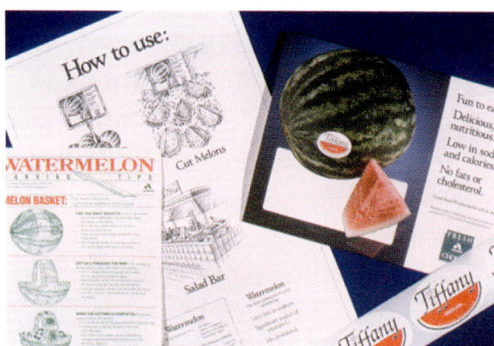

Figure 12.6. Point of purchase materials informs consumers and enhances sales. (Source: L.J. Zanoni.)

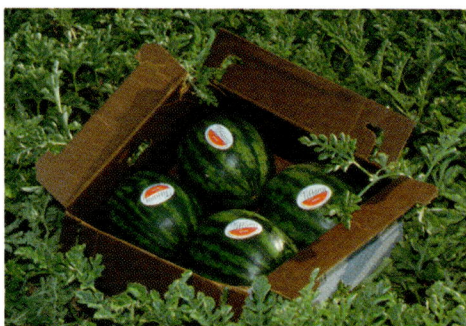

Figure 12.7. Fruit stickers identify the product, provide PLU and encourage repeat sales. (Source: L.J. Zanoni.)

retailers insist that fruits carry a sticker clearly denoting seedless and that the stickers also feature the appropriate price look up (PLU) code to capture the added value in the product, promotion and pricing. These changes have involved a great deal of one-on-one communication from producers and handlers to produce receivers.

Today, some retailers display store posters of the producers with select quotes and poster versions of local newspaper ads. There continues to be a strong desire by today's consumer to want to get closer to nature. The vast majority of today's consumers don't have the time to garden or to drive to a roadside market but they do seek out and support supermarkets with good produce departments where you can now see full size posters of producers by commodity and regionalized by production area.

WATERMELON ASSOCIATIONS

NATIONAL WATERMELON ASSOCIATION. The National Watermelon Association (NWA) promotes the interests of and lobbies for the watermelon industry. Organized in 1914, the original name was the Melon Distributors Association but in 1945 the name was changed to the National Watermelon Growers and Distributors Association and in 1979, the current name was adopted. NWA has members in 30 states and Canada, with individual chapters in North and South Carolina, Maryland/Delaware, Georgia, Alabama, Missouri- Arkansas, Florida, Texas/Oklahoma, California/Arizona, and Indiana/Illinois. The purpose of the Association is to promote the best interests of the watermelon industry from production to consumption. The NWA consistently seeks improvements in the growing, grading, handling, transporting, distribution, and sale of watermelon.

Over the past 30 years and continuing as a tradition today, the NWA sponsors watermelon queen contests and tours to promote and increase consumption of watermelons. Queens selected by each state association, compete for the title of National Queen at the annual NWA convention. The National Queen represents the Association for media appearances, in store promotions, county and state fairs, educational and retail seminars, and other functions where watermelons are featured.

NATIONAL WATERMELON PROMOTION BOARD. Watermelon producers, handlers and importers fund and operate the National Watermelon Promotion Board (NWPB) to increase consumer demand for watermelon through promotion, research and educational programs. About 5,200 commercial watermelon producers, handlers and importers fund the nonprofit NWPB through crop assessments. The NWPB is governed by a Board of Directors, comprised of watermelon producers, handlers, importers and one member who represents the public. Directors decide how to invest the board's multi-million dollar budget in board programs. They work with an administrative staff based in Orlando and led by an Executive Director to enact board campaigns, programs and research.

Established in 1989, the NWPB has launched multifaceted campaigns designed to increase consumer awareness about watermelon. NWPB retail promotions keep watermelon's profile high in supermarket chains and restaurants throughout the United States and Canada, while public relations campaigns raise watermelon's visibility with consumers and the media. NWPB programs teach consumers about watermelon's nutritional benefits and encourage them to add melons to their daily diets. The NWPB also works with scientists at land-grant universities and the USDA to conduct production research to prevent crop damage and to further improve varieties.

Board programs have developed with significant advances in the industry, including the introduction of new seeded and seedless hybrids innovations in packaging and shipment of watermelons and the development of in-store refrigerated areas to display fresh-cut watermelons.

The NWPB has developed targeted marketing and public relations campaigns with continuity from one year to the next. Their campaigns are tailored in response to trends, such as healthy eating, snack foods, entertaining and fresh-cuts. The NWPB has made significant contributions in the retail marketplace, performing retail promotions with leading retailers in the U.S. and Canada. Through these promotions, the NWPB offers consumers free samples of watermelon in produce departments, and provides retailers with proven strategies for successfully marketing watermelon to consumers.

The NWPB is providing retailers with market research, merchandising strategies and handling tips designed to help sell more watermelon in produce departments. As a result, the board's retail seminar program and resource guides have helped make great strides in educating retailers about the value of watermelon to their produce sales.

The NWPB participates in numerous trade conventions and meetings including the Produce Marketing Association convention that is widely attended by retailers and food service vendors. Through a concentrated media campaign, the NWPB reaches millions of consumers with the message to take home a watermelon today. The board funds a media campaign that includes consumer and trade print and broadcast media as well as a web site.

SUMMARY

Through promotion and merchandising (Table 12.1), we have witnessed a transition in the old fashioned image of watermelon being promoted as a

Table 12.1. Watermelon merchandising and promotion.

Activity

Event promotions (Fig. 12.2)

Method

Outdoor displays. Huge watermelon piles or bins in open air or under cover which may be refrigerated. Icing of whole fruits can be used to attract impulse buyers.

Activity

Supermarket promotion of nonrefrigerated whole fruits

Method

Truckload displays outside stores in parking lots, store entrances and in other high traffic areas outside the produce department.

Activity

Produce department displays

Method

Whole fruit are stacked outside the bins and in cartons for consumers to maneuver through with their shopping carts.

Activity

Bin displays (Fig. 12.3)

Method

Use of bins with decorative color graphics to attract buyers.

Activity

Cut fruit in refrigerated displays (Fig. 12.4, Fig. 12.5)

Method

Fruit cut in 1/2, 1/4, and layered wedge-shaped slices are displayed.

Fresh cut watermelon in bite-size chunks alone or in combination with other fruit are displayed.

Watermelons are cut in oval, square, or rectangle shapes following the contours of the fruit and packaged in shrink-wrap film for retail or food service sales.

Activity

Point of purchase materials (Fig. 12.6)

Method

Posters, ads, consumer leaflets, and recipes are developed for use in stores and restaurants and by produce distributors. Information on watermelon carving, selecting a ripe fruit, and nutritional information can be conveyed in point of purchase materials.

Activity

Fruit stickers (Fig. 12.7)

Method

Provide information on variety, brand, and PLU which is required (4032) for seedless watermelons.

Activity

Print and broadcast ads

Method

Provide information on availability, selection, carving and recipes.

Activity

Product tie-ins

Method

Watermelon included with the purchase of a grill or other picnic-related items.

locally produced fruit for summertime picnic consumption to a versatile fruit grown and shipped long distances and available to consumers every day of the year. However, watermelon consumption is still low in the United States compared to many other countries (see Table 1.3). So, there is still a long way to go.

Mark Twain was one of the industry's earliest spokespersons when he wrote of watermelons in 1894: "When one has tasted it, he knows what the angels eat."

General References

Asgrow Seed Company. 1980. Seed for today, A descriptive catalogue of vegetables varieties, 23. Asgrow Seed Company.

Asgrow Seed Company. Date unknown, early 1900s. Jerome B. Rice seed catalogue. Asgrow archives. Asgrow Seed Company.

National Watermelon Association (NWA), P.O. Box 38, Morven, GA 31638-0038.

NWA web page address: www.watermelon.org; www.surfsouth.com/~nwai/.

National Watermelon Promotion Board (NWPB), Orlando, Fla. 32814-0065.

NWPB web page address: http://www.-watermelon.org.

Redman, Emily (ed.). 1999. Produce availability and merchandising guide. The Packer. Vance Publishing Corp., Lenexa, Kans.

Rosen, Harvey. 1999. Melon garnishing. International Culinary Consultants, Elberon, N.J.

WATERMELON ORGANIZATIONS

National Watermelon Association
P.O. Box 38
Morven, GA 31638
Phone (229) 775-2130
Fax (229) 775-2344

Nancy Childers
Executive Secretary-Treasurer

National Watermelon Promotion Board
P.O. Box 140065
Orlando, FL 32814-0065
Phone (407) 895-5100
Fax (407) 895-5022

William Watson
Executive Director

Alabama Watermelon Association
376 Cope Road
Chipley, FL 32428
Phone (850) 638-1310
Fax (850) 638-1646

Carolyn Prescott
Secretary-Treasurer

California-Arizona Watermelon Association
P.O. Box 606
Piru, CA 93040
Phone (805) 521-1756
Fax (805) 521-1528

Dana Abercrombie
Executive Secretary

Florida Watermelon Association
808 East Main Street
Immokalee, FL 34142
Phone (941) 658-1442
Fax (941) 658-1448

Patty Swilley
Secretary-Treasurer

Georgia Watermelon Association
P.O. Box 39
Morven, GA 31638
Phone (912) 775-2580
Fax (912) 775-2344

Nancy Childers
Secretary-Treasurer

Illinois-Indiana Watermelon Association
715 S. 6th St.
Vincennes, IL 47591
Phone (812) 886-0766
Fax (812) 886-1333

Anita Field
Secretary-Treasurer

Maryland-Delaware Watermelon Association
RD 3, Box 228
Laurel, DE 19956
Phone (302) 875-2819

Dawn Collins
Secretary-Treasurer

Missouri-Arkansas Watermelon Association
P.O. Box 1029
Jonesboro, AR 72403
Phone (870) 932-0578
Fax (870) 932-1982

Debbie Johnson
Secretary-Treasurer

North Carolina Watermelon Association
8600 Crowder Rd.
Raleigh, NC 27603
Phone (919) 772-2204
Fax (919) 779-1685

Bonnie Holloman
Secretary

South Carolina Watermelon Association
P.O. Box 175
Barnwell, SC 29821
Phone (803) 259-3486

Allison Forehand
Secretary-Treasurer

Texas-Oklahoma Watermelon Association
P.O. Box 903
Weatherford, TX 76086
Phone (817) 596-0927
Fax (817) 594-1045

Wanda Letson
Secretary-Treasurer

WATERMELON SEED SOURCES

Primary seed producers

Companies listed in this category have plant breeding programs that develop proprietary hybrids for direct sales to growers or sales through dealers.

American Takii, Inc.
301 Natividad Road
Salinas, CA 93906
Phone (831) 443-4901
Fax (831) 443-3976

Asgrow Vegetable Seeds
2700 Camino del Sol
Oxnard, CA 93030
Phone (800) 234-1056
Fax (805) 918-2410

D.V. Burrell Seed Growers Co.
P.O. Box 150
Rocky Ford, CO 81067
Phone (719) 254-3318
Fax (719) 254-3319

Harris Moran Seed Co.
P.O. Box 4938
Modesto, CA 95352
Phone (800) 320-4672
Fax (209) 527-5312

Hazera Seed Ltd.
2250 E. Imperial Hwy.
Suite 200
El Segundo, CA 90245
Phone (805) 473-3452
Fax (310) 648-6753

Hollar Seeds, Inc.
P.O. Box 106
Rocky Ford, CO 81067-0106
Phone (719) 254-7411
Fax (719) 254-3539

Hungnong Seed America, Inc.
3065 Pacheco Pass Hwy.
Gilroy, CA 95020
Phone (408) 848-5354
Fax (408) 848-5349

Known-You Seed Co., Ltd.
26, Chung Cheng 2nd Road
Kaohsiung, Taiwan
Republic of China

Orsetti Seed Co., Inc.
2301 Technology Parkway
P.O. Box 2350
Hollister, CA 95024-2350
Phone (831) 636-4822
Fax (831) 636-4814

Petoseed Co., Inc.
2700 Camino del Sol
Oxnard, CA 93030
Phone (800) 647-7386
Fax (805) 656-4818

Sakata Seed America, Inc.
P.O. Box 880
Morgan Hill, CA 95038-0880
Phone (408) 778-7758
Fax (408) 778-7768

Seeds by Design
130 N. Butte St., Suite L
Willows, CA   95988
Phone (530) 934-8086
Fax (530) 934-7672

Shamrock Seed Co.
3 Harris Place
Salinas, CA 93901
Phone (831) 771-1500
Fax (800) 351-4443

Sugar Creek Seed, Inc.
P.O. Box 508
Hinton, OK 73047
Phone (405) 542-3920
Fax (405) 542-3921

Sunseeds
P.O. Box 2078
Morgan Hill, CA 95038-2078
Phone (408) 776-1111
Fax (408) 776-9375

Syngenta Seeds, Inc.
P.O. Box 4188
Boise, ID 83711
Phone (208) 322-7272
Fax (208) 322-1413

United Genetics Seeds Co.
8000 Fairview Rd.
Hollister, CA 95023
Phone (831) 636-4882
Fax (831) 636-4883

Willhite Seed Inc.
Box 23
Poolville, TX 76487
Phone (817) 599-8656
Fax (817) 599-5843

Zeraim Gedera Ltd.
P.O. Box 103
Gedera 70750
Israel
Phone (972-8-8594605
Fax (972-8-8594576

Secondary seed producers

Companies listed in this section sell proprietary hybrids, but do not have internal plant breeding programs.

Abbott & Cobb, Inc.
P.O. Box 307
Feasterville, PA 19053-0307
Phone (215) 245-6666
Fax (215) 245-9043

D.V. Burrell Seed Growers Co.
P.O. Box 150
Rocky Ford, CO 81067-0150
Phone (719) 254-3318
Fax (719) 254-3319

Otis S. Twilley Seed Co., Inc.
P.O. Box 4000
Hodges, SC 29653
Phone (864) 227-5118
Fax (864) 227-5108

SeedWay
1225 Zeager Rd.
Elizabethtown, PA 17022
Phone (800) 952-7333

U.S. Seedless, L.L.C.
7618 Leonard Drive
P.O. Box 3066
Falls Church, VA 22043

Willhite Seed Inc.
P.O. Box 23
Poolville, TX 76487
Phone (817) 599-8656
Fax (817) 599-5843

Seed dealers

A large number of local, state, regional, and national companies act as seed dealers especially for primary seed producers but also for secondary seed producers. Agricultural publications, the local Extension Service Office, neighbors, and the state watermelon association are good sources of information on seed dealers serving your area.

APPENDIX 3

CUCURBIT PUBLICATIONS

Periodicals

Cucurbitaceae. Proceedings of a meeting held every two years alternating between the United States and Europe and environs.

Proceedings Cucurbitaceae '94. Evaluation and enhancement of cucurbit germplasm. 1994. G.E. Lester and J.R. Dunlap (eds.). Gateway Publishing, Edinberg, TX 78539.

Cucurbits towards 2000. Proceedings of the VI Eucarpia meeting of cucurbit genetics and breeding. 1996. M.L. Gómez-Guillamón, C. Soria, J. Cuartero, J.A. Torés, and R. Fernández-Muñoz (eds.). Estación Experimental La Mayora, Malaga, Spain.

Cucurbitaceae '98. Evaluation and enhancement of cucurbit germplasm. 1998. J.D. McCreight (ed.). ASHS Press, Alexandria, VA 22314-2851.

Proceedings of 7th Eucarpia meeting on cucurbit genetics and breeding. 2000. N. Katzir and H. S. Paris (eds.). Acta Horticulturae 510. ISHS, Leuven, Belgium.

Cucurbitaceae 2002 to be held 8–12 Dec. 2002, Naples Beach and Golf Club, Naples, Fla. Contact: Donald N. Maynard, University of Florida, 5007 60th St. E., Bradenton, FL 34203.

Cucurbit Genetics Cooperative. Contributed brief research reports published annually on genetics of cucurbits. Direct inquiries to: 2118 Plant Sciences Building, University of Maryland, College Park, MD 20742-4452.

The Cucurbit Network News. Brief articles on current happenings of watermelon and other cucurbits. Issued twice a year. Contact: The Cucurbit Network, P.O. Box 560483, Miami, FL 33256.

The Vineline. National Watermelon Association, Morven, Ga.

Books

Biology and Utilization of the Cucurbitaceae. 1990. David M. Bates, Richard W. Robinson, and Charles Jeffrey (eds.). Cornell University Press, 124 Roberts Place, Ithaca, NY 14850. ISBN 0-8014-1670-1.

Cucurbits. 1998. N.M. Nayar and T.A. More (eds.) Science Publishers, Inc., P.O. Box 699, Enfield, NH 03748. ISBN 1-57808-003-7.

Cucurbits. 1997. R.W. Robinson and D.S. Decker-Walters. CAB International, 198 Madison Ave., New York, NY 10016-4341. ISBN 0-85199-133-5.

Cucurbits. Botany, Cultivation, and Utilization. 1962. Thomas W. Whitaker and Glen N. Davis. Interscience Publishers, 440 Park Avenue South, New York, N.Y.

PRODUCTION COSTS

Table A4.1. Income and cash operating summary. Triploid watermelons. Arizona, 1998. (Source: ag.arizona.edu/pubs/marketing/vegetable/central/watermelons_seedless98pdf.)

COUNTY: Maricopa; FARM: Maricopa Veg 98; WATER SOURCE: Roosevelt Water; TILLAGE: Conventional; CROP: Watermelons; ACRES: 1.0; IRRIGATION SYSTEM: Flood Furrow; SOIL: Sandy Loam; AREA: Roosevelt WCD; YIELD: 13.3 Tn/Acre; PREVIOUS CROP: Wheat, Winter
DATE: 12/10/98

Item	Unit	Quantity	Price/ unit	Budgeted/ acre	Total/ acre
INCOME = MELONS	TON	13.25	$156.92	$2,079.19	$2,079.19
CASH LAND PREPARATION AND GROWING EXPENSES					
(INCLUDING SALES TAX)					129.01
Paid Labor (including benefits)					
Tractor/self-propelled				54.90	
Irrigation				67.62	
Other/contract				6.50	139.19
Chemicals and custom applications					
Fertilizer				82.43	
Insecticide				41.64	
Herbicide				15.12	56.21
Farm machinery and vehicles					
Diesel fuel				19.13	
Gasoline				3.65	
Repairs and maintenance				33.42	133.33
Irrigation water (excuding labor)					
Water assessment[z]				962.31	
Other purchased inputs					
Seed/transplants				333.11	
Other services and rentals				243.00	
Other materials				386.20	
TOTAL CASH LAND PREPARATION AND GROWING EXPENSES					1420.05
CASH HARVEST AND POST HARVEST EXPENSES					116.98
Paid labor (including benefits)					
Tractor/self-propelled				116.98	64.75
Farm machinery and vehicles					
Diesel fuel				21.53	
Repairs and maintenance				43.22	140.00
Custom harvest/postharvest					399.73
Other materials					
TOTAL HARVEST AND POSTHARVEST EXPENSES					721.47
OPERATING OVERHEAD = PICKUP USE					15.29
OPERATING INTEREST AT 10.0%					50.04
TOTAL CASH OPERATING EXPENSES					$ 2,206.85
RETURNS OVER CASH OPERATING EXPENSES					$ (127.66)

[z]A water assessment charge of $17.00 per acre is included as an ownership cost.

Table A4.2. Drip irrigated triploid watermelon production costs. Arizona, 1998-99. (Source: ag.arizona.edu/pubs/marketing/vegetable/central/watermelons seedless98pdf.0 Hand labor at $7.50 per hour ($5.75 plus Social Security) unemployment insurance, transportation, supervision and fringe benefits. Yield = 20 tons per acre, 2/3 bin container.

Operation	Rate	Materials Type	Cost	Hand labor Hours	Dollars	Cost/ acre
LAND PREPARATION						
Stubble disc	20.00					20.00
Disc 2×	11.00					22.00
Spread fertilizer	8.00	500 lb 11–52–0	67.50			75.50
List beds	20.00					20.00
Rerun beds 2×	12.50					25.00
Total						162.50
GROWING PERIOD						
Install drip irrigation		Drip system	500.00	12	90.00	590.00
Install plastic mulch	55.00	Plastic mulch	82.00			137.00
Metam sodium via drip		Metam sodium	145.00			145.00
Seedless transplants		S-transplants	840.00	Includes labor		840.00
Pollinator transplants		P-transplants	74.00	Includes labor		74.00
Cultivate 2×	12.25					24.50
Irrigate 10×		Water 3 ac/ft	40.50	10	75.00	115.50
Fertilize via drip		200lb. N @ .35	70.00			70.00
		100# phosphate	35.00			35.00
Drip maintenance		Chemicals	25.00			25.00
Hand weed 2×						90.00
Pollination		1.5 hives@ 22.00	33.00	12	90.00	33.00
Vine turn 2× (hand)						105.00
Insect control 6×	8.50	Insecticides	177.50	14	105.00	228.50
Remove plastic mulch						75.00
Disc out beds	13.00			10	75.00	13.00
Total						2600.50
GROWING PERIOD AND LAND PREPARATION COSTS						2763.00
Land Rent (net acres)						225.00
Cash Overhead		17% of preharvest costs & land rent				507.96
TOTAL PREHARVEST COSTS						3495.96
HARVEST						
Pick, load, haul, sort, sell		20 tons/acre,$100/ton[z]				2000.00
TOTAL OF ALL COSTS						5495.96

[z]Harvest cost may vary substantially depending upon the melon type, container packed, resorting and yard fees.

Table A4.3. Estimated watermelon production costs in north central, Florida, 1997-98. *(Source: Smith, S.A. and T.G. Taylor. 1998. Production costs for Florida vegetables.)*

Category	Avg. Acre	Cwt
Yield (cwts)	300	
OPERATING COSTS	Dollars	
Seed	25.18	
Fertilizer and lime	157.00	
Fungicide	127.64	
Labor	76.07	
Machinery	132.97	
Interest	24.19	
Miscellaneous		
Aerial spraying	21.00	
Bee rental	4.00	
Farm vehicles	19.33	
Total	587.40	
FIXED COST		
Land rent	50.00	
Machinery	61.88	
Overhead	81.01	
Total	192.89	
TOTAL PREHARVEST COST	780.29	2.60
HARVEST AND MARKETING COSTS		
Harvest and pack	375.00	1.25
Packing material	9.00	0.03
Selling	300.00	1.00
Marketing and Promotion Assessment	6.00	0.02
Total	690.00	2.30
TOTAL COST	1,470.29	4.90

Table A4.4. Estimated watermelon production costs for the following crop of a double-crop system in west central, Florida, 1997–98.[z,y] (Source: Smith, S.A. and T.G. Taylor. 1998. Production costs for Florida vegetables.)

Category	Avg. Acre	Cwt
Yield (cwts)	320	
OPERATING COSTS	Dollars	
Seed	24.44	
Fertilizer and lime	105.00	
Fungicide	54.17	
Herbicide	33.87	
Insecticide	53.39	
Labor	338.11	
Machinery	206.46	
Interest	37.02	
Miscellaneous		
Scouting	25.00	
Bee rental	3.60	
Farm vehicles	19.33	
Plastic removal and disposal	75.00	
Total	975.39	
FIXED COST		
Machinery	63.14	
Management	200.30	
Overhead	250.38	
Total	513.82	
TOTAL PREHARVEST COST	1,489.21	4.65
HARVEST AND MARKETING COSTS		
Harvest and pack	480.00	1.50
Packing material	9.60	0.03
Selling	320.00	1.00
Marketing and Promotion Assessment	6.40	0.02
Total	816.00	2.55
TOTAL COST	2,305.21	7.20

[z]Cost attributed to second crop as a result of double-crop production practices following tomatoes.

[y]Costs exclude field and bed preparation, plastic mulch, and fumigant.

Table A4.5. Estimated watermelon production costs in north Florida, 1997–98.[z] (Source: Smith, S.A. and T.G. Taylor. 1998. Production costs for Florida vegetables.)

Category	Avg. Acre	Avg. Cwt
Yield (cwts)	325	
OPERATING COSTS	Dollars	
Seed	65.06	
Fertilizer and lime	105.00	
Fumigant	464.00	
Fungicide	95.67	
Insecticide	9.33	
Labor	164.81	
Machinery	209.66	
Interest	57.64	
Miscellaneous		
Plastic mulch	127.16	
Frost protection	101.10	
Wells	50.00	
Farm vehicles	19.33	
Total	1,468.77	
FIXED COST		
Land rent	50.00	
Machinery	105.93	
Overhead	235.06	
Total	390.99	
TOTAL PREHARVEST COST	1,859.76	5.72
HARVEST AND MARKETING COSTS		
Harvest and pack	406.25	1.25
Packing material	9.75	0.03
Selling	325.00	1.00
Marketing and Promotion Assessment	6.50	0.02
Total	747.50	2.30
TOTAL COST	2,607.26	8.02

[z]Production using plastic mulch and overhead irrigation.

Table A4.6. Estimated watermelon production costs for the following crop in a double-crop system for southwest Florida, 1997–98.[z,y] (Source: Smith, S.A. and T.G. Taylor. 1998. Production costs for Florida vegetables.)

Category	Avg.	
	Acre	Cwt
Yield (cwts)	340	
OPERATING COSTS	Dollars	
Transplants	120.00	
Fertilizer and lime	162.00	
Fungicide	200.72	
Herbicide	18.23	
Insecticide	147.73	
Labor	439.15	
Machinery	245.75	
Interest	40.86	
Miscellaneous		
Ditch maintenance	17.00	
Plastic removal and disposal	156.82	
Bees	30.00	
Farm vehicles	16.12	
Total	1,594.36	
FIXED COST		
Machinery	108.28	
Management	332.36	
Overhead	415.45	
Total	856.08	
TOTAL PREHARVEST COST	2,450.45	7.21
HARVEST AND MARKETING COSTS		
Harvest and pack	656.20	1.93
Marketing and Promotion Assessment	6.80	0.02
Selling	340.00	1.00
Total	1,003.00	2.95
TOTAL COST	3,453.45	10.16

[z]Cost attributed to second crop as a result of double-crop production practices following tomatoes.

[y]Costs exclude field and bed preparation, plastic mulch, and fumigant.

Table A4.7. Irrigated, mulched watermelon budget. Georgia, 1994. (Source: www.ces.uga.edu/agriculture/agecon/vegetables/plastic/plastic6/html.)

Item	Unit	Quantity	Price ($)	Amt/Acre ($)	Total ($)
VARIABLE COSTS					
Seed or plants	lb	2.00	11.00	22.00	22
Lime, applied	ton	0.50	24.00	12.00	12
Fertilizer	cwt	10.00	7.40	74.00	74
Sidedressing	acre	1.00	85.00	85.00	85
Insecticide	appl.	1.00	6.70	6.70	7
Fungicide	appl.	10.00	2.70	27.00	27
Nematicide	acre	1.00	45.00	45.00	45
Herbicide	acre	1.00	13.44	13.44	13
Plastic	roll	2.80	65.00	182.00	182
Plastic removal	acre	1.00	0.00	0.00	0
Machinery	acre	1.00	17.87	17.87	18
Labor	acre	1.00	14.52	14.52	15
Land rent	acre	1.00	0.00	0.00	0
Irrigation (sprinkler)	appl.	6.00	4.26	25.56	26
Interest on op. cap.	$	525.09	0.09	23.63	24
PREHARVEST VARIABLE COSTS				548.72	549
HARVEST AND MARKETING COSTS					
Harvest and hauling	cwt				
Total Harvest and marketing		400	1.75	700.00	700
				700.00	700
TOTAL VARIABLE COSTS				1248.72	1,249
FIXED COSTS					
Machinery	acre	1.00	45.09	45.09	45
Irrigation	acre	1.00	69.01	69.09	69
Land	acre	1.00	0.00	0.00	0
Overhead and management	$	548.72	0.15	82.31	82
TOTAL FIXED COSTS				196.41	196
TOTAL BUDGETED COST PER ACRE				1445.12	1,445

Table A4.8. Irrigated, bareground watermelon budget. Georgia, 1994. (Source: www.ces.uga.edu/agriculture/agcon/vegetables/plastic/plastic6/html.)

Item	Unit	Quantity	Price ($)	Amt/Acre ($)	Total ($)
VARIABLE COSTS					
PREHARVEST					
Seed or plants	lb	2.00	11.00	22.00	22
Lime, applied	ton	0.50	24.00	12.00	12
Fertilizer	cwt	10.00	7.40	74.00	74
Sidedressing	acre	1.00	14.85	14.85	15
Insecticide	appl.	1.00	6.70	6.70	7
Fungicide	appl.	10.00	2.70	27.00	27
Nematicide	acre	1.00	45.00	45.00	45
Herbicide	acre	1.00	13.44	13.44	13
Machinery	acre	1.00	17.49	17.49	17
Labor	acre	1.00	14.52	14.52	15
Land rent	acre	1.00	0.00	0.00	0
Irrigation	appl.	3.00	4.26	12.78	13
Interest on oper. cap.	$	259.78	0.09	11.69	12
TOTAL PREHARVEST				271.47	271
HARVEST AND MARKETING COSTS					
Harvest and hauling	cwt	250	1.50	375.00	375
Total				375.00	375
TOTAL VARIABLE COSTS				646.47	646
FIXED COSTS					
Machinery and irrigation	acre	1.00	73.61	73.61	74
Land	acre	1.00	0.00	0.00	0
Overhead and management	$	271.47	0.15	40.72	41
TOTAL FIXED COSTS				114.33	114
TOTAL BUDGETED COST PER ACRE				760.80	761

Table A4.9. Summary of estimated costs per acre, watermelons (early), hybrid, transplants, plastic mulch, one-row equipment. Louisiana 1997. (Source: agecon.lib.umn.edu/lsu/lsuae155.pdf.)

Item	Unit	Price ($)	Quantity	Amt ($)
DIRECT EXPENSES				
Fertilizer	acre	80.56	1.00	80.56
Fungicides	acre	79.60	1.00	79.60
Hired labor	acre	150.00	1.00	150.00
Insecticides	acre	14.56	1.00	14.56
Plastic	acre	162.00	1.00	162.00
Plants	acre	135.00	1.00	135.00
Harvest labor	acre	300.00	1.00	300.00
Operator labor	hour	7.50	30.73	230.44
Diesel fuel	gal	0.85	5.25	4.46
Gasoline	gal	1.10	38.62	42.49
Repair & maintenance	acre	55.68	1.00	55.68
Interest on oper. cap.	acre	41.34	1.00	41.34
TOTAL DIRECT EXPENSES				1296.13
TOTAL FIXED EXPENSES				68.63
TOTAL SPECIFIED EXPENSES				1364.76

Table A4.10. Summary of estimated costs per acre, watermelons, fresh market, one-row equipment, average yield. Louisiana, 1997. (Source: agecon.lib.umn.edu/lsu/lsuae155.pdf.)

Item	Unit	Price ($)	Quantity	Amt ($)
DIRECT EXPENSES				
Fertilizer	acre	70.31	1.0000	70.31
Fungicides	acre	19.14	1.0000	19.14
Herbicides	acre	27.74	1.0000	27.74
Hired labor	acre	165.00	1.0000	165.00
Insecticides	acre	10.64	1.0000	10.64
Seed	acre	12.50	1.0000	12.50
Harvest labor	acre	300.00	1.0000	300.00
Operator labor	hour	7.50	27.7810	208.36
Diesel fuel	gal	0.85	4.6170	3.92
Gasoline	gal	1.10	42.9000	47.19
Repair & maintenance	acre	56.77	1.0000	56.77
Interest on oper. cap.	acre	20.27	1.0000	20.27
TOTAL DIRECT EXPENSES				941.83
TOTAL FIXED EXPENSES				68.91
TOTAL SPECIFIED EXPENSES				1010.75

Table A4.11. Estimated watermelon costs per acre. Mississippi, 1999. (Source: www.agecon.msstate.edu//budgets.)

Item	Unit	Price ($)	Quantity	Amt ($)
DIRECT EXPENSES				
FERTILIZER				
Lime (Spread)	ton	28.98	1.5000	43.47
Amm Nitrate (34%)	cwt	9.15	2.0000	18.30
FUNGICIDE				
Benlate WP	lb	16.57	2.0000	33.14
Bravo-720	pt	6.81	6.0000	40.86
HERBICIDE				
Curbit	pt	4.65	4.0000	18.60
INSECTICIDE				
Thiodan 3EC	qt	9.09	2.0000	18.18
Asana XL	oz	0.96	6.0000	5.76
SEED/PLANTS				
Watermelon	lb	10.00	2.2000	22.00
OTHER				
Plastic Mulch	roll	50.00	2.0000	100.00
Harvest Melons	cwt	1.05	100.0000	105.00
Hauling	trip	25.00	1.0000	25.00
OPERATOR LABOR				
Implements	hour	8.31	0.7000	5.82
Tractors	hour	8.31	3.3000	27.42
HAND LABOR				
Labor (planting)	hour	6.91	2.0000	13.82
DIESEL FUEL				
Tractors		0.65	12.7380	8.28
REPAIR & MAINTENANCE				
Implements	acre	2.58	1.0000	2.58
Tractors	acre	9.13	1.0000	9.13
INTEREST ON OPER. CAP.	acre	11.71	1.0000	11.71
TOTAL DIRECT EXPENSES				509.08
FIXED EXPENSES				
Implements	acre	5.36	1.0000	5.36
Tractors	acre	22.29	1.0000	22.29
TOTAL FIXED EXPENSES				27.65
TOTAL SPECIFIED EXPENSES				536.73

Note: Cost of production estimates are based on last year's input prices.

Table A4.12. Watermelon production budget. Oklahoma, 1997. (Source: www.okstate.edu/budgets.) Watermelon, small farm machinery complement. Sandy loam soils, irrigated. Cwt. bulk, FOB packing plant, 18 ft row spacing.

Operating inputs	Units	Price ($)	Quantity	Value ($)
Herbicide	Acre	6.250	1.000	6.25
Vegetable seed	Lbs	150.000	1.000	150.00
19–19–19 Fertilizer	Cwt	11.650	2.500	29.13
Potash (K20)	Lbs	0.130	50.000	6.50
RNTFERTSPRD/Acre	Acre	2.500	1.000	2.50
Herbicide	Acre	3.750	1.000	3.75
Insecticide	Acre	10.250	3.000	30.75
Fungicide	Acre	200.000	2.000	400.00
Hoeing labor	Hr.	6.500	9.000	58.50
Prunning labor	Hr.	6.500	4.000	26.00
Harvest labor	Hr.	6.500	28.000	182.00
Grading & Mktg.	Cwt.	0.890	140.000	124.60
Annual operating capital	Dol.	0.088	186.694	16.34
Machinery labor	Hr.	6.500	7.704	50.07
Irrigation labor	Hr.	6.500	1.797	11.68
Machinery, fuel, lube, repairs	Dol.			18.12
Irrigation, fuel, lube, repairs	Dol.			49.30
TOTAL OPERATING COSTS				1165.49

Fixed Costs	Amount	Value
Machinery		
Interest at 9.100%	145.66	13.26
Depr, taxes, insurance		16.15
Irrigation		
Interest at 9.100%	350.27	31.88
Depr, taxes, insurance		51.00
TOTAL FIXED COSTS		112.28

Assumed herbicide preplant prefar 5 lb ai per acre actually treated, 3 ft band over row; postemergence Treflan 0.5 lb ai, insecticide Asana 0.05 lb. ai, fungicide Ridomil/Bravo 2.5 lb ai

COMMON NAMES IN 15 LANGUAGES

Common Names in 15 Languages

Language	Name
English	watermelon
Arabic	bateekh
Chinese (Mandarin)	xi gua
Danish	vandmelon
Dutch	watermeloen
French	pastèque
	melon d'eau
German	Wassermelone
Hindu	tarbuj
	tarbuz
	kharmuja
	tarmuj
Italian	cocomero
	anguria
	melone d'acqua
Japanese	suika
Malay	tembikai
	sikoi
Portuguese	melancia
Russian	arbuz stolovyj
Spanish	sandia
Tagalog	pakwan

Source: S.J. Kays and J.C. Silva Dias. 1996. Cultivated vegetables of the world. Latin binomial, common names in 15 languages, edible part, and method of preparations. Exon Press, Athens, GA 30608-0803.

INDEX

A

Agrobacterium tumefaciens 76
Alternaria leaf blight 109
Animal pests 97
Anthracnose 41, 111, 163
Aphid 132

B

Bacterial fruit blotch 43, 113, 162
Bacterial rind necrosis 44, 112
Bailey, L.H. 28
Bees 10, 45, 94, 96, 132
Beet armyworm 138
Beneficial insects 132
Biotechnology
   Agrobacterium tumefaciens 76
   genetic transformation 76
   microparticle bombardment 76
   molecular markers 75
   tissue culture 74
Black rot 119, 163
Blossom-end rot 44, 79, 129
Bottleneck 129
Breeding
   backcross 60
   hybrid testing 62
   inbred development 61
   mechanization 67
   objectives 54
   pedigree 59
   plan 56
   pollination 50
   recurrent selection 57
   seedless variety development:
   tetraploid production 63
   triploid evaluation 66
   variety development 55
°Brix 19, 37, 156, 160, 163

C

Cabbage looper 138
Cancer risk reduction 20
Cercospera leaf spot.. 116
Chilling injury 46, 162
Citrullus colocynthis 22, 28, 29, 38, 46
Citrullus lanatus 9, 22, 27, 28, 46, 47
Citrullus lanatus var. *citroides* 22, 29
Classification of varieties 30
Colchicine 64
Collins, G. 56
Consumer preferences 18
Consumption
    United States 16, 27
    world 16
Cowpea aphid 132
Crabgrass 150
Crop establishment
    field seeding... 89
    transplanting 88
    transplant production 87
Crop production
    animal pests 96
    bees 95
    drip irrigation 95
    frost protection... 93
    irrigation 93
    mulching 91
    pollination 95
    row covers 93
    spacing 90
    triploid 89
    windbreaks 90
Crop rotation 78
Cross stitch 44, 129
Cucumber beetles 139
Cucumber mosaic virus 77, 126
Cucurbitacin 25, 28
Cucurbit Genetics Cooperative 47
Cucurbit publications... 203

D

DeCandolle 46
Direct marketing options 186
Diseases
    alternaria leaf blight 109
    anthracnose 111
    bacterial fruit blotch 113
    bacterial rind necrosis 112
    cercospera leaf spot 116
    downy mildew 116
    fusarium wilt 118
    gummy stem blight 119
    monosporascus 121
    phytophthora 122
    powdery mildew 124
    pythium 123
    southern blight 125
    virus 126
Disease resistance
    anthracnose 41
    bacterial fruit blotch 43
    bacterial rind necrosis 44
    fusarium wilt 40
    gummy stem blight 42
    physiological 44
    powdery mildew 42
    seedling tests 39
    virus 44
    yellow vine 42
Distribution 22
Downy mildew 116
Drip irrigation 95
Fertilizer injection 82

E

Egusi 22, 28, 29
Ethylene sensitivity 162

F

Fertilizer 80

Field seeding 89
Flavor
   bitter 37
   caramel 38
Flea beetles 144
Flowers 10, 29, 53, 68
Fresh cut 163
Frost protection 94
Fruit maturation 11
Fusarium fruit rot 163
Fusarium wilt 40, 78, 118

G

Gene list 32–33
Genetics
   inbreeding depression and heterosis 49
   qualitative traits 49
Genetic transformations 76
Germplasm resources
   centers of diversity 47
   centers of origin 46
   repositories 47
Goosegrass 150
Grades and standards 19, 159
Grasshoppers 144
Greasy spot 130
Greenhouse whitefly 134
Green peach aphid 132
Growth enhancement 93
Guinness Book of Records
   largest fruit 24
   seed spitting record 24
Gummy stem blight 42, 119

H

Hardin, M. 35
Harvest
   maturity determination 25, 156
   procedures 156
Herbicide labels 154

History 23, 27, 189

Hollowheart 44, 128, 162

Hopkins, D.L. 43

Horticulture 10

Horticultural traits

    earliness 34

    fruit characteristics

        external quality 36

        internal quality 37

        size, shape, rind pattern 35

        seeds and seedlessness 38

        sex expression 31

        vines 31

        yields 34

Horticultural types

    citron 29

    egusi 29

    watermelon 30

I

Insects

    beet armyworm 138

    beneficial 132

    cabbage looper 138

    cowpea aphid 132

    cucumber beetles 139

    flea beetles 144

    grasshoppers 144

    greenhouse whitefly 134

    green peach aphid 132

    leafminers 142

    melon aphid 132

    melon thrips 143

    mole crickets 148

    rindworms 137

    seedcorn maggot 145

    silverleaf whitefly 134

    southern mole cricket 148

    squash bug 136

    tawny mole cricket 148

    thrips 143

    tobacco thrips 143

    whitefly 134

    whitefringe beetle 147

    white grubs 147

    wireworms 146

Insect resistance 44

International marketing 184

IR-4 154

Irrigation 93

J

Javanese root-knot nematodes 98

Jefferson, Thomas 23

Johnson, M.W. 55

K

Kolb, R. 55

L

Layton, D.V. 42

Leafminers 142

Lime and calcium 79

Livingston, David 21, 46

Lycopene 19, 27

M

Male sterility 34

Marketing

    advantage 176

    competition 175

    developing a plan 180

    direct options 186

    international 184

    options 167

    preparing a strategy 170

    research 172

    successful 166

    window analysis 178

Maturity 11, 156

Maynard, D.N. 48
Measles 46
Melon aphid 132
Melon thrips 143
Microparticle bombardment 76
Mole crickets 148
Molecular markers 75
Monosporascus 121
Morphology 10, 28
Mites 141
MRI 11
Mulch culture fertilization 82
Mulching 91

N
National Seed Storage Laboratory 47
National Watermelon Association 193, 197
National Watermelon Promotion Board 17, 18, 193, 197
Nematodes
    biology 102
    disease complexes 103
    economic importance 102
    host races 100
    javanese root knot 98
    life cycle 101
    management
        biological control 107
        cultural practices 106
        host resistance 106
        nematicides 106
        population assessment 105
        northern root knot 99
        peanut root knot 98
        population dynamics 102
        southern root knot 98
        symptoms 99
        northern root knot 99
        southern root knot 98
Nightshade 151
Nutritional composition 17

Nutsedge 151

O

Organizations
    National Watermelon Association 193, 197
    National Watermelon Promotion Board 17, 18, 193, 197
    State associations 197–198
Origin 21, 46
Orton, W.A. 41

P

Papaya ring-spot virus 77, 126
Peanut root-knot nematode 98
Pest management
    disease 109–130
    insect and mite 131–149
    nematode 98–108
    weed 150–155
Petiole sap testing 84
Physiological disorders
    bottleneck 129
    blossom-end rot 44, 79, 129
    cross stitch 129
    greasy spot 130
    hollowheart 128, 162
    sunburn 129
    target spot 130
Phytophthora 122
Phytohthora fruit rot 163
Pigweed 150
Plant characteristics 10, 28, 31
Plant tissue analysis 84
Planting dates 86
Pollination 50, 45, 96
Polyethylene mulch 82, 91
Postharvest disease
    anthracnose 163
    bacterial fruit blotch 162
    black rot 163
    fusarium fruit rot 163

phytophthora fruit rot 163
Postharvest disorders
    chilling injury 162
    ethylene sensitivity 162
    hollowheart 162
Postharvest handling
    bulk shipment 158
    fresh cut 163
    grades and standards 19, 159
    inspection requirements 160
    packaging techniques 160
    packing 159
    precooling 160
    storage 161
    transportation 161
    washing 158
Powdery mildew 42, 124
Production
    China 13
    world 12
    United States 13
    by county 15
Production costs
    Arizona 204–205
    Florida 206–209
    Georgia 210–211
    Louisiana 212–213
    Mississippi 214
    Oklahoma 215
Promotion
    history 189
    quality 191
    triploid 191
Publications 203
Pythium 123

Q
Quality 11, 86, 191

R

Regional Plant Introduction Center 47
Rind characteristics .... 10, 30 ,36
Rindworms 137
Root-knot nematodes 98–108
Root-knot nematode resistance 44
Rotation 78
Row covers 11, 93

S

Seed
    color 10, 25, 28
    count 10
    fermentation 71
    germination temperature 29
    hybrid production 68
    producers 199–201
    production systems 69
    size 10, 39
    sources 199–201
    treatment 72
Seedcorn maggot 145
Silverleaf whitefly 134
Soil
    fertilization 80
    insects 145–149
    liming 79
    pH 79
    preparation 84
    rotation 78
    testing 79
Southern blight 125
Southern mole cricket 148
Southern root-knot nematode 98
Spacing 90
Spider mite 141
Squash bug 136
Squash mosaic virus 77, 126
Storage 161
Stress resistance 45

Sunburn 129, 158
Sweetness 19, 160, 163

T
Target spot 130
Tawny mole cricket 148
Thoreau, Henry David 24
Taxonomy 9, 27
Temperatures for growth 46
Thrips 143
Tissue culture 74
Tissue testing 84
Tobacco ring spot virus 126
Tobacco thrips 143
Total soluble solids 19, 25
Transplanting 88
Transplant production 87
Transportation 161
Triploid field arrangement 89
Tunnels 11, 93
Twain, Mark 24, 196
Twospotted spider mite 141

U
Uses
    livestock feed 24
    medicinal 25
    pickled 24
    seed 23, 24
    water source 22
United States
    consumption 16
    production 13–15
    standards for grades of watermelons 19, 159

V
Variety
    classification 30
    currently important 48
    development 55

selection 85

W

Wagner, R.F. 42
Watermelon in 15 languages 216
Watermelon mosaic virus-2 .... 77, 126
Weeds
    goosegrass 150
    large crabgrass 150
    nightshade 152
    smooth pigweed 150
    yellow nutsedge 151
Weed competition 150
Weed control
    cultural 152
    herbicides 153
    mechanical 151
Wehner, T.C. 47
Whitaker, T.W. 47
Whitefly 134
Whitefringed beetle 147
White grubs 147
Windbreaks 90
Wireworms 146
World production 12

Y

Yeager, A.F. 35

Z

Zucchini yellow mosaic virus 77, 126